Readings in Primary School Development

Dedication: for Ben

Readings in Primary School Development

Edited by

Geoff Southworth

 The Falmer Press

(A member of the Taylor & Francis Group)

London • Washington, D.C.

UK   The Falmer Press, 4 John Street, London WC1N 2ET
USA   The Falmer Press, Taylor & Francis Inc., 1900 Frost Road, Suite 101,
        Bristol, PA 19007

First published in 1994

**A catalogue record for this book is available from the British
Library**

**Library of Congress Cataloging-in-Publication Data are
available on request**

ISBN 0 7507 0355 5 cased
ISBN 0 7507 0356 3 paper

Jacket design by Caroline Archer

Typeset in 10/12 Bembo by
Graphicraft Typesetters Ltd., Hong Kong.

*Printed in Great Britain by Burgess Science Press, Basingstoke on paper
which has a specified pH value on final paper manufacture of not less than
7.5 and is therefore 'acid free'.*

Contents

Contents

Acknowledgments

The publishers are grateful to the following for permission to reproduce copyright material:

The editor and publishers of *School Organisation* for SOUTHWORTH, G.W. (1993) 'School Leadership and School Development: Reflections from research'.

The editor and publishers of *Education 3–13* for SOUTHWORTH, G.W. (1993) 'Trading Places: Job rotation in a primary school'.

Introduction: From Management to School Development and Improvement

Geoff Southworth

Some years ago I edited a book for Falmer Press entitled *Readings in Primary School Management* (1987). That volume is in some respects a companion to this book. However, since the first book the world of education has changed quite markedly. As I began to think about this collection of chapters I recognized that amongst all the changes we were facing in education, there was one which was occurring relatively unnoticed. This change concerns a shift in emphasis away from management and towards school development or school improvement as it is increasingly being called.

The 1980s might be described as the decade of school management. During that period a great deal of attention was devoted to school administration. The roles of headteachers, middle managers and curriculum specialists were researched, analysed and discussed, although most of this effort was focused upon secondary schools rather than primary. Indeed, primary schools continue to be relatively under-researched organizations. As school management theorizing developed and practice in schools was shaped by central government, a new technical language was introduced. Some heads and teachers began to speak about targets, goals, appraisals, audits, customers and delivery. Others were uncomfortable that the language of commerce and accountancy was being applied to schools.

The influence of commercial and industrial management thinking was strong during the 1980s. Ideas were often imported from business settings and applied to schools. Indeed, increasingly the principles of the market place were imposed upon schools. Autonomous, locally managed schools were created, partly to reduce the role of the LEAs and partly to move decision making closer to those to whom the decisions applied. By moving many more decisions to the school site it was thought that schools would be able to make better use of their finite resources. At the same time competition was introduced between schools with the advent of open enrolment. All of these ideas and many more, were promoted by central government which believed that competition and efficiency were two of the ways of raising standards in

1

schools. Yet underneath all of these initiatives lay the fact that each had to be managed. Management as an activity grew in scope and significance throughout the 1980s.

Yet management was not the only meta-theme of the 1980s. In education the search for effective schools began to grow as a field of study. Many studies were published during the 1980s which tried to identify the key characteristics of successful schools, such as Mortimore *et al.*, 1988. These studies attempted to identify the secrets of success by examining high performing schools. It was believed that by looking at schools which were doing well it would be possible to detect those factors which accounted for their success. The research has provided some useful insights. Moreover, across many of the studies some common characteristics have appeared such as: staff collaboration; shared values; a strong focus on teaching and learning; a positive school climate and leadership. The latter one is especially interesting since what the effectiveness studies point to is leadership rather than management.

The effective schools research can in some ways be regarded as a bridge between the theme of management in the 1980s and the theme of school improvement in the 1990s. The effective schools research showed that leadership was important to the health and vitality of the organization. Moreover, the research suggests that schools do need to be efficiently managed in respect of resources, time, communications, decision making, parental involvement and so on. Yet the research also shows that in addition to leadership and management there needs to be a persistent emphasis upon teaching and learning. In particular, staff need to consider what the children are doing and to take note of the pupils' learning outcomes. In short, the effective schools research shows that management is not a panacea but only one condition of a successful school.

At the same time the school effectiveness research, while useful in identifying the characteristics of successful schools, is singularly unhelpful in explaining how these schools got to be like that. In other words, the research fails to show how to become effective. As a result, a parallel field of study has developed, namely the school improvement research. These studies are interested in managing changes which are explicitly introduced to improve the school.

Of course, the rise of a specific field of enquiry does not constitute a new theme in education. Rather, it is this research in conjunction with certain other features which marks a theme. Therefore, it is necessary to note that adjacent to the school improvement research are some other related developments. Three interrelated developments serve to support my argument.

First, there is the current interest in total quality management (TQM). In business and in education managers are being encouraged to focus on *quality*. It is no longer sufficient for managers to keep the organization running smoothly, they must also strive to improve the quality of their products or services.

Second, in education the establishment of the Office for Standards in

Education (OFSTED) has further increased and accelerated the attention to be paid to quality. Central government has now mandated that every school can expect to be regularly inspected by independent teams of trained and approved inspectors, whose reports are made public. Significantly, while the inspectors examine many aspects of the school, they are devoting the greatest amount of inspection time, and space in their published reports, to the quality of the teaching and learning in the school. OFSTED inspections firmly place an emphasis upon pupil outcomes, standards of achievement and the quality of teaching.

Third, recent work on the assessment of pupils' learning has, over a seven year period of intense activity, channelled heads' and teachers' attention in this area. Moreover, threats about published results and league tables have also had a similar effect. So saying, I am not justifying the means by which this development has taken place, only noting the ends. Yet, however the effect has occurred, it does appear that staff in school have become more aware of and focused more directly upon pupils' learning than, say, ten years ago.

These three developments suggest that in recent years attention has been increasingly drawn to considerations of quality in general and the pupils' experience and outcomes in particular. In many ways we are now embarked on a quest for quality. This quest for quality is not a search for some educational nirvana. Quality is not about arriving at a fixed point, rather it is a neverending journey in which teachers are forever striving to develop their practice, individually and collectively. In this sense, quality is not a once and for all time position rather it is a state of mind. Attention to quality is about constantly trying to improve one's practice. Quality is the outcome of the improvement process.

In noting this change away from management and towards improvement there are two other points to add. First, I do not want to suggest that teachers have only recently become interested in quality or improvement; they have not, as the school self-evaluation movement in the early 1980s showed. That movement helped many teachers to evaluate their work and to devise ways of developing their classroom practice. Indeed, the great majority of teachers wish to enhance their classroom skills and understandings which is why so many continue to undertake in-service education and training, often at their personal expense both financially and in terms of giving over their precious personal time. Yet, the shift I am referring to here is somewhat different because the focus on quality is not only a matter of individual practice, but also to do with the overall performance of the whole school. This wider attention means that teachers, especially in primary schools, must look to sharing their strengths, supporting one another's limitations, and developing whole school practices which provide some unified approaches, (for example, behaviour, discipline, contact with parents, rewards and incentives, special educational needs and equal opportunities). Quality is now a matter both for the individual teacher and for the whole staff.

Second, in saying that there is a movement away from management I am not implying that we are approaching the end of school management. The movement is really a matter of degree. Whereas until recently management was paid a lot of attention, now it needs to be seen as having a part to play alongside many other concerns, the most important of which are pupils' learning and the quality of teaching. The part management has to play is a multi-faceted one. Heads and other senior staff need to bring colleagues together, to preserve some of their hard pressed time for monitoring what the children are doing and for providing opportunities for other colleagues to do likewise. They need to ensure, in lots of different and often subtle ways, that they and their colleagues' are frequently and regularly focusing on teaching and learning in every classroom and across the whole school.

The challenge for school management in the 1990s is to enable the school as an organization to move forward qualitatively. School management is not just about keeping the school going, it is about taking the school somewhere better. There is a lot of material currently around which relates to the school improvement theme sketched out here, (such as Holly and Southworth, 1989; Fullan, 1991; Fullan and Hargreaves, 1992; Hargreaves and Hopkins, 1991; Louis and Miles, 1990) and no doubt there is more to come. Yet across this burgeoning literature there is little on primary schools. In many ways, we know surprisingly little about *how* primary schools have actually developed. There are few descriptive, longitudinal studies which track the growth of a school. We know very little about the time scales and timelines of the improvement process in primary schools.

We do know that a number of characteristics appear to be important if the school is to develop. These characteristics include:

- school leadership
- curriculum development
- pupil assessment
- staff development
- school culture

In varying ways each of these characteristics is addressed in this volume. They form the focus of this book because, given the lack of explicit attention to primary school development, I felt it would be timely to put together a set of readings which, in a number of ways, addressed the theme of improving primary schools. Moreover, such a book needs to be based upon sound knowledge of primary education and an awareness of what is happening in primary schools. Therefore, the contributors to the book are all experienced primary school practitioners and all work closely with primary teachers and schools. Each has something of value to say about primary schooling.

The book is organized into three parts. Part I looks at school leadership, in particular considering the work of headteachers, deputies and their development. Part II focuses on managing the curriculum. The three chapters here consider a headteacher's part in curriculum development, managing assessment and manageability and the National Curriculum. The third part is called Development and the four chapters look at teacher development, lessons from school improvement studies, the stories of three developing primary schools and the implications of school inspections for primary school development. In the next section I offer a brief résumé of each chapter.

The Chapters in this Book

Chapter 1: School Leadership and School Development:
　　　　　　Reflections from Research
　　　　　　Geoff Southworth

In this chapter I draw upon the insights and findings of two funded research projects I have worked on. The two projects are the Primary School Staff Relationships Project and the Whole School Curriculum Development Project. Each was a school-based enquiry which took me back into school to observe what the staff groups actually did. In both projects attention was given to school leadership. In this chapter I summarize the findings of both projects with regard to leadership and then go on to examine five reflections: the complexity of school leadership; instrumental and expressive leadership; the pace of school development; headteacher motivation; vision, ownership and community. I conclude by suggesting that we urgently need more studies into primary school leadership and offer some tentative thoughts as to the directions these studies might take.

Chapter 2: Headteachers and Deputy Heads
　　　　　　Geoff Southworth

For a long time I have been interested in the role of the primary school deputy. In fact, my interest pre-dates the time when I was one in a primary school in East Lancashire. In this chapter I try to synthesize my current thinking about deputy heads. The chapter begins by noting a shift in the occupational culture of teachers. I argue that over the last twenty-five years teaching has gradually been reconceptualized. Teaching is no longer viewed as an independent activity but as an interdependent one. I then suggest that this shift is mirrored in the idea that heads and deputies should work as partners. I next go on to explore partnership by looking at two studies which throw some light on the practice of heads and deputies. Then I examine more recent investigations. From the empirical work I draw out some common themes but also suggest that the existing work is limited in a number of respects. The severest weakness is that all of the studies are preoccupied with the managerial work of headteachers and deputies and overlook the school improvement perspective. In the fourth section I draw upon current thinking on school culture and argue that heads and deputies need to work together as partners in order to promote a collaborative culture. In the concluding section I pull together the main ideas in the chapter and suggest that the deputy head should be seen as an assistant head who works closely with the head where both are critical friends to one another and their colleagues and where the pair model professional interdependence.

Chapter 3: Trading Places: Job Rotation in a Primary School
Geoff Southworth

This chapter reports upon an initiative I was invited to observe in a local primary school. The headteacher, wanting to have direct experience of teaching the National Curriculum decided, with the support of the governors, to return to class teaching for a year and delegate the running of the school to the deputy head. Furthermore, another senior teacher was temporarily promoted to the position of acting-deputy. In the chapter I set out the background to the initiative and then present a term-by-term account of how the three main protagonists, the head, acting-head and acting-deputy, described to me how they were individually experiencing their new roles. Having presented the interview data I collected I next go on to discuss four themes which emerge from the enquiry. The four themes are: headship is hard work; the role of the deputy is poorly defined and teachers can be ill-prepared for the job; individuals need time to learn new roles; the head's return to the classroom increased his awareness of teaching in the 1990s.

Chapter 4: A Primary Headteacher In Search of a Collaborative Climate
Denis Hayes

As in the previous chapter Hayes draws upon a school based enquiry he conducted in a primary school where he observed a primary head at work. In particular he recorded how she attempted to develop a *collaborative climate* in the school to deal with the heavy demands of national reform, especially a delegated budget and the requirements of the National Curriculum. The chapter focuses on the head's time management, the development of decision-making structures and how efforts were made to maintain staff enthusiasm for involvement. Hayes closes the chapter by considering the benefits and costs of collaboration and the implications for staff development. Throughout Hayes paints a picture which captures the messy reality of life and work in a primary school and touches on some of the tensions and contradictions inherent in staff groups, especially at times of change and upheaval. Hayes shows how challenging managing and developing a primary school in the 1990s can be. It is also worth noting that Hayes' chapter acts as a bridge between the first and second parts of the book and is in several ways a useful trailer for the next chapter.

Chapter 5: Manageability and Control of the Primary Curriculum
Jim Campbell

In this chapter Jim Campbell critically reviews the introduction of the National Curriculum in primary schools. He focuses upon three problems: curriculum time allocation; teacher expertise; and resources in primary schools. Campbell then goes on to examine the Dearing Review of the National Curriculum and argues that the arithmetic about teaching time in Dearing's report is mishandled and does not solve the problem of time, let alone the other two. Next, Campbell looks at the management implications for schools. He sketches out some possible ways of alleviating these problems but is aware that what he offers are only treatments and not cures. In the conclusion Campbell suggests that the task for school management over the next 5 years is to establish curriculum priorities with which the governors and staff agree, which seek to raise standards while offering a broad curriculum within the national curricular framework and yet avoids covering content in a superficial way. Throughout the chapter Campbell draws upon his own recent research and that of others in the primary field. The chapter is built upon a deep understanding of what is happening in schools in the 1990s.

Chapter 6: Managing Assessment: Have we Learned any Lessons from the Experience of National Curriculum Assessment?
Colin Conner

Conner's chapter looks at the issue of pupil assessment in primary schools. Drawing upon his extensive knowledge of the topic and his close contact with primary schools in the Eastern region of England, the author examines recent developments in pupil assessment. He begins by looking at the Dearing Review and by noting 'the significant gains which have been made as a result of the assessment expertise developed in primary education' and more particularly in key stage one. Conner goes on to draw upon the research he has been working on which looks directly at how schools have managed their assessment activities. He includes two case studies of work and developments in primary schools. In line with many other contributors in this book his insights and thinking are grounded in actual practice in real primary schools. Following the presentation of these two case studies Conner sets out four main conclusions: the importance of evidence to support judgements about children's achievements; the need for teachers to collaborate to develop greater consistency amongst themselves; the role of the LEAs; involving the learner in assessment.

> *Chapter 7*: Becoming Someone Other: Teacher Professional Development and the Management of Change Through INSET
> *Marion Dadds*

This chapter traces in detail how an INSET course contributed to a deputy head's professional development and to her school's development by examining how she sought to develop the use of pupil profiling and pupil self assessment in her school. While the chapter has much to say about development it also connects to the previous section on managing the curriculum. The chapter draws upon interview data and captures some of the highs and lows and the uncertainties of individual and institutional development. In particular the study shows how there is an emotional dimension to development, that a collaborative culture is an enabling context for school growth, that the support of the head is important and that resistance to development is common, if not natural. In other words, the processes of development are demanding, situationally specific and dynamic. Moreover, a change agent needs to be a learner since the deputy in this case was learning about herself, her school and how to manage change. The chapter is a valuable contribution to our understanding of school and teacher development.

> *Chapter 8*: School Development: Lessons from Effective Schools and School Improvement Studies
> *Dick Weindling*

This chapter provides an overview of the research on school effectiveness and of efforts to utilize this work in respect to school improvement projects. Weindling begins by reviewing school effectiveness research. He draws extensively upon studies in elementary schools in the USA and compiles a valuable summarizing list of the key characteristics associated with school effectiveness.

In the second section Weindling goes on to look at how a number of projects have tried to apply some of the school effectiveness insights to schools which either wish to or need to improve. He sets out what a typical school improvement project in the USA looks like and then goes on to describe in greater detail two initiatives in this field in the USA. In the fourth section Weindling reviews school improvement projects in the UK, including the IQEA project (which is also described in Chapter 9 in this book). The final part of the chapter is devoted to identifying the lessons from this research and what it means for staff in a school. The chapter condenses a great deal of research and study into a valuable and manageable whole. The lessons

Weindling identifies support many of the points raised earlier in this Introduction and should be of benefit to all in school.

Chapter 9: Understanding the Moving School
Mel Ainscow and David Hopkins

In this chapter the authors highlight some of the lessons they have learned from an on-going school improvement project based at the University of Cambridge Institute of Education. The first part of the chapter describes and analyses how three primary schools have attempted to improve their practice. Each school's efforts are described and, by themselves, these provide valuable insights into how staff in primary schools go about making their schools more effective for the pupils. In the second part of the chapter the authors pull together the insights from each of these schools. They set out some of the general findings from the improvement project. In particular they note that staff in schools need to pay attention to the internal conditions of the organization since these can enhance or impede development. In several ways the chapter relates to others in this volume. For example, the importance of leadership is stressed, the need to cope with external change and the National Curriculum is implied throughout, while the issues of resistance (to change) and of 'internal turbulence' resonate with Dadds' chapter. Ainscow and Hopkins offer an all too rare glimpse into the processes of primary school development.

Chapter 10: School Inspection for School Development?
Geoff Southworth and Michael Fielding

This final chapter looks at the question of whether regular school inspections will enable schools to develop. The authors examine the work of the Office for Standards in Education (OFSTED) and briefly highlight four concerns: the fact that there is little evidence to support the proposition that inspections aid development; inspections do not show the pace and direction of school development; inspections do not encourage dialogue between the staff and the inspectors; OFSTED's handbook for inspection presents an overly tidy and unproblematic view of pupil learning. Given these strong reservations the authors move on to discuss how inspections might be yoked to school development. Four points are discussed. First, inspection needs to be seen as playing only a part in school development. Second, staff must help one another to deal with the emotional impact of an inspection. Third, staff need to recognize that it is the school which is being inspected and so they need to look at their collective practice across the whole school. Fourth, staff, especially senior staff, need to look closely at the teaching and learning in the school. The chapter closes with some practical advice about preparing for and managing inspections.

References

FULLAN, M. (1991) *The New Meaning of Educational Change*, London, Cassell.

FULLAN, M. and HARGREAVES, A. (1992) *What's Worth Fighting For in Your School?*, Buckingham, Open University Press.

HARGREAVES, D. and HOPKINS, D. (1991) *The Empowered School*, London, Cassell.

HOLLY, P. and SOUTHWORTH, G. (1989) *The Developing School*, London, Falmer Press.

LOUIS, K. and MILES, M. (1990) *Improving the Urban High School; What Works and Why*, New York, Teachers' College Press.

MORTIMORE, P., SAMMONS, P., STOLL, L., LEWIS, D. and ECOB, R. (1988) *School Matters: The Junior Years*, Wells, Open Books.

SOUTHWORTH, G. (1987) *Readings in Primary School Development*, London, Falmer Press.

Part I

Leadership

Chapter 1

School Leadership and School Development: Reflections from Research

Geoff Southworth

Introduction

Between 1985 and 1990 I was involved in two school-based research projects. The Primary School Staff Relationships Project (PSSR) was funded by the Economic and Social Research Council (ESRC) (ESRC ref. no. C09250003) and Cambridge Institute from 1985 to 1987. The Whole School Curriculum Development Project (WSCD), 1988–1990, was also funded by the ESRC (ref. no. R000231069). Each project has been written up in detail with the main findings and their implications for primary school development discussed (Nias *et al.*, 1989; Nias *et al.*, 1992).

Both projects focused, in part, upon leadership in primary schools. We observed heads, deputies and co-ordinators at work. Separately and together, both projects have much to say about school leadership.

In this chapter I want to reflect upon what these two projects reveal about leadership. In a sense I want to try to draw together what I have learned about leadership in English primary schools of median size. I shall set out in this chapter my insights, ideas and speculations about leadership and how these relate to school development and improvement.

The chapter is divided into four sections. The first section outlines the research methods used on the two projects. The second section presents the main findings from the PSSR project, and the third section focuses on the WSCD project. In the fourth section I present my reflections on these two projects.

Research Methods

The projects shared a common methodology. The researchers (Jennifer Nias, Robin Yeomans and myself for PSSR; Jennifer Nias, Penelope Campbell and myself for WSCD) acted as participant observers in five schools per project.

For one academic year we each worked, one day a week, as part-time teachers in the project schools. We used standard ethnographic methods — observation and interviews. At the end of our time in school we wrote individual case studies for each of the schools, using themes suggested by what we had seen and heard. These case studies were subsequently cleared by the staff groups. Each project team then compared and contrasted the validated case studies, looking for themes and overarching concepts. From those analyses came the two sets of findings and the subsequent books.

The findings of these two projects are based upon accounts of what we saw happening in the schools. The resulting ideas are grounded in what the heads did. Our work essentially describes what we saw rather than prescribes what should be done.

Primary School Staff Relationships Project

The main concept to emerge from this research was that of organizational culture where culture was loosely defined as 'the way we do it around here', that is, as a set of norms about ways of behaving, perceiving and understanding underpinned by jointly held beliefs and values.

The research team found that each of the five schools involved in the project had its own culture embodying strongly held beliefs about the social and moral purposes of education. These beliefs originated with the headteachers. In three of the schools the heads had worked for over 10 years to develop and sustain an organizational culture which enabled the teaching and ancillary staff to work closely together. The project team described this as a 'culture of collaboration' (Nias *et al.*, 1989: 46–74). In the other two schools the heads were endeavouring to develop a similar culture but were impeded by conflicting values held by long-established staff members.

The culture of collaboration rested upon four interacting beliefs:

1 individuals should be valued;
2 since individuals are inseparable from the groups of which they are a part, groups too should be fostered and valued;
3 the most effective way of promoting these values is by developing a sense of mutual security; and
4 fostering openness amongst staff.

In respect of leadership PSSR found that the head was the culture founder (see also Schein, 1985) and the person who most prominently sustained it. To establish and sustain a collaborative culture the heads did the following things:

- provided an educational vision which had become the school's mission;
- articulated their individual philosophies;
- actively and self-consciously exemplified their philosophies when they taught, took assemblies and met with staff face-to-face;

- used themselves as role models, teachers and coaches;
- developed extensive communication networks to know what was happening in the school;
- worked hard at not forgetting individuals and their contributions to the school;
- toured the school, visiting everyone in their work places;
- were accessible to staff, being approachable and available;
- sought out news and information;
- were very perceptive;
- used positive reinforcement to increase teachers' confidence and self-esteem;
- were considerate of others.

As a result of their actions the heads were greatly respected figures in their own schools. This respect enhanced the heads' authority and influence. The combination of exemplary behaviour and respect meant that the heads were educative leaders. They talked about the need to create opportunities for individuals to grow. Similarly, teachers spoke about learning from their heads.

The heads managed to behave in these ways as part and parcel of their everyday tasks. For example, they coped with numerous unexpected incidents; dealt with accidents and unannounced visitors wanting to see them. They responded to parents' concerns, which could be anything from lost property to the statementing of pupils. They also had to oversee the school site, handle the administrative tasks and communicate with a multitude of external agencies.

These heads' leadership, then, was not simply about keeping the school running on a day-to-day basis. Nor was it merely a matter of development planning and producing policy documents. Leadership meant infecting colleagues with one's educational beliefs. These heads worked on two levels: a high level of abstraction (e.g. defining their beliefs about the social and moral purposes of education); and at the most mundane and detailed level (see also Coulson, 1986: 85). On the one hand these heads were value-shaping leaders, offering visions for their staffs and fulfilling a pathfinding role. On the other hand, it seemed the only way to instil enthusiasm for the vision was through scores of daily events. The value-shaping leader:

> is a bug for detail and directly instils values through deeds rather than words: no opportunity is too small. So it is at once attention to ideas and attention to detail.
>
> (Peters and Waterman, 1982: 287)

While the PSSR project yielded some important insights, it raised questions about which aspects of school organization and staff interaction made it possible for productive working relationships to co-exist with an explicit commitment to whole school curricular development. The WSCD project was devised to examine these questions.

Whole School Curriculum Development Project

The major finding to emerge from this project is that teachers' learning is the key to whole school curriculum development. We found teachers were motivated to learn because they felt individually responsible for the children's learning and therefore the curriculum. Generally, teachers wanted to develop in order to improve their teaching and the pupils' learning. Yet these teachers also needed to learn to become active members of the school communities of which they were a part. They needed to do this because the instincts of teachers and the organizational characteristics of schools favour self-reliance and independence rather than mutual support and interdependence.

The teachers in the WSCD project schools described whole schools as being characterized by:

- a strong sense of community;
- staff sharing the same educational beliefs and aims and interpreting them in similar ways in their own classrooms;
- teachers exercising autonomy in their classrooms, able to play an individual role in the school and call upon one another's expertise;
- staff relating well to one another;
- staff able to work together;
- teachers' knowledge of the school not limited to matters of immediate concern to themselves or their classes;
- staff valuing the leadership of the headteacher.

(Nias *et al.*, 1992: 56)

In terms of leadership we saw the heads acting in ways similar to those reported in the PSSR project. The heads attempted to develop a sense of whole school and an organizational culture that supported collaboration. Yet we also saw, more clearly than before, that these heads and other leaders were committed to seeing the schools' policies put into practice. These heads wanted to make things happen and this they did by way of a blend of positional authority and interpersonal influence.

Most often the heads relied upon their influence to alter and affect how staff worked. They encouraged staff rather than told them what to do. We saw the heads using an array of tactics to develop a sense of whole school. Sometimes the heads were direct, sometimes indirect. They could, on occasions, be explicit, at others their intentions were implicit and could be perceived only from prolonged observation and analysis. The heads' ability to use a range of tactics and to exercise their power in different ways usually made them hard to resist. Moreover, the heads were prepared to be patient with colleagues and worked gradually and steadfastly over long periods of time.

The tactics the heads used to develop a sense of whole school can be summarized as follows:

- careful selection of staff when the opportunity to appoint teachers arose, plus ensuring there was an active process of induction for the newcomer;
- speaking openly about their own educational beliefs;
- stating explicitly what they expected and wanted to see in the school and inside the classroom. Some of the heads described this as 'pushing' what they wanted;
- being constructively critical of teachers' proposals for curriculum change;
- occasionally speaking frankly to a colleague whose beliefs or behaviour differed markedly from their own. Such frankness was intended to make it clear that there were minimum standards below which individuals should not fall, and if they did, the heads would not be able to tolerate it;
- demonstrating what they wanted and expected by teaching classes, small groups, leading assemblies and putting up displays;
- using assemblies, especially 'showing assemblies', to acknowledge the achievements of colleagues;
- touring the school, monitoring the work of the teachers and children — undertaking what Ball (1987: 93) calls 'benevolent surveillance';
- meeting informally with individual teachers in their classrooms, after school, to take an interest in their work and to offer advice, support, practical help;
- joining in with working parties, projects, concerts, productions, preparations for parents' evenings etc. Such action modelled collaboration and signalled the heads' desire to see staff sharing, co-operating, and participating with others;
- openly praising individual teachers in the presence of colleagues;
- leading formal meetings, such as staff meetings and curriculum discussions;
- valuing informal discussions and meetings;
- being active in the micropolitics of the school, and occasionally being manipulative, especially when they encountered competing interests of individuals and/or groups.

In utilizing these tactics we also noted that the heads relied upon three professional attributes. First, as noted in PSSR, these heads were *educators*. They saw their work as being concerned with developing their staff. Moreover, the heads themselves were also learners. They all had impressive records of participating in, and continuing to be involved with in-service education and training (INSET) of one kind or another. The heads valued learning and showed an appreciation for new ideas, reflection and professional growth. Stated another way, these heads were receptive to fresh ways of thinking about teaching and learning.

The second attribute was *patience*. Although not necessarily personally patient these heads recognized that there was 'no end to development', as one head said, and that whole school curriculum development was a long haul. Thus the heads tended to be tenacious, assiduous and very persistent in striving to see their beliefs put into practice across the school. Third, they could synthesize and *link* ideas and information. In addition to seeing and knowing a great deal about what was happening around the school, they could make connections between individuals and see where support was needed. We likened this attribute to 'weaving', that is, the heads were like a running thread stitching together the individual parts of the school and making it cohere.

Reflections on these Findings for School Leaders and School Development

Research is valuable not only for what one finds but also for what it leads one to think about. Certainly these two projects have spurred me on in my thinking about leadership and in this section I shall outline five of my reflections.

Complexity

The first concerns the complexity of leadership. Leadership in action is more dynamic and complex than the analyses of it in the literature. Indeed, at present our understanding of leadership in school may be hidebound by the categories we use to understand leadership. While some categories have been useful it is also the case that they can be overly tidy and restrictive. For example, at present there is much interest in Burns's (1978) transactional and transformational categories (for example, Foster, 1986; Beare *et al.*, 1989; Leithwood and Jentzi, 1990). While these categories help us to classify heads as transactional or transformational, they do not capture the character and nature of leadership in action. They are too abstract and omit the vigorous quality of headteachers at work. Rather, researchers should seek more grounded interpretations of school leadership, so that they do not leave behind the very essences they are trying to portray.

There is another aspect to this issue of complexity. The PSSR project suggested that heads work on two levels; a high level of abstraction, where they are concerned with values and beliefs, and a more mundane level, where they are dealing with day-to-day tasks and system maintenance. The WSCD project broadly supports this view. The idea that heads work on an abstract level of beliefs and values and wish to shape the values of their colleagues suggests that they are transformational leaders. They are leaders with a vision and are able to project it in such a way that others become committed to it (Beare *et al.*, 1989: 114). The second, and seemingly mundane level, is that of the transactional leader who is fixing things, managing and coping in order to maintain the smooth operation of the organization. Time studies present this side of headship, showing heads dealing with crises, poorly-understood problems and dilemmas (Coulson, 1990: 103–4):

> During the working week the [four observed primary] heads undertook a multitude of activities . . . the level of work activity displayed an unrelenting pace throughout the day . . . characterised by brevity, variety and fragmentation.
>
> (Davies, 1987: 44)

This portrayal does not suggest that these heads were reflective, transformational leaders. Rather, they were chronically busy, reactive as against proactive, and caught up in, and tied down by the unceasing demands of others for their attention.

Now although we saw the heads in the projects' schools sometimes coping with a multitude of varied tasks, it is wrong to infer they were only transacting and not transforming. These categories are based on a false sense of separation. What we saw the heads doing was both simultaneously. The two need to go hand-in-hand since, as Duignan says:

> leadership is filtered, transacted and transformed through the myriad brief, fragmented, everyday routines or 'chores' that are part and parcel of complex organizational life. (1988: 3)

Expressed another way, the seemingly ordinary and 'little stuff' of management is the vehicle for the leader's messages. The interruptions, decisions on the run, and chance encounters in corridors are the media for the message. That they occur fleetingly only means that the messages of leadership are transmitted in micro-seconds, as well as in staff meetings. The transactions are particles of the transformations the leader seeks. Thus, transformational leadership is dependent upon transactional leadership. And one is not better than the other, rather the two are mutually dependent and complementary. Although some writers presently portray transformational leadership as a superior option (see Sergiovanni, 1990; Leithwood and Jentzi, 1990; Foster, 1991), I believe we need to see transformational leadership as mediated by transactional leadership.

This suggests that leadership is more complex, subtle and interactive than our analytical categories convey. Given our relatively meagre understanding of leadership, not only do we need more descriptions of leaders in action, we also need richer and detailed descriptions of them at work. What we need are more studies of the kind Hall *et al.* (1986) and her colleagues have undertaken of headteachers at work. We especially need them of primary heads in action since there is a paucity of material to work on. Such descriptions might then facilitate fine-grained interpretations of their leadership and what it means for their schools. PSSR and WSCD suggest that some primary heads are sophisticated leaders. Until we expand our knowledge of primary heads, our understanding of how they lead will remain simplistic and perhaps, superficial.

Geoff Southworth

Instrumental and Expressive Leadership

One of the WSCD project findings was that the heads were persistent and tenacious professionals. Indeed, they were determined individuals; passionate in their desire that the pupils for whom they were responsible did well. Like their teacher colleagues the heads wanted the very best for the children. The heads were unhappy about poor practice and, if necessary, could be blunt with those whom they regarded as performing below acceptable levels. We saw little of this but heard about it because stories of such behaviour by the heads were part of the schools' staffroom folklore. Yet these heads were also overwhelmingly considerate and caring leaders being sensitive to colleagues, kind and thoughtful.

In other words, these heads could be both tough and tender leaders. Their leadership was both instrumental and expressive (where 'instrumental' refers to task definition and accomplishment and 'expressive' encompasses the affective and pastoral aspects of interactions in the organization, see Etzioni, 1964; Nias, 1987). These heads did not hold a wholly instrumental view of their staff. An instrumental outlook is one which regards staff as subordinates, people to be directed and instructed and reduces persons to objects denying subjectivity and a sense of self. Instrumentality takes a functionalist approach, being preoccupied with goals and ends. It is driven by a bureaucratic-managerial rationale which sees leadership as essentially getting the employees to do what management wants them to do (Foster, 1989: 43). It is, according to some, the rationale which generally underpins school management theorizing (see Smyth, 1989).

By contrast, the project heads saw staff as persons in their own right, hence they were concerned to avoid trespassing upon their teachers' sense of individuality and autonomy. When the heads sought to balance the needs of individuals and their obligations to the group, the heads were sensitive towards teachers' sense of worth.

The mix of instrumental and expressive leadership means that, although concerned with the effectiveness of the school, these heads did not drive relentlessly towards it regardless of the human costs. They understood that schools are not machines but social systems. They tacitly recognized that management which adopts an unyielding approach and takes no account of human creativity is not only mechanical and inflexible but is also inappropriate for developing and improving schools.

The latter point is especially important. School improvement relies, in part, upon teachers learning from one another (Fullan *et al.*, 1990). Such learning is not always amenable to being programmed because it is not entirely predictable, as we saw during the WSCD project. Consequently, leaders need to be receptive to the learning needs of their colleagues, aware that learning is sometimes painful and alert to its erratic nature (Nias *et al.*, 1992: 240). Staff need to develop in an atmosphere which is supportive since without it some teachers may not learn at all.

Expressive leadership is not soft-centred or inefficient. It is a necessary part of creating a collaborative culture in which teachers and leaders can learn with and from one another. Unless leadership has an expressive dimension schools may not become communities of adult learners and so may not improve at all.

The Pace of School Development

These heads were committed to improving their schools. Yet they understood that this was a time-consuming business. It also required their personal attention because they understood that change relies primarily upon personal contact (Fullan, 1991: 132) because change is essentially concerned with altering colleagues' subjective realities (pp. 34–6).

The heads regarded change as a slow process. They spoke of edging forwards and making gradual progress (Nias *et al.*, 1992: 108–11). However, this should not be interpreted as meaning the heads were leisurely in the quest for improvement. Quite the reverse, these heads were intensely active for two reasons. First, they all had much to do. The tasks of managing a school or teaching a class are full time and demanding. No one was ever at a loss for something to attend to. Indeed, quite the reverse. They saw no end to their work and even when exhausted felt there was something else they should be getting on with.

Second, because school, teacher and curriculum development are interrelated (Nias *et al.*, 1992: 151–97) improvement rests upon moving forward on a broad rather than narrow front (Holly and Southworth, 1989). School development requires that: policies be discussed and agreed; implementation plans be produced and resourced; INSET opportunities be integrated with the plans; school and classroom organizational arrangements be reviewed and adjustments made; parents and governors be informed and involved; pupils' views and reactions be noted and monitored; unexpected developments and mandates be dealt with; allowances be made for personnel changes; the emotional reactions to the change and the change process be dealt with; and the whole enterprise be kept under review and the validity of the original plan considered from time to time.

Moreover, within and across each and all of these activities there are likely to be interpersonal differences, personal doubts and resourcing difficulties which all need to be resolved. In other words, everyone needs to understand what Fullan (1991: 4–5) calls the small and the big picture of change. Everyone needs to attend to and learn about the *what* and the *how* of change (Nias *et al.*, 1992: 168–76). At the same time, heads need to deal with any arising interpersonal differences and any organizational difficulties.

It is not surprising, then, that heads are very busy dealing with all these tasks. Heads are actively engaged on a broad range of issues. Moreover, because the relationship of many of these tasks is lateral, that is, they need to be done at the same time and alongside one another, heads and their colleagues are busy across a broad front. Yet while there is much industrious activity laterally, the apparent forward progress may be relatively small. The relationship of gains in improvement to energy expended may be disproportionately small.

If this is true it means that the charismatic and innovative leader is not necessarily the person who will move the school and develop its culture (Fullan and Hargreaves, 1992: 69). Leaders need to be hard-working, painstaking and dogged as well as subtle and sophisticated. Importantly, change needs to be understood not as a Damascus Road but as an endurance race. Leading and managing school development is a marathon not a sprint.

Headteacher Motivation

Given that headship is hard work, demanding and unrelenting, one needs to ask what motivated these heads to work as hard as they did? In truth we lack any definitive answer to this question since there are no studies of headteacher motivation. Nor have we examined headteachers' feelings of work success and job satisfaction. While Lortie (1975) has advanced the notion of 'psychic rewards' for teachers (p. 101), and to the extent that heads regard themselves as teachers this is also likely to relate to headteachers' work rewards, there has been no comparable study in this country of primary headteachers' notions of occupational success.

Anecdotal evidence, derived from working with heads at the Cambridge University Institute of Education and elsewhere, suggests that what motivates them is their belief that they can make a difference to the schools they lead. They see themselves as having a contribution to make to *their* school. As Coulson (1980: 275–6) suggests, this tends to mean that heads believe they should set the philosophy for the school. Like the elementary principal in the study of Smith *et al.* primary heads regard themselves as 'true believers' (1985: 116–42) holding 'strong but not dogmatic views regarding the way children learn' (p. 121), and it is the heads' wish to see their beliefs put into practice which accounts for why they work so long and hard — 'beyond the call of duty' as Smith *et al.* claim (p. 127).

Further support for this claim comes from Mortimore and Mortimore (1991). From the personal reports of seven headteachers Mortimore and Mortimore draw together a number of common themes, one of which is the heads' educational philosophies:

> The seven heads have been guided, to a greater or lesser extent, by what they hold to be their philosophies shaped over many years and by a number of influences . . . The importance of having a personal philosophy cannot be overstated.
>
> (Mortimore and Mortimore, 1991: 123–4)

Another theme is 'the sustaining power of the feeling that, as a head, they can achieve change: they can get things done' (p. 130). In other words, what appears to motivate heads is their wish to pursue their educational visions.

Now this insight has particular significance because of contemporary developments in education. Given the recent changes in schools in England and Wales, will heads continue to feel they can pursue their individual educational visions? The imposition of a National Curriculum, as some heads see it (Sedgwick, 1989; Stone, 1989), coupled with the need to be more responsive to the wishes of governors and parents, may have the effect of reducing headteachers' feelings of autonomy, and individuality. Indeed, where the heads regard the developments as antithetical to their educational beliefs these heads may find it difficult to wholeheartedly manage the developments. Perhaps, then, this interpretation of what motivates heads leads on to another question: can visionary leaders implement the wishes of others? Mortimore and Mortimore (1991) regard heads' philosophies as offering a raft of support when their schools are subjected to orchestrated changes (p. 124); maybe they are right. More than anything, we need to investigate this whole issue to find out what a larger sample of heads believe motivates them, what gives them a sense of success and how they are approaching and managing the implementation of the National Curriculum, local management of schools, and other initiatives in their schools.

Vision, Ownership and Community

If it is true that heads are motivated to work hard because their leadership is a pursuit of their individual visions, it means that heads are the owners of the vision and teachers are not. This suggests that teachers' educational beliefs are not as important as those of their heads. It also suggests that teachers are expected to be less assertive about their beliefs and compliant to the wishes of their leaders: only heads are 'prescient enough to guide us' (Foster, 1989: 39).

The idea that heads are the owners of the schools' visions has implications for the meaning of collaboration. Where heads hold the vision and encourage teacher collaboration the head, tacitly or otherwise, may only be developing teacher interaction as a vehicle for the implementation of his or her wishes. Not only were there traces of such an arrangement in the project schools, but it also has wider support. For example, within the effective schools movement there is advocacy of strong, visionary leadership (Angus, 1989: 65). Moreover:

> Shrewd leaders are expected to manipulate people and situations so that the leader's vision is willingly shared by followers in schools; teachers in schools will work earnestly and purposefully to do well that which the leader of vision wants them to do.
>
> (Angus, 1989: 67)

Such an outlook sustains a managerial model of leadership since it assumes teachers are followers and treats them as workers and subordinates and not as professionals and colleagues (see Codd, 1989: 159).

The idea that schools must be led and directed by heads who are strong, potent figures in their schools and who control much that happens in the organization, has been roundly condemned, particularly by critical theorists (see Bates, 1983; Smyth, 1989). Yet the two projects reviewed here suggest that the managerial model of leadership continues to work in schools. For example, we noted in PSSR how the heads were the owners of the schools (Nias *at al.*, 1989: 99). In WSCD we said the heads were central, powerful figures who exercised a controlling influence upon the school and its development (Nias *et al.*, 1992: 247). Although both projects showed that primary heads can be visionaries, at the same time, they also showed that the heads tended to create the conditions for teachers to be dependent upon them. As such their leadership may be 'effective' in an instrumental sense but it is ethically questionable since it overrides teachers' professionality.

Alexander (1984: 207) argues that 'managerialism' sustains the unquestioned power of the head, maintains top-down control and assumes an 'employee' view of the teacher. Such a model circumscribes staff discussion and debate, severely inhibits intellectual autonomy in questioning, or scepticism towards authority, and denies teachers' professional status (pp. 168–205). More recently, Rivzi (1989, in Smyth, 1989) has argued that an instrumental view of leadership is injurious to more broadly-based participation in educational decision-making and thus democracy (p. 206). Although others (Coulson, 1980; Campbell, 1985; Southworth, 1987) have touched upon these issues with reference to primary schools, they remain in need of further and fuller analysis. We may have discovered some seemingly effective ways of developing schools, but are they ethically just ways in terms of treating teachers as professional colleagues?

So saying, let me make it clear that I am not personally accusing these heads of being unjust. Indeed, I overstate the position to develop a more general case. Rather, I regard them as caught up in a pervasive web of assumptions about organizations and leadership which underwrites a managerial outlook. Our society favours efficiency and the right of management to manage before workplace democracy. Also, educational management reflects these assumptions by generally facilitating the control of organizations (Bates, 1989: 135).

Moreover, these heads were themselves individually caught up in the managerial web of ideas because they had never been offered a substantial opportunity to critically reflect upon their own assumptions about leadership. It is a feature of promotion in primary schools in this country, as compared to, say, the USA, that an individual is not prepared for headship in any formal sense. There are few opportunities for deputies and heads to examine over-time and in a planned way, alternative approaches to headship and different conceptions of leadership and power in organizations. Equally, there are few opportunities for individuals to formally review how she or he is actually leading the school. While headteacher appraisal offers some hope in this direction, without awareness of alternative approaches, the process may prove to be inherently conservative. Heads, deputies and others need to reflect upon alternatives to the orthodoxies of school leadership.

In seeking alternatives these heads and others might consider choosing between schools-as-organizations and schools-as-communities. This idea comes from Sergiovanni who sees the two in this way:

> Organizations use rules and regulations, monitoring and supervising, and evaluation systems to maintain control over teachers. Leadership in organizations, then, is inevitably control driven.
>
> In this system, principals and supervisors, by virtue of their rank, are presumed to know more than teachers . . . Command and instructional leadership as they are now understood in schools are products of this logic. All this would change if community became the metaphor for schools. Communities are not defined by instrumental purposes, rationally conceived work systems, evaluation schemes designed to monitor compliance, or skilfully contrived positive interpersonal climates. Communities are defined by their centres . . . They answer questions like, What is this school about? What is our image of learners? How do we work together as colleagues?
>
> (Sergiovanni, 1992: 41)

Sergiovanni suggests that communities unite around a common set of *shared* values. These values create the community's vision and enable everyone to follow the vision rather than a person (p. 42).

At the risk of oversimplifying, the project heads appear, in Sergiovanni's terms, to be regarding their schools as both communities and organizations. While on the one hand, they believe in shared goals, consideration for others, and professional collaboration, on the other hand they continue, albeit in a muted form to direct and control teachers. Furthermore, while the two types of institution co-exist, they may not be equal. The latter overrides and inhibits the former because the heads are predominant. Subtle, sensitive and sophisticated leaders they may be, but they were also sovereign in their individual schools. Yet it is also possible to regard these schools as travelling on a journey away from *organization* and towards *community*. For one thing these heads were not autocrats, ruling by dictat. Differences were sometimes openly voiced. Also, they had 'left behind' a wholly instrumental view of individuals and embraced an expressive one. Moreover, the journey towards community will take time. As Fullan and Hargreaves (1992: 77) say, building collaborative cultures involves a long developmental journey.

One step on the way might be what Hargreaves (1991) has called contrived collegiality, which can be a preliminary phase in setting up more enduring collaborative relationships between teachers. Indeed, some contrivance is virtually essential (Fullan and Hargreaves, 1992: 78); whole staff collaboration is unlikely to occur by spontaneous combustion. Yet although heads may be the prime movers of staff collaboration, they should avoid over-managing collegiality (p. 81). Possibly this is the point reached in some of the project schools.

It is, however, a crucial and difficult point, for now the staff, and especially their headteachers, need to rethink leadership. In order to develop healthy communities these and other heads will have to recognize they must relinquish strong leadership. Although these heads may have brought the schools some way towards becoming communities, so long as the process of development remains dependent upon the head, the destination can never be reached. Achieving a sense of community rests upon empowered teachers and for this to be brought about the status of the head needs to alter (see Jenkins, 1991: 48) and so too the teachers. All staff need to become leaders and visionaries. This will mean an end to deference towards and dependence upon the head.

This will not be easy for heads. It means heads must recognize their reluctance to give staff power (Jenkins, 1991: 54). Yet, from what we know about managing and implementing change, teacher empowerment is necessary (Fullan, 1992: 41). If we want schools to be just, participative and productive communities rather than organizations where there is a lack of equity and much rests on the wisdom and competence of a single person — the head — empowerment becomes essential. Indeed, teacher empowerment is both efficacious and ethical.

Conclusion

Clearly there is much more to explore here. A crop of concepts have been raised each of which requires a more thorough exegesis. Yet, perhaps, for too long primary school leadership has been discussed on the basis of a limited knowledge base and conceptualized from within a single, bureaucratic paradigm. The time may now be opportune for a radical revision to our thinking about leadership. As a contribution to that review process I suggest:

1 We need more detailed, close-up studies of heads in action to show the complexity of their work in greater relief. We also need to investigate what motivates heads and where they find job satisfaction.
2 Heads need to think about being both (a) transformational and transactional leaders and (b) instrumental and expressive leaders.
3 Heads must recognize that school development involves slow forward progress despite considerable industry across the school. Developing a school requires subtlety, tenacity and persistence.
4 Visionary leadership can be synonymous with powerful and controlling headship, which, in turn, means teachers are only ciphers for their heads' wishes. Heads need to reflect upon: alternative approaches

to leadership; whether staff follow a collective vision or a person; whether the school is an organization or a community; and whether as heads they can let go of their power and empower staff.

Leadership is a key factor in developing schools and managing change. As leaders in school cope with all the educational and organizational changes which recent legislation has created, they may also need to contemplate changing the way they lead.

References

ALEXANDER, R. (1984) *Primary Teaching*, London, Holt, Rinehart and Winston.

ANGUS, L. (1989) '"New" leadership and the possibility of educational reform', in SMYTH, J. (Ed) *Critical Perspectives on Educational Leadership*, London, Falmer Press, pp. 63–92,

BALL, S. (1987) *The Micro-politics of the School*, London, Methuen.

BATES, R.J. (1983) *Educational Administration as a Technology of Control*, Geelong, Deakin University Press.

BATES, R.J. (1989) 'Leadership and the rationalization of society', in SMYTH, J. (Ed) *Critical Perspectives on Educational Leadership*, London, Falmer Press, pp. 131–56.

BEARE, H., CALDWELL, B.J. and MILLIKAN, R.H. (1989) *Creating an Excellent School*, London, Routledge.

BURNS, J.M. (1978) *Leadership*, New York, Harper and Row.

CAMPBELL, J. (1985) *Developing the Primary School Curriculum*, London, Holt, Rinehart & Winston.

CODD, J. (1989) 'Educational leadership as reflective action', in SMYTH, J. (Ed) *Critical Perspectives on Educational Leadership*, London, Falmer Press, pp. 157–78.

COULSON, A.A. (1980) 'The role of the primary head', in BUSH, T. GLATTER, R. GOODEY, J. and RICHES, C. (Eds) *Approaches to School Management*, London, Harper and Row, pp. 274–92.

COULSON, A.A. (1986) *The Managerial Work of Primary School Headteachers*, Sheffield Papers in Education Management No. 48, Sheffied City Polytechnic.

COULSON, A.A. (1990) 'Primary school headship: A review of research', in SARAN R. and TRAFFORD, V. (Eds) *Research in Education Management and Policy: Retrospect and Prospect*, London, Falmer Press.

DAVIES, L. (1987) 'The role of the primary school head', *Educational Management and Administration*, **15**, 1, pp. 43–7.

DUIGNAN, P.A. (1988) 'Reflective management: The key to quality leadership', *International Journal of Education Management*, **2**, 2, pp. 3–12.

ETZIONI, A. (1964) *Modern Organizations*, Englewood Cliffs, NJ, Prentice Hall.

FOSTER, W. (1986) *Paradigms and Promises: New Approaches to Educational Administration*, New York, Prometheus Books.

FOSTER, W. (1989) 'Towards a critical practice of leadership', in SMYTH, J. (Ed) *Critical Perspectives on Educational Leadership*, London, Falmer Press, pp. 39–62.

FOSTER, W. (1991) 'Moral theory, transformation and leadership in school settings', paper presented at *American Educational Research Association* annual conference, Chicago.

FULLAN, M. (1991) *The New Meaning of Educational Change*, London, Cassell.

FULLAN, M. and HARGREAVES, A. (1992) *What's Worth Fighting for in Your School?*, Milton Keynes, Open University Press.

FULLAN, M., ROLHEISER-BENNETT, C. and BENNETT, B. (1990) 'Linking classroom and school improvement', *Educational Leadership*, **47**, 8, pp. 13–19.

HALL, V., MACKAY, H. and MORGAN, C. (1986) *Headteachers At Work*, Milton Keynes, Open University Press.

HARGREAVES, A. (1991) 'Contrived collegiality', in BLASE, J. (Ed) *The Politics of School Life*, San Francisco, CA, Sage.

HOLLY, P. and SOUTHWORTH, G. (1989) *The Developing School*, London, Falmer Press.

JENKINS, H. (1991) *Getting It Right: A Handbook for Successful School Leadership*, Oxford, Blackwell.

LEITHWOOD, K. and JENTZI, D. (1990) 'Transformational leadership: How principals can help reform school cultures', paper presented at the *Annual Meeting of the Canadian Association for Curriculum Studies*.

LORTIE, D. (1975) *Schoolteacher: A Sociological Study*, Chicago, IL, University of Chicago Press.

MORTIMORE, P. and MORTIMORE, J. (1991) *The Primary Head: Role Responsibilities and Reflections*, London, Paul Chapman.

NIAS, J. (1987) 'One finger, one thumb: A case study of the deputy head's part in the leadership of a nursery/infant school', in SOUTHWORTH, G.W. (Ed) *Readings in Primary School Management*, London, Falmer Press, pp. 30–53.

NIAS, J., SOUTHWORTH, G. and CAMPBELL, P. (1992) *Whole School Curriculum Development in the Primary School*, London, Falmer Press.

NIAS, J., SOUTHWORTH, G. and YEOMANS, R. (1989) *Staff Relationships in the Primary School*, London, Cassell.

PETERS, T. and WATERMAN, R. (1982) *In Search of Excellence*, London, Harper and Row.

SCHEIN, E. (1985) *Organizational Culture and Leadership*, San Francisco, CA, Jossey-Bass.

SEDGWICK, F. (1989) *Here Comes the Assembly Man: A Year in the Life of a Primary School*, London, Falmer Press.

SERGIOVANNI, T. (1990) 'Adding value to leadership gets extraordinary results', *Educational Leadership*, May, pp. 23–7.

SERGIOVANNI, T. (1992) 'Why we should seek substitutes for leadership', *Educational Leadership*, **49**, 5, pp. 41–5.

SMITH, L., KLEINE, P., PRUNTY, J. and DWYER, D. (1985) *Educational Innovators: Then and Now*, London, Falmer Press.

SMYTH, J. (Ed) (1989) *Critical Perspectives on Educational Leadership*, London, Falmer Press.

SOUTHWORTH, G. (1987) 'Primary school headteachers and collegiality', in SOUTHWORTH, G. (Ed) *Readings in Primary School Management*, London, Falmer Press, pp. 61–75.

STONE, C. (1989) 'All that remains is ambivalence: A headteacher's reflections', *Education 3–13*, **17**, 3, pp. 4–9.

Chapter 2

Headteachers and Deputy Heads: Partners and Cultural Leaders

Geoff Southworth

Introduction

Since the late 1970s there has been a strong interest in effective schools. Researchers, HM Inspectors, LEA staff and heads and teachers have become increasingly interested in the trying to identify the characteristics which account for some schools being more effective than others. There is now a large literature which reports upon and discusses the implications of this research (see Reid *et al.*, 1987; Mortimore *et al.*, 1988; Ainscow, 1991; Reynolds and Cuttance, 1992). While the studies have generated much debate and a range of interesting findings, they have also highlighted two common themes which are central to this chapter: *leadership* and *collaboration*.

Almost without exception school effectiveness studies show that the leadership which occurs in some schools contributes positively to the effectiveness of the school (see Southworth, 1990). In certain cases the leadership of the headteacher is singled out for attention, while in some other studies the leadership roles of other staff are emphasized along with the head. Undoubtedly, the studies have been instrumental in establishing the now widely held belief that school leaders, especially headteachers, can and do make a difference to the effectiveness of the school (Southworth, 1990).

At the same time a number of studies, along with the work of HM Inspectors, have drawn attention to the importance of the staffs' capacity to work together. Teachers, more than ever before, are being urged to work together. Teamwork is now regarded by many teachers, heads, inspectors and advisers as the way to build a healthy school. Indeed, the image of a modern primary school is traced by a number of key words which teachers, heads, researchers and others use in a seemingly taken-for-granted way. These words are: co-operation, communication, continuity, co-ordination, collaboration, consistency, coherence and collegiality. For example, teachers need to co-operate to share resources. They must also communicate with one another to ensure that the curriculum is continuous and their teaching plans and projects co-ordinated. Such teacher collaboration is assumed to help create a more coherent curriculum for the pupils and will, at the same time, foster among staff a sense of collegiality. Moreover, as some now argue, in management terms we may be moving from a time when we thought of schools as organizations, to a time when we think of them as *communities* (Sergiovanni, 1992; Southworth, 1993).

While many of these terms have been around for some time (see Blyth and Derricott, 1977; Coulson, 1976), they nevertheless serve to show that amongst all the changes with which staff in schools are presently dealing, there is also a long term and pervasive shift taking place in the nature of teaching. I believe that over the last twenty years or so, teaching has gradually changed from being thought of as an autonomous activity, to being understood as a more *interdependent* enterprise. The professional norm of teacher autonomy has been supplanted by a belief in teacher collaboration (see Fullan and Hargreaves, 1992).

This shift in occupational norms has not only been gradual, it has also been uneven, erratic and non-linear. In some schools there is already a tradition of staff working together (see Nias *et al.*, 1989). Yet, in others, staff remain fastened to working in relative isolation and find collaboration uncomfortable. Furthermore, in some schools, there is evidence that previously established patterns of working together have not survived changes in staff. As the Whole School Curriculum Development (WSCD) project shows, teacher collaboration is a fragile exercise and once established it continues to need nurturing, otherwise collaboration can halt and teachers can retreat to their classrooms (Nias *et al.*, 1992).

For sure, collaboration, even with dynamic leadership, is not always easy to accomplish. Yet, we now find evidence of primary school staffs being described as 'combined teaching units' (HMI, 1987). In a sense, the effective schools research, along with the findings of school improvers (Fullan, 1991; Hopkins *et al.*, 1994) and HM Inspectors, suggests that the quality of primary schooling now rests not only on the efforts of individual class teachers, but also on the quality of the ways in which they combine their respective expertise and interests so that they complement one another and supplement their individual weaknesses. Without doubt, one of the attainment targets heads and deputies are working towards in the 1990s is that of teacher collaboration. School leaders must strive for staff to work together.

I have emphasized leadership and collaboration because they are central to an understanding of how heads and deputies might work together. In a sense, the drift away from teacher independence and towards professional interdependence finds its parallel in the ways heads and deputies regard their ways of working together. In the past, particularly the 1970s and 1980s, it was common to hear deputies describing their role as that of a 'go-between'. They saw themselves as providing a link between the head and the staff, and regarded themselves as having a foot in both camps. However, as an ILEA (1985) report noted, this gave deputy headship a 'Janus-like quality', by which the author meant that deputies had to be able to look two ways at once, or, perhaps, be two-faced about their workplace relationships!

Such a role convention arose, perhaps, because heads during that time were themselves rather remote and independent figures in the school. The go-between role assumes that heads are somewhat distant from the staff; not a member of staff, but a leader over them. As heads have become more consultative (Lloyd, 1985) and become more active members of the staff group (Nias *et al.*, 1989), then the notion of heads and deputies working in partnership has taken over from the go-between arrangement. In other words, the drift from teacher independence to interdependence has been mirrored by a change in deputies seeing their work as a go-between to now regarding their work as a partnership with the head.

In this chapter I will examine the idea of partnership. In the next section I will look at two studies which have highlighted, and, to some extent, examined the idea of partnership. In the third section I will go on to review the more recent literature concerned with heads and deputies. This review is necessary because the earlier work in section two may have become dated with the advent of the 1988 Education Act and other developments in the 1990s. I shall follow up this review with a fourth section which synthesizes some of the ideas emerging from the literature. I will also argue that we need to take account of certain recent insights from school improvement studies. These have important implications for how heads and deputies might proceed and I will offer a prescription for their partnership.

Two Studies of Partnership

The idea of heads and deputies working as partners has not been thoroughly investigated by researchers. Indeed, the work of the primary deputy is relatively under-researched. At best, we have some comments about deputies, but very few school-based enquiries which show us what deputies actually do and why.

In this section I will look at two studies which have focused on deputy heads in action. The first study is Mortimore *et al*'s (1988) work on effective junior schools and departments in London. The second is Nias' (1987) ethnographic study of a single deputy head. Mortimore and his colleagues identified twelve characteristics which they associated as contributing to a school's effectiveness. In terms of this chapter the first two characteristics are the most pertinent. The first was 'purposeful leadership of the staff by the head'. Such leadership occurred where the head understood the needs of the school, was actively involved in the school's work and did not exercise too much control over the staff:

> In effective schools, headteachers were involved in curriculum discussions and influenced the content of guidelines drawn up in the school, without taking complete control. They also influenced the teaching strategies of teachers, but only selectively, where they judged it

necessary. This leadership was demonstrated by an emphasis on the monitoring of pupils' progress, through teachers keeping individual records.

(Mortimore, *et al.*, 1988: 250)

These heads also knew what went on in classrooms, were concerned about the progress of individual pupils and encouraged staff to attend INSET activities which were relevant to the needs of the school (p. 251).

While there is a lot in Mortimore's work which demands close attention, with reference to heads I think the study's findings suggest two general points. First, heads need to know what is happening in the school in terms of teaching and learning. In a sense, Mortimore's study demonstrates that primary heads need to be aware of what teachers and children are doing. Second, in monitoring the quality of teaching and learning, heads should not become meddlesome or dominating. They should be supportive of staff, selective as to when and how they should intervene, and trust teachers as professionals. In short, heads should offer direction, but also recognize that teachers are colleagues who need support.

The second characteristic of effective schools noted by Mortimore *et al.* was 'the involvement of the deputy head':

> Our findings indicate that the deputy head can have a major role to play in promoting the effectiveness of junior schools. Where the deputy was frequently absent, or absent for a prolonged period [due to illness, attendance on long courses or other commitments], this was detrimental to the pupils' progress and development. Moreover, a change of deputy head tended to have negative effects. The responsibilities undertaken by deputy heads also seemed to be significant. Where the head generally involved the deputy in policy decisions, it was beneficial to the pupils. This was particularly true in terms of allocating pupils to classes. Thus it appears that a certain amount of delegation by the head and a sharing of responsibility, promoted effectiveness.
>
> (Mortimore *et al.*, 1988: 251)

Clearly, there is much here to discuss about delegation and shared responsibility, but given the confines of this chapter, I will concentrate upon just four points.

First, the finding that the involvement of the deputy head is advantageous to the effectiveness of the school is an especially valuable one for the continuation of the position of deputy head. Until Mortimore *et al.*'s study was published there was no research evidence to justify the position of deputy. In fact, in the early 1980s the view had been expressed that primary deputy headship was a 'position without a role' (Bush, 1981: 83). Bush, drawing upon the work of Coulson (1974), argued that because primary heads tended to monopolize responsibility, their deputies were left with very little to do (other than class teaching, which the majority of deputies continue to do as well as try to undertake their managerial duties). All that deputies did, which was noticeably different from other teachers, was cover for the head in her/his absence and undertake some administrative tasks on behalf of the head. Instrumental leadership, such as curriculum development, school improvement, was not a significant part of the role of the deputy. Overall, this pattern meant 'little room was left for the development of a distinct rationale for deputy headship' (Bush, 1981: 84). Consequently 'The position of deputy head in primary schools has little substance or meaning' (Bush, 1981: 84). This interpretation of the role of the deputy is a damning one and no doubt caused some to question the need for deputy heads in primary schools. Bush himself argued that it made better sense to develop an organizational structure, in medium and larger schools, based upon department heads rather than continue with deputies (p. 84).

If the position of deputy was under question in the 1980s, it is possible to argue that, with the advent of local management of schools (LMS) the position may be under even greater threat in the 1990s. School governors and heads themselves may ask whether the role and performance of the deputy is worth the finance invested in the post. Deputies are paid the second highest salary in the school and when school budgets are tightly constrained, it is not too fanciful to predict hard questions being asked about the best salary structure and value-for-money. In short, heads and deputies need to able to justify the deputy head's position and role.

Given these threats to the position of deputy, Mortimore *et al*'s research offers an important counter to them. It shows that when heads do delegate and share responsibilities, the school as a whole benefits. Mortimore *et al*'s work provides strong evidence that the work of the deputy can make a difference. The study provides a justification for deputy heads.

Second, it is implicit to Mortimore *et al*'s findings that what influences the work of the deputy most is the attitude of the head to delegation and sharing. As others have noted (e.g. Coulson, 1974; Bush, 1981; Whitaker, 1983; Southworth, 1987; 1988; 1993), what deputies do is largely contingent upon what the head allows them to do. If deputies are to perform a role which has substance and meaning, then heads must be prepared to devolve some of their responsibilities and must delegate to their deputies.

Third, and following from the second point, since it has been shown that the involvement of the deputy makes a difference to pupils' progress, then the work of the deputy needs to be looked at very carefully. Although sharing out tasks between head and deputy makes sound managerial sense, Mortimore *et al*'s work suggests that the contribution of the deputy goes beyond making workloads tolerable for the head and meaningful for the deputy. According to Mortimore *et al*., the deputy's participation can actually enhance the development of the pupils. Such a finding surely moves the idea of delegation onto a different level. Involvement of the deputy becomes not so much a managerial matter, as a teaching and learning issue. Heads and deputies need to work together to make the school more effective and to enhance pupil progress. Delegation is therefore not an option for heads to adopt when they feel the deputy is ready for it. Rather, delegation is a professional obligation. Heads must share and involve the deputy; and deputies must recognize that by accepting the position they must take on the extra tasks and responsibilities. Neither player can treat these matters as options, they are professional necessities because they improve the quality of provision for the pupils.

Fourth, I find it intriguing that out of all the specific responsibilities deputies might undertake, Mortimore and his associates emphasized the deputy having a say in the allocation of teachers to classes. I suspect there are many stories connected with this observation. However, I think it signals that the deputy knows some things which the head may be unaware about teacher colleagues' preferences. In my experience, as a former head and deputy and now working with large numbers of deputies on school management courses, some members of staff will share confidences with the deputy and not the head (of course, the reverse is also true). This suggests that the 'go-between' aspect of the role continues even when the head and deputy are working in partnership. Yet, if my interpretation is accurate, it also suggests that when heads are making plans for the school, they will be wise to include the deputy because the deputy will be plugged into the micropolitics of the staff group. Deputies know some things heads do not. Working together will help them to use their shared knowledge to the benefit of the school.

The second study I want to discuss in this section is Nias' (1987) observational study of a head and deputy head at work in an infant and nursery school. In addition to providing much valuable detail Nias' account makes a series of important points. First, the study shows that while these two women worked closely together it was not a partnership of equals. The head was always the senior partner and the deputy deferred to the head. Second, a great deal of the deputy's work could be described as informal. She devoted a lot of time to, and placed great emphasis on, keeping open the informal communication channels in the school. She toured the school, listened to colleagues' concerns and provided a lot of pastoral care for the staff. Yet, although her work was largely informal, she was influential. She helped to keep staff morale high and her concern for others meant she was well liked and respected. Moreover, because of this and through her constant interaction with colleagues 'she was able to affect the way they thought and behaved, with consequent implications for school policy and the way it was carried out' (Nias, 1987: 50). The deputy also performed some formal tasks such as taking assembly, being responsible for a curriculum area and undertaking certain administrative duties. Yet these were relatively less prominent on a day-to-day basis than her informal activity. Third, the deputy essentially complemented the work of the head. The head was more of an instrumental leader, concerned with the management of teaching, curriculum and school development, and the deputy was more an expressive leader concerned with care and consideration for people (see Nias, 1987: 50–1).

In addition to these three points Nias' study also touches on another feature. From her case study it can be seen that this partnership was built upon two 'rules'. The first rule was that the school belonged to the head. It was quite clear from the deputy's testimony that she would not usurp the head. The deputy saw the school as belonging to the head and did not believe she should reduce the head's proprietal feelings for the school. The second rule was that the deputy should be loyal to the head and stemmed from a wish to avoid either of them being seen by parents or staff to be divided on matters of policy.

Nias' study raises three general issues for me. First, the deputy's lack of instrumental leadership is a concern. If deputies are to be deputy *headteachers* then they need to play a part in all aspects of school leadership. The partnership which had evolved, overtime, in Nias' case study may be too limited and narrow a view of deputy headship. Second, the 'rule' that the school belongs to the head casts the deputy in a supporting role. Consequently, the deputy can only act on behalf of the head. The deputy is but an agent of the head; the deputy is the head's deputy and not deputy head of the school. Such a role may be stifling for many deputies because they may be overly constrained by the head's preferences and wishes. For sure, the rule does not empower deputies. Third, I have suggested elsewhere (Southworth, 1987) that the idea of loyalty means that differences between heads and deputies are allowed to surface only in private. Deputies are therefore rarely seen to be questioning the head's ideas. Now this may help create a sense of unity, but it also means that there is little scope for the creative use of difference. Differences are kept out of view. In turn, other staff may implicitly follow this pattern thereby ensuring that professional differences of opinion and value are submerged. If this submergence becomes a norm, it could mean that the very differences between staff which are preventing the school from becoming more holistic are not being openly addressed, but kept hidden. The rule of loyalty may foster privacy and inhibition rather than openness.

Together, the Mortimore *et al.* and Nias' studies help to cast some light on the idea of partnership, yet neither offers a comprehensive review of the issues. Therefore, it is necessary to look at other commentaries on, and studies into, deputy headship. Moreover, Mortimore *et al.* and Nias' investigations were conducted before the 1988 Education Act; since then there have been so many changes in schools that account needs to be taken of more recent enquiries. In the next section I will review such work as has been undertaken in the 1990s.

Recent Investigations

In this section I will review six pieces of work which, in varying ways, examine the work of deputy heads. The first is Reay and Dennison's research into deputy heads' perceptions about their position with a particular emphasis upon the managerial partnership they might have formed with the head. Using a questionnaire approach the views of thirty deputies in one LEA were collected. The findings echo some of the points raised in the previous section. At least half the deputies who responded to the questionnaire felt they shared expressive and instrumental responsibilities with the head. Others saw deputy headship as an apprenticeship to headship, or thought deputies were subordinate to the head. Three-quarters of the respondents felt they worked in a team with the head, but many also felt the head was senior to them and that the team was not made up of equal members. When they were asked to comment on relations with staff, over half implicitly saw themselves as go-betweens (1990: 43).

In summarizing their findings Reay and Dennison say that the following represents an appropriate portrait of the deputies' work in their sample:

> The deputy is a teacher whose main function is to deputise for the head during any absence. The main duties are as go-between (keeping the head and staff informed of what the other side is thinking), as a counsellor of staff and as organiser doing those jobs no-one else thinks are part of their responsibilities. Only a minority seem accountable for major areas of school activity, and while a majority claim a working partnership with the head it is on the basis of the deputy as subordinate member.
>
> (Reay and Dennison, 1990: 44)

In the light of this view, Reay and Dennison go on to say that the emerging picture of the work of the deputy is of a person who is highly dependent on what the head allows (p. 45). Moreover, when heads see it as their job to personally involve themselves in all aspects of the school and to always give a lead, then 'there is little left for the deputy other than to deputise and do some administrative work' (p. 45). The conclusions drawn by these researchers are that the partnership of a head and deputy does not demonstrate interdependence, only subordination and that many deputies are denied 'a real job' (p. 46).

The second study to review is Pay's (1992) brief and personal account of what it is like to be a deputy head in the 1990s. This account is one of the few published pieces of writing by a deputy about deputy headship. One of the weaknesses in the existing literature is that very few deputies have been invited to write about their experience of the position. Pay begins her description of what it is like to be a deputy by saying it is hard to find some things a deputy does not do! (p. 6). Pay states that deputies need to be able to handle any crisis at the same time as teaching a class, managing meetings and communications with staff, playing a part in planning the school's curriculum and deputizing for the head (pp. 6–7). Such responsibilities mean that deputies need to be able to give a lead, be enthusiastic and listen to others' ideas. Pay also believes that, in the 1990s, the role of the deputy has altered. The advent of both the National Curriculum and LMS have had implications for deputies and heads. According to Pay: 'Headteachers have LMS to deal with, which appears to take an inordinate amount of their time and energy, leaving less time for curriculum leadership' (p. 8).

In turn, this has led to an increased role in planning and implementing the curriculum for deputies. Moreover, it is now deputies, rather than heads 'who truly know the difficulties surrounding these new initiatives and are thus better suited to providing the curriculum support and leadership all staff need at this demanding time' (pp. 8–9). While Pay acknowledges that this arrangement might be a temporary one, as heads became accustomed to LMS, nevertheless, it points to deputies beginning to play a more central role in managing the curriculum than hitherto.

A similar picture emerges from research undertaken by Purvis and Dennison (1993). This study sought to investigate in detail the extent to which the 1988 Education Reform Act had affected the position and responsibilities of deputy heads (Purvis and Dennison, 1993: 16). From the responses of just under half the deputies in a single LEA the following findings were identified. First, opportunities for many deputies to play a major part in instrumental leadership were curtailed because these deputies had fulltime teaching responsibilities (p. 16). Second, since 1988, deputies felt that the managerial burdens in school were rising and thus their overall workloads. Consequently, 'the vast majority of replies were from individuals who seemed to view themselves as busy people, in demand, with too much to do in too short a time' (p. 18). Third, over 75 per cent of the respondents felt they worked as a team with their headteacher (p. 19). Fourth, while busy and active, these deputies did not appear to have a clear rationale for their position. Fifth, the working patterns adopted by the head continued to provide a major feature influencing the constitution of the deputies work (p. 19).

Purvis and Dennison next go on to make an important point. Since many deputies teach a class, have little, or no, non-contact time and now find themselves having to deal with an increased workload, deputies have to come to terms with these constraints, as well as with what the head expects. Indeed:

> expectations hold the key; yet always two way — what the head expects of the deputy and also, equally important, what the deputy expects of the head. When a pair are clear about the nature of the commitment to one another, the basis for sound communication exists and there is a good chance that shared leadership can be offered to the rest of the school.
>
> (Purvis and Dennison, 1993: 20)

The new managerial demands upon primary schools in the 1990s make it imperative that heads and deputies work together. Yet, partnerships must be built upon an awareness of the constraints imposed upon teaching deputies. Furthermore, heads and deputies need to openly discuss their expectations of each other and frame their work accordingly.

The perspectives of both Pay and Purvis and Dennison are broadly supported by Webb's (1993) research. Webb has surveyed fifty schools across thirteen LEAs to examine the introduction of the National Curriculum in Key Stage 2. Her study has cast light not only on the implementation of the National Curriculum, but also on the work of heads, deputies and co-ordinators. Webb describes the heads as being caught up in greater administrative tasks and thus less involved than formerly in curriculum development. Many heads felt they were less knowledgeable about the curriculum orders than their teacher colleagues and also less experienced at teaching the National Curriculum. Heads were also concerned about the heavy demands placed upon teachers by the recent legislation and sought to protect staff from unnecessary pressures.

Turning to the data on deputies Webb says that most of her respondents were teaching deputies. They all fulfilled the deputy's 'traditional nuts and bolts jobs', such as organizing sports day, arranging school visits (p. 7). Many were also curriculum leaders, most for one or more subjects, some for all of Key Stage 2 or the whole school. All talked about the expansion in their workload since the implementation of the National Curriculum and identified three particular concerns as a result of this growth. First, the burden of work was making it difficult to maintain the quality of their teaching which they considered important for their self-image and in order to maintain credibility with the staff (p. 8). Second, 'classroom bound' deputies were finding it hard to keep up to date with developments. At best, heads were briefing deputies in snatched moments during the school day. Consequently, deputies felt they would find it 'extremely difficult to take over the running of the school' in the absence of the head (p. 8). Also, the deputies felt there were insufficient INSET opportunities for them. Third, the deputies saw themselves as assuming the role of assistant head rather than that of a go-between.

The idea of deputies becoming assistant heads is probably consistent with the notion of partnership. As such, Webb's research suggests that heads and deputies are trying to work together. However, they are being prevented from achieving the goal of shared leadership because of both the scale and pace of the changes faced by heads and deputies, and primary deputy heads' work conditions.

The fifth study to review is Bolam *et al*'s (1993) enquiry into effective management in schools. This cross phase study of self-selected schools was conducted on behalf of the DfE and all the national professional associations and the findings have been published in a major report. I shall draw upon just one section of the study, Part 3, which deals with leadership and management. Bolam and his colleagues, while acknowledging the major part heads play in the leadership of the school, also state that 'it is increasingly rare for heads to manage alone' (p. 37). Indeed, the researchers say that 'it quickly became apparent that many of the headteachers in the sample of schools were operating in close conjunction with one or several colleagues' (p. 37). This finding was as true for primary schools as for secondary. For example, Bolam *et al.*, felt there was 'clear evidence of a management team in five of the seven primary schools to which visits were made' (p. 38). The management team typically comprised the head, deputy and teachers with senior allowances.

The above finding was largely explained by Bolam and his associates as reflecting the increased complexity, scale and diversity of management tasks, 'which merited some form of collegial management' (p. 45). The researchers also noted how LMS had 'propelled' heads 'toward a role more akin to chief executive' (p. 45). In turn:

> The role of the deputy headteacher would appear to have been considerably enhanced, embracing both new areas of responsibility, greater overall responsibility and more autonomy. In particular, the headteacher's focus having become broader and longer term has led to the deputy headteacher assuming greater control of day-to-day matters within the school. This represents change of considerable magnitude in the primary sector in particular, where, historically, deputy headteachers all too often have remained under-extended in terms of managerial functioning.
>
> (Bolam *et al.*, 1993: 45)

Bolam's study confirms many of the above points from the other studies and points to some consistent themes.

Indeed, from these five studies it is possible to highlight five themes. The first is that of increased management tasks. The devolution of financial management to schools has expanded the amount of work to be done at the school level. In the short term, at least, heads are rather preoccupied with these new tasks and so are giving their deputies more to do. Second, deputies and heads are trying to work together, and the notion of partnership is now well established as an idea and principle. Third, while the notion of partnership now has currency, it is constrained by heads' attitudes, deputy heads' workplace conditions and limited INSET opportunities for deputies. Fourth, deputies are having to accept greater responsibilities in the school but this is impacting upon their teaching role and may be making them, in their own eyes, less effective classroom practitioners. Fifth, some deputies are now being described as assistant heads. Although such a title apparently signifies partnership, it might also mean something more specific than this. Indeed, this is where the sixth study by West (1992) has relevance.

West, building upon his experience and work with primary heads and deputies, has recently argued that the head–deputy relationship be conceptualized as a 'partnership model' (p. 35) with the deputy working as assistant head. West offers this idea in preference to two other ways of conceptualizing deputy headship; the deputy as head's deputy, and the deputy as prospective head. The former, while useful, meant that the deputy was cast in the role of 'commissioning agent' for the head (p. 36). The latter is a future-oriented role which tends to mean some deputies acquire 'information about headship rather than experience it' (p. 36). By contrast, the assistant head conceptualization recognizes that 'all deputy heads have careers, though not all are promoted and that some do not seek preferment' (p. 36).

West's formulation of assistant head has two strengths. First, he sees heads and deputies as needing to work closely together, while also having separate parts to play. Indeed, he sees headship as a professional partnership between head and deputy, rather than in terms of differentiated roles. Headship is a shared role to which both partners contribute. Second, and relatively absent in the discussion so far, West stresses the deputy's need for planned developmental opportunities (PDOs) to move the deputy beyond being a super-ordinate classteacher. Moreover, 'what is being worked towards is the extension of the management repertoires of head, deputy and others' (p. 49). In short, by developing the deputy, the head will also grow and benefit. One reason why this will happen is because West sees the head as a mentor for the deputy and, sometimes, the deputy will mentor the head (p. 52). By mentoring West means an intentional process which fosters the growth and development of another. It involves the sharing of experiential wisdom, guiding, supporting and challenging (pp. 52–3).

West also sees the head–deputy relationship as one which enables the sharing of 'the arts of headship' (p. 54). These arts centre upon two things:

- connoisseurship — knowing how to look, see and appreciate;
- the capacity to engage in educational criticism — the art of disclosing the qualities of education life in a language which is understandable to a range of different stakeholders (p. 54).

Clearly, West has in mind a much richer and dynamic partnership between head and deputy than much of the foregoing suggests. Indeed, this dynamism is made explicit in the following diagram (Figure 1). Essentially, West regards deputy headship as a major position in its own right. It is not merely a way-station to headship in another school. Nor is it only doing those jobs which the head wants the deputy to do. Instead, deputy headship is a *part of headship*. It is an active involvement with the head which enables the deputy to know what is happening in the school and to play a full part in the school when the head is both present and absent. Also, deputy headship means being provided with development opportunities. The head should act as a mentor to the deputy, while the deputy should also contribute to the head's continuing professional growth. West's work is both a useful synthesis of many of the ideas reviewed here and is a valuable extension to them.

What Else?

While West's work has helped to move forward our thinking about deputy headship, in this section I want to argue that we also need to consider deputy headship from another angle. So far all the thinking has emanated from an essentially managerial perspective, that is, deputy headship tends to be

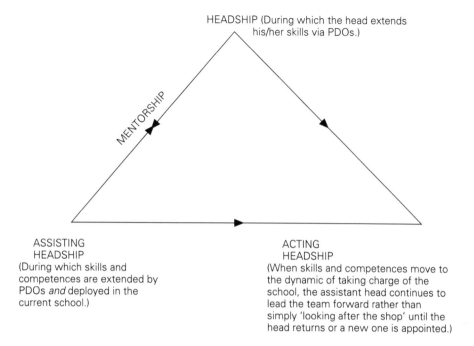

HEADSHIP (During which the head extends his/her skills via PDOs.)

MENTORSHIP

ASSISTING
HEADSHIP
(During which skills and
competences are extended by
PDOs *and* deployed in the
current school.)

ACTING
HEADSHIP
(When skills and competences move to
the dynamic of taking charge of the
school, the assistant head continues to
lead the team forward rather than
simply 'looking after the shop' until the
head returns or a new one is appointed.)

Figure 1:   The head–deputy triangle
Source: West, 1992: 55

conceptualized in terms of delegation, task sharing and how deputies can maintain the smooth running of the school. These are important matters, but they are not the whole picture. Indeed, I now want to argue that there is more to the work of heads and deputies than fulfilling managerial functions. I say this because in addition, we need to look at deputy headship from the perspective of school improvement. Deputy heads are not just managers, they are school developers. As such, we should try to see what contributions they might make to the growth of the school.

From the foregoing, it is clear that deputies can play a part in curriculum and staff development. Both types of development are significant to the improvement of the school. However, in this section I want to emphasize another area where the deputy, along with the head, can make an important, even vital, contribution. The area I have in mind is that of the school's organizational culture and I want to draw upon the work Jennifer Nias and I, along with others, have conducted into school cultures.

Over the last few years a number of studies have drawn attention to the importance of school culture, where culture is understood as 'the way we do things around here' (Nias *et al.*, 1989: 10), and is manifested in customs, ceremonies, rituals and patterns of interpersonal interaction. For example, Nias *et al.* (1989) showed that a collaborative culture in primary schools accounted for healthy and, often productive professional relations, while HM Inspectors have noted the benefits of staff working as a 'combined teaching unit' (HMI, 1987). As acknowledged in the introduction to this chapter, teamwork is now seen as the way to build an effective school and a collaborative culture can be a way of nurturing professional interdependence.

There are various types of school culture. Hargreaves (1991) has argued that there are two main types; independence and collaboration. The culture of independence is characterized by privatism, teacher isolation and professional loneliness. As suggested in the introduction to this chapter, this culture is now less common than formerly. By contrast, teachers are now more collaborative than, say, twenty years ago. However, 'the mere existence of collaboration should not be mistaken for a thoroughgoing culture of it. Some kinds of collaboration are best avoided. Others are wastes of time and limited in their impact' (Fullan and Hargreaves, 1991: 52). Fullan and Hargreaves go on to note three forms of collaboration of which we need to be watchful: balkanization, comfortable collaboration and contrived collegiality (p. 52).

Balkanization refers to a culture which is made up of separate and, perhaps, competing groups of teachers. These groups may be formally constituted, such as key stage one teachers versus key stage two teachers — the old infant and junior teacher rivalries which existed in some primary schools. Here the tensions arise from organizational structures. However, some other groups may be more informally arranged, such as a group of newcomers and a group of long established die-hards. Whichever way groups are formed and constituted, balkanization means that teachers attach their loyalties to the particular groups and not the school as a whole. Consequently, there is poor communication between the groups, indifference and petty squabbles. It becomes important in these schools to defend one's territory and status, hence there is much tension, micropolitical activity and conflict (see Fullan and Hargreaves, 1991: 52–3).

Comfortable collaboration is a relatively superficial form of teacher togetherness. It tends to allow for some professional interaction, but not much. As Fullan and Hargreaves say, such collaboration 'can stick with the more comfortable business of advice giving, trick-trading and material-sharing of a more immediate, specific and technical nature' (p. 55). Consequently, teachers do not share what they are doing in their respective classrooms, nor do they reflect upon their practice in groups or as a whole staff. Little, if any, time is devoted to sharing, exchanging, co-ordinating and questioning their classroom practices (p. 56). Exchanges remain at a more comfortable level. Therefore, while there is much social interaction, there is little professional discourse. The teachers get along together, they like and enjoy one another's company and there is likely to be a sense of comradeship, but there is a lack of enquiry and professional development. This type of collaboration is congenial and cosy (p. 57) and it may also be complacent.

Contrived collegiality occurs because collaborative cultures do not evolve quickly, as both Fullan and Hargreaves and our work at the University of

Cambridge Institute of Education (UCIE) shows (see Nias *et al.*, 1989; 1992). Consequently, senior staff, wanting to increase teacher collaboration, stimulate interaction through wholly formal organizational structures and strategies. Procedures are put in place to increase joint teacher planning, consultation, working parties and mentor schemes. These are essentially 'administrative contrivances designed to get collegiality going in schools where little has existed before' (Fullan and Hargreaves, 1991: 58). They are intended to nurture more sharing, closer associations between teachers and enhance peer learning and involvement.

While there is some sense in legislating for collaboration, it is best to regard contrived collegiality as a necessary and preliminary phase in setting up more durable and natural forms of collaboration. It helps to put teachers in touch with one another, but it also needs to be supported by other more informal patterns of interaction, which, hopefully, will develop from this early phase. However, contrived collegiality can be 'a quick, slick administrative surrogate for collaborative cultures' (p. 58). Moreover, staff can come to mistrust many of the strategies since they regard them as imposed and artificial. Where mistrust develops, contrived collegiality can inhibit and reduce teacher co-operation.

These concerns about some forms of collaboration should be taken as warnings rather than deterents. A culture of collaboration can take time to become established, may for a while become insular, and probably needs to be formally nurtured, but it is also worth working towards. I say this because a culture of collaboration creates a set of workplace conditions which aid school development (Nias *et al.*, 1992).

A culture of collaboration is based upon four interacting beliefs. First, that individuals should be accepted and valued. Individuals are to be welcomed and fostered for their own sakes, but also for the mutual enrichment which comes from diversity. Second, the groups of which these individuals are a part should also be fostered and valued. Interdependence is valued because it celebrates both the social group and the team which ensures the tasks are undertaken. Third, the most effective way of encouraging collaboration is to establish a sense of security amongst staff. Fourth, once there is some security amongst staff inter-professional openness will develop (see Nias *et al.*, 1989, Chapter 4). Collaborative cultures based upon these four beliefs give voice to the teacher's sense of purpose, make allowances for the teacher as a person, empower teachers and create communities of teachers where there is a sense of collective responsibility and enable professsional differences to be worked out from within the security of the staff group (see Fullan and Hargreaves, 1991: 50–1).

There are two other points to make. First, subsequent work at UCIE has gone on to show that another characteristic is needed alongside the collaborative culture, if schools are to develop. The additional factor is that of teachers learning. The Whole School Curriculum Development (WSCD) Project (Nias *et al.*, 1992) has demonstrated that the key ingredient for school development is teacher learning. The existence of a collaborative culture is a necessary condition for whole school curriculum development because it creates trust, security and openness. Yet these are not sufficient conditions for growth. For growth to occur teachers must be constantly learning. 'The challenge for staff in primary schools . . . is to establish a culture which facilitates teacher collaboration whilst, at the same time, enabling teachers to learn from each other and from courses outside the school' (Nias *et al.*, 1992: 247–8). Moreover, these findings are supported by Rosenholtz's (1989) work in the USA. Rosenholtz identified two opposing sets of workplace conditions in the schools she researched. In one group of schools, which she characterized as 'stuck schools', she found teachers predominantly believed that they did not need to continue their professional development. By contrast, in the schools she called 'moving schools' (i.e. developing schools), the teachers believed that there is always something else to know about the work. In the moving schools 'continuous self-renewal is defined, communicated and experienced as a taken-for-granted fact of everyday life' (Rosenholtz, 1989: 74). Teacher learning becomes part of the culture, and when it does, schools 'move' and improve.

The second point is that in both the collaborative culture research and the WSCD project the UCIE reseachers noted the central importance of the headteachers and the deputy heads to the establishment and maintenance of both the culture of collaboration and teacher learning. In other words, heads and deputies are pivotal players in the creation of the conditions and climates which are conducive to school development.

Indeed, I believe it is possible to draw parallels between the ways heads and deputies relate to one another and the cultures of the schools in which they work. I say this because I now believe that the ways in which heads and deputies work and relate to one another often symbolizes the school's organizational culture. Heads and deputies are tacit, or explicit role models for other staff. The partnership of the head and deputy is not simply about a well functioning pair of managers, it is also the active demonstration of how they expect other staff to behave with one another and whether staff can and should work together or not. Heads and deputies can help create a culture which makes it possible for other staff to collaborate.

Let me offer some examples. Where a head and deputy do not work together and no sense of partnership exists then they are demonstrating their independence of one another. Such a lack of partnership signifies that neither or both parties believes that collaboration is necessary or possible. Consequently, it may be very difficult for other staff to collaborate.

Where the head and deputy are in conflict they symbolize a balkanized culture. They show that professional and personal differences take precedence over their professional obligations. Although school effectiveness studies show that schools function better and pupil development is enhanced when heads and deputies work together, when they do not collaborate they are showing that they are not capable of submerging differences for the sake of the health of the school and the benefit of the pupils.

Those heads and deputies who relate well to one another, enjoy one another's company and spend time socializing, but little time working on classroom and curricular matters, are modelling comfortable collaboration. They are showing colleagues that it is pleasant to spend time together rather than necessary to be working together. They prefer congeniality to productive collaboration.

By contrast, those heads and deputies who work together, sharing tasks and discussing setbacks and successes, who look at pupils' learning and teachers' endeavours in classrooms and strive to lead curricular developments are positively indicating that staff need to collaborate. Moreover, where these heads and deputies develop a partnership approach to headship and mentoring is an active component of their relationship, then they are fostering the idea that staff need to keep on learning. Such a partnership with the twin components of collaboration and mutual learning, symbolizes a collaborative school culture which fosters school development and growth.

School culture is crucial to the school's development. School improvement is thwarted or enhanced by the absence or presence of particular forms of organizational culture. Heads and deputies play a central part in the creation of culture, and how they work and relate to each other has a direct bearing upon the nature of the school's climate and the ways in which other staff collaborate. The work of heads and deputies, and the ways they interact with one another, have wider and deeper implications for the growth and character of the schools they lead than might, at first sight, be appreciated. Partnership is not simply about sharing tasks, rather it is also implicated in the development of a collaborative culture which, in turn, enhances the school's capacity to improve.

Conclusions

Heads and deputies are important figures in the school. They make a difference to the effectiveness of the school, as does staff collaboration and teacher involvement. The ways in which heads and deputies work together contributes to the development of pupils, especially when the head delegates and provides the deputy with a role as well as a position. If shared leadership is so important that it enhances the achievements of the children, then the partnership between a head and deputy is a professional obligation and not an option or a matter of luck.

In the recent past, deputies were often given little instrumental responsibilities in contrast to their expressive leadership. In part this can be accounted for by a reluctance, on the part of heads, to delegate and lack of time for deputies to assume greater responsibilities around the school because many are full-time classteachers. Webb's (1993) and Bolam *et al*'s (1993) research, however, suggests that the work of deputies in the last few years is assuming more of an assistant head role. This new role configuration may not yet be applicable to all schools and appears to have developed because the introduction of the National Curriculum and the advent of LMS has increased the complexity, scale and diversity of management tasks.

The assistant head role is also advocated by West. He sees headship as a shared task to which both partners contribute. Also, the head should provide planned development opportunities for the deputy and both should mentor one another. Together they should monitor the work of the school and act as critical friends to each other and their teacher colleagues.

Although much of the thinking about heads and deputies is preoccupied with managerial concerns, West's work also helps to signal the importance of a school development perspective. Indeed, when the work of the head and deputy is considered from the school improvement angle, then their partnership takes on another complexion. Heads and deputies are key players in creating the school's culture, which, in turn, impedes or facilitates the growth of the school and its effectiveness. A productive partnership, along the lines mapped out by West and reinforced in this chapter, will help to establish and sustain a culture of collaboration in which professional learning occurs naturally. Heads and deputies who work together productively are a beacon for all staff. They model professional interdependence and growth. Their partnership lights the way for teamwork and staff development. And where the head and deputy demonstrate strong and persistent interest in teaching and learning, through their monitoring and support, they will be helping the school to move forward.

Heads and deputies are managers *and* school developers. Their partnership sets the tone and signposts the way for staff collaboration in which learning occurs and thus makes the institution a learning organization, a moving and improving school. Heads and deputies must work together, for we now have sufficient evidence to suggest that when they do, they increase the pupils' achievements, enable staff to develop and enhance the school's capacity to improve and become a learning community for both children and adults. The partnership of the head and deputy can create both the conditions and a culture which energizes the work of the school.

References

AINSCOW, M. (Ed) (1991), *Effective Schools for All*, London, Fulton.

BLYTH, A. and DERRICOTT, R. (1977) *The Social Significance of Middle Schools*, London, Batsford.

BOLAM, R., McMAHON, A., POCKLINGTON, K. and WEINDLING, D. (1993) *Effective Management in Schools*, London, HMSO.

BUSH, T. (1981) 'Key roles in school management', Part 3 in Policy-making organization and leadership in schools, Block 4, E323, *Management and the School*, Milton Keynes, Open University.

COULSON, A.A. (1974) 'The deputy head in the primary school: Role conceptions of heads and deputy heads', unpublished M.Ed., thesis, University of Hull.

COULSON, A.A. (1976) 'The role of the primary head', in BUSH, T., *et al.* (Eds) (1980) *Approaches to School Management*, London, Harper and Row, pp. 274–92.

FULLAN, M. (1991) *The New Meaning of Change* (2nd ed.) London, Cassell.

FULLAN, M. and HARGREAVES, A. (1992) *What's Worth Fighting for in Your School?*, Buckingham, Open University Press.

HARGREAVES, A. (1991) 'Continued collegiality' in BLASE, J. (Ed) *The Politics of Life in Schools*, San Francisco, CA, Sage.

HMI (1987) *Primary Schools: Some Aspects of Good Practice*, London, HMSO.

HOPKINS, D., AINSCOW, M. and WEST, M. (1994) *School Improvement in an Era of Change*, London, Cassell.

ILEA (1985) *Improving Primary Schools*, London, ILEA.

LLOYD, K. (1985) 'Management and leadership in the primary school', in HUGHES, M., RIBBINS, P. and THOMAS, H. (Eds) *Managing Education: The System and the Institution*, London, Holt, Rinehart and Winston.

MORTIMORE, P., SAMMONS, P., STOLL, L., LEWIS, D. and ECOB, R. (1988) *School Matters*, Wells, Open Books.

NIAS, J. (1987) 'One finger, one thumb: A case study of the deputy head's part in the leadership of a nursery/infant school', in SOUTHWORTH, G. (Ed) *Readings in Primary School Management*, London, Falmer Press.

NIAS, J. (1989) *Primary Teachers Talking*, London, Routledge.

NIAS, J., SOUTHWORTH, G.W. and YEOMANS, R. (1989) *Staff Relationships in the Primary School*, London, Cassell.

NIAS, J., SOUTHWORTH, G.W. and CAMPBELL, P. (1992) *Whole School Curriculum Development in Primary Schools*, London, Falmer Press.

PAY, F. (1992) 'Deputy Headship — 1990s style', *Primary File* No. 16, pp. 6–9.

PURVIS, J.R. and DENNISON, W.F. (1993) 'Primary school deputy headship: Has ERA and LMS changed the job?', *Education 3–13*, **21**, 2, pp. 15–21.

REID, K., HOPKINS, D. and HOLLY, P. (1987) *Towards The Effective School*, Oxford, Blackwell.

REAY, E. and DENNISON, W.F. (1990) 'Deputy headship in primary schools — is it a real job?', *Education 3–13*, **18**, 1, pp. 41–6.

REYNOLDS, D. and CUTTANCE, P. (1992) *School Effectiveness, Research, Policy and Practice*, London, Cassell.

ROSENHOLTZ, S. (1989) *Teachers' Workplace: The Social Organization of Schools*, New York, Longman.

SERGIOVANNI, T. (1992) 'Why we should seek substitutes for leadership', *Educational Leadership*, **49**, 5, pp. 41–5.

SOUTHWORTH, G.W. (1987) 'Primary school headteachers and collegiality' in SOUTHWORTH, G.W. (Ed) *Readings in Primary School Management*, Lewes, Falmer Press, pp. 61–75.

SOUTHWORTH, G.W. (1988) 'Looking at leadership: English primary school headteachers at work', *Education 3–13*, **16**, 2, pp. 53–6.

SOUTHWORTH, G.W. (1993), 'School leadership and school development: Reflections from research', *School Organisation*, **13**, 1, pp. 73–87. See also chapter 1 of this book.

WEST, N. (1992) *Primary Headship, Management and the Pursuit of Excellence*, Harlow, Longmans.

WEBB, R. (1993) 'Whole school planning: Roles and responsibilities', draft paper for BERA/ASPE Policy Task Group, York University mimeo.

WHITAKER, P. (1983) *The Primary Head*, London, Heinemann.

Chapter 3

Trading Places: Job Rotation in a Primary School

Geoff Southworth

Introduction

One of the main recommendations of the School Management Task Force (SMTF) (DES, 1990) was that management training and preparation should become more school-based. To achieve the objectives outlined in the SMTF report the authors set out a summary of the actions required at school level:

1 Prepare and publish a school management development policy incorporated within the school development plan, which recognizes that staff development is a major area of personal accountability for the head.
2 Establish appropriate management structures to reflect new tasks and responsibilities.
3 Provide adequate supervision and support for staff in their daily tasks.
4 Establish integrated procedures for the review and appraisal of individual, team and institutional performance.
5 Support each teacher in reviewing experience throughout their career.
6 Promote strategies for succession planning and career development providing:

- preparation for and induction to new posts;
- new task, job or project opportunities

(DES, 1990: 30)

These action points, like the report, were aimed at all schools irrespective of their size or phase. While some of these points can be undertaken by all schools, some pose particular challenges for primary schools. I can identify at least two.

First, primary heads traditionally lead their schools by example (Coulson, 1976; Southworth, 1987; Nias *et al.*, 1989, 1992). Indeed, leading by example is frequently a head's preferred strategy for influencing the curriculum (Beare *et al.*, 1989; Mortimore and Mortimore, 1991). However, many heads appointed to non-teaching headships before 1988, presently feel they lack first-hand, sustained teaching experience of the National Curriculum. Consequently, these heads feel disadvantaged in terms of supporting their teacher colleagues in their daily tasks (Laws and Dennison, 1991). Action point 3, therefore, asks many primary heads to do something they presently feel ill-equipped to perform.

Second, the advocacy of succession planning (Action point 6) is not something which primary heads may readily adopt. My work with large numbers of deputy heads indicates that custom and practice in primary schools leaves many of them ill-prepared for headship. Deputies are often inadequately trained by their heads and some are offered very few opportunities for professional development either inside or outside the school. Moreover, deputies are typically full-time class teachers and have no time during the school day to undertake managerial responsibilities. In other words, succession planning is a novel idea in primary schools.

Indeed, school-based management development for senior staff in primary schools is not very common in my experience. If this is true, then for many schools the thrust of the SMTF report will require staff in primary schools to change their ways otherwise the report will be a missed opportunity, or an irrelevance, or both.

Given these observations I was interested to learn that a head of a primary school in East Anglia was planning a job rotation for himself, the deputy and another senior teacher. When I was invited to act as an observer of the plan in action I was only too pleased to record some of the main issues and outcomes.

The Plan: Background and Rationale

In this section I will set out the plan and the reasons for it. I shall draw extensively upon the head's description of it in the school's management plan.

Hardwick school has approximately 300 children on roll taught by twelve teachers plus the head, Alan. The school is situated in a village not far from a large town which provides most of the employment for the parents of the pupils. Hardwick is a purpose built, community primary school.

Alan had been at the school for five years at the start of the project. He was aware that two key members of staff, the deputy Kathleen, and Suzy, a B allowance post holder, were interested in promotion and that this would most probably result in them leaving the school. The promotion of either or both teachers would be a great loss to the school for two reasons. First, two experienced and capable teachers would leave. Second, the teams of teachers they each led would be disrupted and the school's management structure weakened.

Yet Kathleen and Suzy had some reservations about leaving the school because both were happy there, and Alan believed that the school could benefit from starting a year with an unchanged staff, something which had never happened since he had been at the school. Also, after five years of headship he was feeling he should be moving onto another school.

> I have always believed that heads can build schools only to a certain height; they then need to move to another to build higher.
>
> (School Management Development Plan, 1991)

However, Alan was happy at the school and reluctant to leave. He believed if he was to stay at the school and 'build higher' he would need a new perspective. The following plan, therefore, was his attempt to reconcile each of these points for the good of the individuals, himself and the school as a whole.

The plan was that Kathleen become acting head for one school year. Suzy was to become acting deputy head, and Alan would become a class teacher. Alan believed Kathleen and Suzy would gain first-hand experience of the jobs to which they aspired. Also, Kathleen would be able to support the lower school team she normally led without being fully involved. Hence the team would have Kathleen on hand but would learn to work without her day-to-day example. Suzy would continue to be upper school team leader and deputy head, but would relinquish her responsibility for INSET. Alan would teach in Suzy's team, this being for him an 'in-school secondment' to the classroom. The advantages of this plan were:

- increased management experience for Kathleen and Suzy;
- an opportunity for Alan to:

    — teach the National Curriculum;
    — gain a different perspective on the school for future development;
    — work alongside less experienced staff;
    — look closely at early years education in the school;

- increase opportunities for other staff to take a lead (for example, in Kathleen's absence in the lower school team);
- unlike a normal secondment the staff group remains unchanged.

The possible disadvantages noted by Alan were:

- the scheme is so unusual there is no precedent by which to judge it;
- parents' reactions to the change are difficult to anticipate.

I learned all these points when I visited the school early in the spring term 1991. I also heard that Kathleen and Suzy were willing to participate and that the chair of governors was sympathetic to the scheme. However, the governors had not formally discussed the plan, nor had parents or all members of staff been informed of it. At a subsequent meeting with Alan I was invited and agreed to act as an observer of the project, and, at its close, to offer some comments in the light of what I had learned from the three main participants.

Research Methods

It was accepted that I would try to record the views of Alan, Kathleen and Suzy at intervals during the 1991–2 school year. I used semi-structured interviews with each individual. The interviews were reflective in tone with the subjects encouraged to 'think out loud' about their experience and insights concerning the project. I interviewed the participants on a one-to-one basis in the head's office. Early interviews were tape recorded and transcribed. During later interviews I relied on handwritten notes. I was also given copies of both the school's development and management development plans.

At the end of the school year I analysed all the data I had collected searching for themes and topics. These were then organized, data edited and the findings written up and fed back to the three participants for their comments and clearance. This chapter is my report of the project.

Main Findings

I visited the school on four occasions (June 1991, January, March and July 1992), the visits taking up either a morning or an afternoon. On each occasion similar and different issues surfaced. I have decided to group these issues in chronological order. In this way a sense of development during the year can be provided as well as the salient features of the project highlighted.

June 1991

I visited the school at this time to learn what each of the three participants thought about the project and to discover what was taking place in and around the school.

First, Alan updated me on the implementation of the scheme. The governors had formally approved the plan but only after some resistance to it from two governors. The proposal went to a vote which was significant because as Alan explained, it was the 'first time in five years anything has gone to a vote'.

Parents were then notified by letter. Parental reaction was muted. As Alan said,

> hardly got a mention from parents . . . the only comment I got was from those who thought it would be a good idea.

Kathleen also mentioned only positive responses.

> A lot of people were saying how pleased they were. What a nice opportunity for me.

Alan told me that he and Kathleen were very busy trying to transfer responsibilities between themselves. Alan felt he was working full-time as head while simultaneously attempting to give headship to someone else. He needed to do this because he believed a lot of decisions for the autumn term had to be taken in the summer term. Despite the extra work involved Alan felt the changeover was going smoothly. He also recognized that it was a high priority for him to leave things alone in the next school year.

Kathleen also felt she had a lot to attend to in addition to her class.

> I find I am having head's meetings for next year, lower team meetings
> . . . it gets a bit frantic. Alan is already passing documents over
> to me saying, 'You deal with that, that's going to be next year's
> responsibility.'

Kathleen felt that things would improve once Alan was in the classroom and she could begin to make decisions by herself.

In looking forward to the coming year Alan talked about two things. First, he wanted the year to provide a break for him from headship. He enjoyed being a head but he was finding that the amount of time he devoted to the job sometimes made him feel very tired and

> I begrudge feeling I'm not functioning well because I'm tired. It's
> easy to make a mistake when you're tired and just soaked up with
> school.

Alan felt it was the demands of the job which accounted for him feeling fatigued, rather than his inability to manage time. He told me that he had not had a night off work for the last two weeks. He had attended PTA, Governors, Governor sub-committees, and Community Association meetings, plus three nights had been taken up with a school production and one evening he had attended a disco for the pupils. He said,

> What I want to do [next year] is cut down the time I'm here. I'd like
> to be able to go home at 5.30 p.m. without having to be back here
> in the evening . . . Kathleen will have to get used to having less time
> for herself next year. Its starting to come to her attention this term.

Second, Alan was aware that he would have less control in the school but he added,

Deep down I have to say that there are not many people I would have given this opportunity to. If it wasn't for the fact that . . . Kathleen and I think the same way, so I don't feel I'll be out of control because 90 per cent of what she'll do is probably what I'll do. The 10 per cent she will do a different way so I don't feel too bad about that.

Alan might have been handing over headship but while there would be a change of leader there would also be continuity in the direction of the school and the guiding beliefs.

Kathleen was looking forward to the year:

I'm going to make the most of it. Throw myself into it whole-heartedly, and we'll see what happens, and if I find I do like headship, then obviously I'll apply and if I don't then I shall be happy to be deputy again.

During the year Kathleen wanted to try 'to draw the best from people' and to give herself some new challenges such as leading evening meetings for parents. 'I don't enjoy speaking out at meetings so that's something I would like to overcome.'

Kathleen felt there would be occasions when she would want to ask Alan to help her, but she also knew that the chair of Governors was on call.

The chair of Governors has been very supportive. He said if ever I need him I just have to ring him at work or home and he will do his best to help me at any time.

As far as working with Suzy was concerned Kathleen was aware that

I still have to get together with her to do her job description. I think she feels that the deputy head's job is a bit more important than it is . . . I have been trying to tell her that my role as deputy is to support Alan and be a listening ear to him, but also to support the staff and do things that contribute to the smooth running of the school, making everyone's life as easy as possible in the everyday, nitty gritty things. It is very difficult to actually tell anyone what I do do.

In other words, it was not easy for Kathleen to define Suzy's duties in the next school year.

More than anything though Kathleen was excited at the prospect of the coming year:

It's given me a new lease of life in a way. I think its nice to have the opportunity to try the job without committing oneself. I know I can do it, its just whether I want the hassle . . . Its a big compliment to me because I value Alan's opinion very highly, he's done a lot for me.

Suzy was looking forward to the year. She appreciated that the work of a deputy involved a lot of pastoral care for the staff, but she expressed some concerns which centred on the lack of clarity about deputy headship:

> I do feel a little concerned that the role might become a 'nothing' one. I haven't had a job description yet . . . Kathleen says its a difficult job, and I think its going to be more difficult for me than if I was the real deputy head.

Suzy was also preparing for the presence of Alan in her team.

> Although I am looking forward to working with him I think he is quite a loner in his ideas. It will be interesting to see if he can shake off being head.

In broad terms then Kathleen, Suzy and Alan were preparing to take on new roles and throw off old ones. Each of them was looking forward to the coming year, although each had different expectations and hopes.

January 1992

When I next visited the school a whole term had elapsed. For a variety of reasons I had been unable to return to the school although I had spoken to Kathleen on the telephone. The three participants now had a lot to reflect on and share with me. Analysis of their transcripts suggests the following topics were the most prominent ones.

Suzy was now deputy head and to support her work she was attending an LEA management course for deputy heads. She was enjoying the course, generally finding that course members' perceptions supported her own experience that the duties of deputies varied considerably from one school to another. Suzy attributed this to different heads' perceptions of the role. 'It's quite fluid how the person you are working for perceives the role of deputy head.' She saw the work of a deputy as contingent upon the head's assumptions of the role.

She also thought that the role could be that of a 'dogsbody' not least because, 'there are not a lot of huge leadership areas that would be given to a deputy'.

For much of the first term Suzy felt she had not been given enough guidance about her role:

> I felt Kathleen was very, very busy. I think one of the problems is that we are all in a learning role and I'm at the end of the line. Obviously Kathleen has gone into a big role. I felt I was in the wilderness a bit, without direction. I didn't feel I was being directed . . . We [Kathleen

and Suzy] weren't in line as to what we wanted from each other . . . I think I had a difficult term last term because I was sandwiched in between Alan doing a brilliant job [teaching in her team] and I was trying to assert myself as deputy head.

Suzy felt she managed to do many of the mundane duties associated with deputy headship at the school, such as video recordings, timetables, taking assemblies in Kathleen's absence. Suzy was also attending to the

pastoral side of the job. [I've] got round and chatted and listened to problems and talked through problems [with staff].

In addition, to the smooth running of the school Suzy said,

I wanted to have a regular meeting [with Kathleen] and discuss the problems that were arising in school, you know, it might be sort of administration problems.

Moreover, Suzy began to sense 'that Kathleen didn't feel I was being assertive enough'. As the end of term approached, and both became tired there were some tensions between them:

You know what it is like in school at the end of term, everybody is tired and I think there were two or three very small incidents, I think it was the emotional side of things.

As a result the two met and cleared the air. Kathleen outlined her views on deputy headship and this helped Suzy:

Now I know [what] sort of things matter to the person I'm working with . . . [When you know] you obviously change your image. You have got to be yourself, of course, but after that, different heads are going to require different things . . . You've got to be your own person, but you've got to fit in with the particular head, so that you can become a team. You work together. Now I feel a bit clearer.

In short, Suzy had been trying to become a deputy at the same time as Kathleen was becoming a head. While Kathleen was understandably preoccupied with headship this had also resulted in Suzy believing she had not been given the guidance she needed to perform her role.

Yet although there had been a lack of clarity, and Suzy had suffered some uncertainty during the term, she nevertheless remained optimistic. 'I mean it's not made me feel I couldn't be a deputy head . . . I feel positive.'

Kathleen's reflections on the term were also strongly positive. She told me it was 'going well' despite the fact that it was hard work being a head:

Some days you wonder where the time's gone . . . I usually get [to school] at 8.00 and I normally leave after 6.00 unless I am going to a meeting, then it can be 7.00, 8.00 or 9.00 p.m. There was one week when I had four evenings when I was here till 11.00 p.m., Monday to Thursday. I was supposed to be here on Friday for a children's disco and in on Saturday for a bazaar. On the Friday night I said to the chair of the PTA 'sorry, I'm going to excuse myself'. I needed some time.

Although Kathleen had expected to miss her class teaching role she had discovered that headship meant she had now got 'a bigger class'. 'I can walk round the school and go in each classroom.'

Kathleen also spoke about the support she had been offered by the staff and by the chair of Governors. 'He comes in once a fortnight, 8.30 to 9.00 a.m. He's been very good.' She continued to draw some support from Alan. She confessed that the two of them still met, once a month, although this was not known by the rest of the staff.

A proportion of Kathleen's work had been devoted to getting:

to all the staff. I've set out doing job descriptions and visiting classrooms. It was very satisfying getting into the classrooms and observing and being able to talk to staff about what I'd seen. Just giving staff a boost to their confidence by being positive . . . By consulting [with individual teachers] I've changed a lot of the curriculum responsibilities and looked at [teachers'] career development, arranged some free time and got people on courses.

Kathleen saw part of her work as to do with making people feel valued. Yet, at the same time she felt she needed 'to be tough'. 'I've not had to be terribly tough — but I did tell one individual something; sort things out.'

One notable achievement for Kathleen was a successful parents' evening when the teaching of reading had been the focus of the meeting. The evening had gone well and Kathleen felt she had started to overcome her anxieties about public speaking.

Kathleen also commented on her experience of headship:

I always knew it was a very responsible sort of job. I also knew there were niggling little things to deal with, but I didn't realise how niggling . . . I didn't realize how many little things went on in school . . . I didn't appreciate how many things Alan did.

In other words, Kathleen was coming to terms with being a head. She had accepted the mantle of headship and was now feeling how it fitted.

In focusing on the positive, Kathleen was not blind to some of the difficulties she had encountered. She thought there had been a hitch between herself and Suzy:

We were having some problems. I saw her before the end of term
. . . we had a long chat and came to the conclusion we hadn't been
meeting regularly enough. Suzy felt there was a lack of communication between us. So we are going to have regular meetings now.

To stimulate and structure these meetings Kathleen and Suzy had agreed to
trial for the LEA some newly-published distance learning materials for school
management development. These required heads and deputies to work together
on a set of tasks and readings. Kathleen felt it would 'help us to work more
closely together'.

While the two had now resolved their difficulty Kathleen was still reflecting upon what it meant. She said she felt Suzy was now coming towards to
being a deputy, whereas in the autumn term 'I felt she wasn't'.

I'm still trying to work out whether its my expectations of her as a
deputy or her expectations. We did sit down before we started and
talked about the sort of things I'd done in my role as deputy. But I
think you've got to find your own niche, because its a very peculiar
job.

Kathleen was quick to recognize that Suzy was very hard-working and a very
good class teacher, yet:

when you are deputy you can't give as much to your class as you did
before. You have to balance the deputy's job with the teacher's job.
You have to say to yourself the children will sometimes have to take
a back seat. It shouldn't be, but there are days when you have to
attend to the staff as well as the class. I think that's been one of the
hardest things [for Suzy] . . . I see the deputy's role as helping in the
smooth running of the school . . . Suzy seems a lot more relaxed now.
We've got off to a good start [this term].

When I interviewed Alan he raised five points. First, he felt the initiative
was going well from his point of view. He felt much more relaxed compared
to being a head. He also thought he had more personal time than as a head.

Second, during the autumn term he had had to adjust to 'how accommodating everyone was to Kathleen'. He had found this slightly difficult:

It was staggering how people praised her . . . if she picked up a piece
of paper she'd get praised. It was almost like a jealousy that someone
else had the job and was getting heaps of praise for just breathing and
I used to work really hard to do things and no one would mention
it!! . . . That was something I didn't expect. [At the same time] I was,
of course, quite flattered that people were telling me how brilliant she
was . . . they could obviously see how well [the project] was working.

As Alan recognized in some of his other comments, there was an 'ego problem' to overcome in switching jobs. Kathleen's efforts were being recognized and praised whereas his efforts had become taken for granted.

Third, Alan understood that Suzy and Kathleen 'were both growing into new jobs' and:

> It was quite interesting to see a deputy who needed help and a head who was learning the job and trying to cope with a new deputy . . . It is quite difficult for any deputy in a primary school . . . and I didn't see Suzy getting a great deal of recognition at all.

When Alan reflected upon what Suzy had gained so far from the experience he said:

> I think she's learned some of the negative aspects of deputy headship. That must now turn into learning some of the positive aspects.

Alan was not uncomfortable with the idea that so far Suzy had seen the down side of being a deputy. However, he hoped she would see that as a learning experience on which to build.

Fourth, Alan believed that Kathleen had so far gained the most from the initiative:

> Its making her realize what headship is all about, to the point where I'll be surprised if she doesn't express doubts about whether she wants to be a head. She must now realize if she does become a head a good chunk of personal life will disappear, because you can't leave headship, you can't get rid of it . . . you're on call virtually all the time.

Fifth, Alan himself had gained something other than a sense of relaxation. He was developing a new set of insights into the school. For one thing he was finding teaching the National Curriculum difficult. 'There's enough content in each subject area to last a whole year.' He was also thinking about the school's system of reporting children's progress to parents. Moreover, he was concerned about 'the level of maths teaching' across the school.

More than anything else though, Alan was thinking about the use of time in the school. While he speculated on a number of ideas he appeared to have decided that, 'the deputy needs one afternoon a week, and I'll make that time available'. He believed the deputy needed some time to 'be on call' and to learn to cope with whatever cropped up in the school without recourse to himself as head.

Easter Time

I next visited the school at the end of March. The first thing Kathleen told me was that she had completed the school's development plan and the budget.

She said, 'It was such a relief when I sent off the budget last Friday.' Kathleen also felt that presenting the budget to the governors had been an important exercise for her.

Kathleen said Suzy was now applying and being interviewed for deputy headships in other schools. Kathleen felt their relationship was good. Kathleen also reflected upon the lessons to be drawn from the first term:

> I keep trying to weigh up in my own mind how fair this has been for Suzy . . . The worst thing was the lack of communication in the first term . . . Maybe it would have been better if Suzy had been Alan's deputy, then she would have been paired with an experienced head.

Kathleen felt that because she and Alan had an established rapport as head and deputy, it was difficult for Kathleen and Suzy to emulate such a close association so quickly. In a sense, the rotation not only altered professional relations, it temporarily dislocated them.

Kathleen again spoke about her experience of headship. She said the pressures were different from those of a teacher. Although she claimed to love teaching she felt there was 'a freedom' to headship. 'You never know what's going to happen which can be stimulating or threatening.' To illustrate the latter part of this remark Kathleen described an incident at the recent annual meeting for parents and governors:

> A parent asked a question and I didn't understand the question at all.
> At that moment I thought this is why I didn't want to be a head.

In front of an audience made up of governors, parents and staff she felt terribly exposed, 'naked' was her term. 'If I'd not been able to answer I'd have let the staff down. That was the worst moment of the year.' That episode apart, Kathleen continued to enjoy being a headteacher.

Kathleen felt the rotation was 'brilliant'. The experience had:

> Made me feel different about myself— more confident, more assertive — because I've faced so many challenges. I now feel I've got the knowledge of headship . . . I now feel I know what's going on in the job compared to September.

Indeed, I made a note to this effect in my own jottings. I noticed she spoke much more about what she had done and mentioned Alan much less. She looked and sounded more confident.

The last point Kathleen made was that she thought that while she and Alan would slot back into their original roles quite easily in the next academic year, they now planned for her to be more involved than formerly in the school's management.

When I talked to Suzy she told me she now felt a lot better than when we had last met. 'Its all come together; we now talk. I'm more in touch . . .

I feel more in tune.' Suzy attributed this harmony to the fact that she and
Kathleen were meeting on a regular basis.

> The talking is ever so important. We are both busy and it can easily
> work out that you don't see each other. Its essential for a head and
> deputy to meet. You need a definite, programmed business meeting.

Suzy also felt that she and Kathleen were now working productively together
because she 'had learned the ropes'. Suzy said she now had a knowledge of
how things in the school worked and that the mystique was less.

Like Kathleen, Suzy believed she had learned a lot.

> I feel different inside myself . . . I feel I'm moving on. Its not status,
> its a feeling of progression. A kind of development.

Moreover, she felt she could now apply for deputy headships with her eyes
open; she had rehearsed the part:

> I now really want to be a deputy. I want to now go and do the job
> somewhere else. I don't want to revert to being a team leader.

Not surprisingly, Suzy said she would recommend job rotation in other schools
since she felt she had gained a lot. However, she also thought it took a 'special
head' to create such an opportunity.

When I spoke to Alan he told me that he felt such a scheme needed to be
undertaken for longer than a single term because it took a year for the individuals to develop. He thought both Kathleen and Suzy had developed, but
drew particular attention to Suzy's progress. 'I've seen Suzy develop, perhaps
the hard way because she's had the most difficult role.'

Alan also spoke about how the year had enabled him to be 'detached
from headship and see anew'. He continued to recognize that he needed to try
to regularize his hours when he became head again. He felt that he wanted to
introduce some specialist teaching into the upper years to help staff cope with
the demands of the National Curriculum and he wanted to provide some free
time for teachers to complete pupil records. Alan spoke with some certainty
about these ideas for the future, so it was no surprise that he had built them
into plans for the next year when he and I spoke in July.

July

The scheme had almost run its alloted time when we next met. Without hesi-
tation Alan told me he would do it again. He felt refreshed and relaxed. Also,
Kathleen and Suzy had gained 'lots of insights'. As a result of the project Alan
was now planning what he called phase two management development.

First, he had to cover for Suzy's departure. She had been appointed to a deputy headship in another school and would leave at the end of term. He described her departure as 'an enormous loss', and it was one which raised conflicting feelings:

> I'm sorry she's going; she's irreplaceable. She's magnificent in the classroom . . . but I'm glad she's going — she's ready to go. It's good for her.

Second, Alan had decided to buy in specialist teaching for Design and Technology, from the neighbourhood high school. This would have the effect of releasing teachers who could then cope better with their additional responsibilities in the school and the paper work of the National Curriculum.

Third, Alan now wanted Kathleen to teach for only four days a week. He wanted to capitalize upon Kathleen's development and he intended that she should still have 'ownership of the school'.

Overall Alan thought that the year had been a training programme, 'in a dramatic way', for Kathleen and Suzy. He now thought everyone else in the school should have some training and the introduction of both some non-contact time and specialist teaching would contribute to that training.

Alan also readily acknowledged that he had learned some things. For one thing he told me that he was now more aware of teachers' problems. For another, from watching Kathleen, he was more 'conscious of the pastoral role in headship'. He said Kathleen had certainly noticed when others were under pressure.

Suzy was also upbeat about the experience. She thought it had been a 'good year'. Working with Alan had gone well and, in terms of the unit, he had shaken off being a head. She believed she had 'learned a lot' and went on to talk about becoming more confident and professionally assertive, seeing beyond her classroom and dealing with staff's problems.

As to the salient features of the year Suzy felt that it was only as Kathleen grew into her role as head that she, as deputy, had then been able to develop her role. While she acknowledged that they had 'both been on a learning curve',

> Kathleen had to deal with her role first. When she became familiar with her work we began to communicate more productively.

It should also be added that Suzy, while sad to be leaving the school, was nevertheless excited and enthusiastic about becoming a permanent deputy head.

Kathleen had arrived at the end of the year 'with mixed feelings' about headship. She had greatly enjoyed being the head of *this* school but, 'I'm not so desperate for the power of headship that I'm prepared to be a head anywhere'.

During the year she had sometimes experienced the loneliness of headship, of feeling that decisions were 'all up to me'. Also, the demands of the job were physical as well as mental:

> I lost a stone in weight in the first half-term; I tried to be all things to all people. You just can't be . . . [but] you need to be fit . . . [and] you do get very tired.

At times Kathleen said she had been 'bombarded by things' and at those times she felt the job was 'impossible for one person to do'. However, she had learned to tell herself that 'in a few days things will be alright again'. Also, as the year wore on things got easier.

Kathleen also felt people treated her differently once she was a head. She said there was 'an aura about being head'. There was also:

> a lot of freedom in the job in terms of organizing how you work, even where you work. You have options. It's the power to choose how you want to do the job.

Looking forward, Kathleen knew Alan wanted her to have a higher profile in the next year, even though she would be reverting to the position of deputy. She admitted that part of her didn't want to give the job back to Alan. However, another part of her recognized that headship involved so many tasks that she was glad to let someone else have the responsibility. 'I'm not afraid of responsibility but sometimes you feel you wish you could pass things onto another person.' I suspect this statement betrays some ambivalence on the part of Kathleen about becoming deputy again. However, one thing is clear, no one could suggest she was afraid of responsibility. She had, with Suzy's assistance, kept the school on its planned course and maintained the support of governors, parents and staff alike. Moreover, there had been no major mishaps during the year. Kathleen had steered the school on its charted course.

Discussion of the Emerging Themes

In this section I want to focus upon four themes which stand out from the data.

The first concerns headship. It is clear from many of the comments of Alan and Kathleen that primary school headship is hard work. The job consists of a wide variety of responsibilities, such as managing personnel, curriculum, site and plant, budgets, performed before a number of different audiences — staff, governors, parents, pupils. As time studies of heads at work show

(Clerkin, 1985; Davies, 1987), they are often dealing with a multiplicity of tasks, some of which are trivial and mundane, or as Kathleen said, there are a lot of little, niggling things to do which take up a head's time. Moreover, from the testimonies of both Kathleen and Alan it seems heads can spend long hours at work. When I asked Kathleen to account for her hours she estimated that she worked *at least* sixty hours a week, and sometimes many, many hours more. Kathleen spent a lot of time in school during the evenings, usually attending meetings. Headship is a day job with a night shift.

Indeed, the commitment of Kathleen and Alan to their work was such that each felt it was at the expense of their personal lives. Yet the literature concerned with primary headship barely mentions this feature of the job. Certainly prospective applicants for headship need to be aware, as Kathleen and Alan were, that headship is not only hard work, but that it has personal costs.

The second theme focuses upon deputy headship. There are three points to make. First, all three participants regarded the role of the deputy as poorly defined. Moreover, Kathleen and Suzy understood that the work of a deputy was almost wholly contingent upon what the head allowed them to do. Although deputies are senior figures in their schools, being second in the school's organizational hierarchy and, after the head, earning the next highest salary, they can be very junior to the head.

The second point follows from the first. There appears to be a gulf between being a head and being a deputy. The former is responsible for everything, seemingly on call to everyone, making key decisions, intensely active and working at the centre of the school. By contrast the deputy can be confined to the margins and less centrally involved in the management of the school as an organization. Consequently, deputies can be less knowledgeable about what is going on in the school, unless and until their heads share with them what they are doing and why. If heads are the senior partners, with that goes a need, perhaps an obligation, to share with the deputy their knowledge about the school. If heads do not share what they know with the deputy, then they will have restricted the deputy's capacity to play a full part in the school. Certainly what this scheme shows is that when Kathleen and Suzy began to meet regularly in the spring term, talked about each other's expectations and shared information, Suzy began to feel she was becoming a deputy.

Third, it seems to me that Suzy had the most to learn upon taking up her new role. Kathleen had been acting head on occasional days before the start of the year, and anyway Alan had previously involved her in some of the management of the school. By contrast Suzy had not been involved very much in school management. In these circumstances the step from year leader to deputy may be as great, or greater, than that of deputy to head. Furthermore, deputies have to learn their new role while remaining full-time classteachers. Suzy learned to be a deputy in the relatively few moments available to her when not attending to her teaching responsibilities. By contrast, Kathleen could learn to be a head by doing headship. All her time was devoted to learning the new role. Together, this means that deputies may be struggling to take great strides in their professional development in a context which severely constrains their opportunities for such learning. Deputies may only learn to be deputies in the cracks between their class teaching duties. Deputies may have a full-time job but only part-time opportunities to learn and develop the role.

Clearly this means heads need to think carefully about the induction of deputy heads. Somehow, time must be found for deputies to have some space in which they can learn to become a deputy, and not simply to be the highest paid teacher.

The third theme is closely related to the second one. From this rotation of jobs it can be seen that it takes time for individuals to learn new roles. Even without needing to find out much about the school and its setting, it still took Kathleen at least one term to adjust to the role, while Suzy may have taken longer. It follows then, that new heads and deputies cannot be expected to perform to a high degree of competency in the early phase of their appointment. Allowances must be made for them to learn about their responsibilities, to become accustomed to their new contexts, and for them to grow into their roles. Taking on a new job may occur suddenly, at the start of a term, but it actually occurs over a period of professional transition. Becoming a head or a deputy is not an event, it is a process.

It seems, therefore, that recent initiatives in the mentoring of headteachers are wholly appropriate. Kathleen undoubtedly benefitted, sometimes, from having Alan on hand to turn to. He was her mentor, albeit in a discreet way. While it is encouraging that mentoring is now being promoted for heads, it should be recognized that deputies also need to be mentored. One possible weakness in this project, as all three participants recognized, was that until Kathleen had made her transition, it was difficult for her to help Suzy. Until that help became available from Kathleen, Suzy's role was inhibited. One finding from this scheme is that heads need to mentor their newly appointed deputies.

The fourth theme centres upon the insights Alan developed during the year he spent back in the classroom. Although Alan had been closely concerned with the curriculum during his five years of headship, when he returned to full-time teaching his appreciation of the demands of the National Curriculum increased. For one thing he recognized how much time teachers needed to devote to completing pupil records and reports. He also now understood how time for staff meetings could compete with other calls on teachers' time. In short, Alan was more sensitive to the classroom concerns of teachers as a result of his time back in the classroom.

This increased sensitivity seems to me to be an important outcome from the project. It enabled Alan, along with Kathleen, to determine fresh ways of marshalling resources and supporting teachers in the classroom. Teaching and learning are the key tasks of schools, and heads must remain in close touch with classrooms, as others (Alexander *et al.*, 1992: 46–8) have argued.

Conclusions

There is no doubt that the experience of these three teachers shows that job rotation is a worthwhile exercise. All three participants individually benefitted from the experience. Suzy gained experience of deputy headship and her career subsequently advanced. Alan returned to headship feeling refreshed and more relaxed. Kathleen became fully aware of the workings of the school and was ready to play a larger role in the management and development of the school. Each had fulfilled his or her expectations at the outset. Moreover the advantages Alan articulated in the school's management development plan had been realized. There had been some small strains along the way, largely arising from Kathleen and Suzy simultaneously needing to learn their new roles and rehearse their parts. Yet, at the end of the year, the school as a whole had undoubtedly benefitted. Other colleagues would now be developed during the second phase of management development. All staff would have greater amounts of non-contact time. Kathleen would now take a more leading role in the school. Indeed, the school might now have two headteachers, and as the old adage has it, two heads are better than one.

Acknowledgments

I should like to acknowledge the support I was given by the Cambridge Institute Research and Development Fund. An award from the fund enabled me to conduct the work in school and to prepare this article.

More than anything, I should like to thank Alan, Kathleen and Suzy. First for admitting me into their project. Second, for sharing with me their thoughts and observations. Third, for allowing this report to be made public. Like them, I learned a great deal from the project.

References

ALEXANDER, R., ROSE, J. and WOODHEAD, C. (1992) *Curriculum Organisation and Classroom Practice in Primary Schools: A Discussion Paper*, London, DES.

BEARE, H., CALDWELL, B.J. and MILLIKAN, R.H. (1989) *Creating An Excellent School*, London, Routledge.

CLERKIN, C. (1985) 'What do primary school heads actually do all day?', *School Organization*, **5**, 4, pp. 287–300.

COULSON, A.A. (1976) 'The role of the primary head', in BUSH, T. *et al.*, (Eds), (1980) *Approaches to School Management*, London, Harper Row.

DAVIES, L. (1987) 'The role of the primary school head', *Educational Management and Administration*, **15**, 2, pp. 43–7.

DES, (1990) *Developing School Management: The Way Forward; a Report by the School Management Task Force*, London, HMSO.

MORTIMORE, P. and MORTIMORE, J. (1991) *The Primary Head: Roles, Responsibilities and Reflections*, London, Paul Chapman.

NIAS, J., SOUTHWORTH, G.W. and YEOMANS, R. (1989) *Staff Relationships in the Primary School*, London, Cassell.

NIAS, J., SOUTHWORTH, G.W. and CAMPBELL, P. (1992) *Whole School Curriculum Development in the Primary School*, London, Falmer Press.

SOUTHWORTH, G.W. (1987) 'Primary school headteachers and collegiality', in SOUTHWORTH, G.W. (Ed) *Readings in Primary School Management*, London, Falmer Press.

Part II

Managing the Curriculum

Chapter 4

A Primary Headteacher in Search of a Collaborative Climate

Denis Hayes

Introduction

As a child, I can recall the excitement generated by watching a weekend variety show hosted by a number of energetic personalities. In particular, I loved to watch the plate-spinner as he danced about the stage, wiggling a number of bamboo sticks with cleverly designed plates wobbling drunkenly on top of the spikes. Sometimes, it appeared impossible to keep them all rotating at the same time; the prospect of a plate falling from its lofty position and crashing to the floor created a kind of hysteria among the audience, who called out, cheered, gasped and screamed advice to the apparently beleaguered performer.

Of course, it was a professionally managed act; the purpose was to engage the audience and convince them that 'together', artist extraordinaire and gaping crowd could keep control of those confounded sticks and saucers. By the time the last plate had been whipped triumphantly from its stand, the gasp of relief was genuine and ecstatic applause broke out across the auditorium. I remember sitting back, shaking my head in disbelief and sighing contentedly, reassured that all was well. Such are the vagaries of youth! Why is it, I wonder, that thirty-five years on, through a serious study of the role of a primary headteacher during a time of rapid change, these memories should return so vividly? The following account may help to explain . . .

Patter's Primary (pseudonym) is an inner-city primary school in the southwest of England and characterized by many of the familiar problems and achievements associated with a challenging situation: high population mobility, a small but dedicated group of closely involved parents, multi-ethnic intake, involvement of social services, and the ups-and-downs of keeping a busy ship afloat during a time of great pressure with a keen but over-stretched workforce of fifteen teachers (including the head). Pupils number around 300, but are liable to fluctuate considerably from week-to-week, even day-to-day, as families arrive, stay, leave, and sometimes return a few months later. About one-third of the school population is mobile across the academic year, throwing a great administrative and emotional burden upon all the staff as they cope with children facing new circumstances and attempt to absorb newcomers into the school system.

Mary Tyler (pseudonym) had been at the school for about three years when this study began, following earlier experience as the headteacher of a smaller school. When she arrived at Potter's in 1988 the full weight of statutory change was hitting education; over the next three years, there were many innovations to interpret, discuss, and implement that were common, no doubt, to all maintained schools. In 1991, the school was already facing the heavy demands of national reform and one of Mary's strategies to cope with the mounting tide of legislation, delegated budget and National Curriculum requirements was to develop and enhance the degree of collaboration within the school. She was anxious to involve staff in decision-making, delegate curriculum responsibilities and develop a staff structure that facilitated the processing of documentation and protected classroom teachers from unnecessary overload. She established a senior management team (SMT) composed of herself, the deputy and the three allowance holders, and for the purpose of discussion divided teachers into two age-group 'phases' (Early Years and Upper School) to consider matters particular to Key Stages 1 and 2 respectively.

To a large degree, the account that follows traces Mary's efforts to use these structures to develop a collaborative culture in school (Nias *et al.*, 1989; Hargreaves and Hopkins, 1991; Fullan and Hargreaves, 1992). The data was collected by weekly attendance at staff meetings and SMT meetings, occasional attendance at 'phase' meetings, interviews with all staff (including at least half-termly with the headteacher), and general observations in the staff-room and school. Over the two years of the study, three issues associated with Mary's attempts to establish a collaborative climate in the school became strikingly evident:

- Mary's time management;
- Developing decision-making structures;
- Maintaining staff enthusiasm for involvement.

Each of these factors influenced her efforts to establish and maintain a collaborative climate in school. I will now look at each of these in turn.

Mary's Time Management

Plate spinning on a weekend variety show seemed relatively straightforward in comparison with the persistent demands under which Mary Tyler laboured (Blease and Lever, 1992). Everyone, it seemed, needed her attention, approval, comment or signature for a form. Potter's Primary seemed, on occasions, to be full of visitors: prospective parents, local authority officers, community workers, university lecturers and students, publishing company representatives and the like, all wishing to speak to her or at least wave a cheery greeting. The hard-pressed secretary did her best to offset some of the pressure, but demands upon Mary's time were constant (Stone, 1989; Kirkpatrick, 1990). Breaktimes and lunch breaks offered little solace, for this was the occasion when teachers needed access to her, often to share news of a child or report some item of concern. During lunchtimes, meal-time assistants used the door of her office as an isolation area for miscreants; sometimes, a child who had been particularly troublesome in class worked at a table in the corridor.

These interactions characterized Mary's day-to-day work. In addition, there was the regular contact with the school secretary to negotiate the seemingly endless volume of post, telephone calls, form-filling and messages. A short absence from school meant that the accumulated paperwork mounted, waiting for attention on her return (Sullivan, 1990).

Every Monday, a regular meeting of the senior management team took place during the lunch break, which Mary chaired and for which she produced an agenda. The full staff meeting was held every Wednesday after school. Each week, she produced a staff bulletin outlining coming events: times when members of staff would be absent, names of supply teachers (when known) and any other key points of information. The significant number of children in the school from distressed home situations produced regular meetings with child care officers, case conferences and discussions with LEA staff. Attendance at governors' meetings, both full and sub-committee, took place after school or in the evenings and she spent time liaising informally when she felt that she needed to gain specific advice.

In addition, there was the important interaction with teaching and non-teaching staff, and with children. When she was in school, Mary tried to free herself from responsibilities during breaktimes to be available for casual conversations with staff, though opportunities were sometimes constrained by the need to offer pastoral support in private to both teaching and non-teaching staff. Her contact with adults therefore relied quite heavily upon the round of formal meetings together with chance encounters in the staff room or about the school (Ball, 1987; Nias *et al.*, 1989). However, these informal chats and opportunity for sharing general gossip or lighthearted exchanges were rare. The inexorable chase to stay abreast of the heavy demands sometimes resulted in Mary adopting a reclusive role in which communication with teachers outside formal meetings relied heavily upon memos.

She also tried to maintain a regular teaching commitment of a day per week to ensure that she didn't become remote from the demands faced by classroom teachers ('I'm afraid that if I don't I might lose touch') though in practice this proved difficult to maintain. Otherwise, her interaction with the children tended to fall within one of three situations:

- during assembly times;
- when children were sent to her by staff for approval or scolding;
- when prospective parents arrived with their children to look around the school.

One way and another, Mary's working life was complicated by the variety of demands upon her; some unpredictable and diverse, others (like assemblies and her teaching commitment) regular and systematic (Laws and Dennison, 1991). This scenario will, no doubt, be recognized by many primary headteachers who, like Mary, have struggled through a time of unparalleled national change characterized by fast-moving multiple innovation. And like Mary, senior staff in school will doubtless have quickly reached the conclusion that it is neither wise nor realistic to shoulder alone the burden of whole school management and curriculum leadership. The time pressure reinforced the need to press ahead with fuller staff involvement but concomitantly reduced Mary's opportunity to promote and monitor the success of the collaborative process.

Developing decision-making structures

Mary did not attempt to carry the full weight of responsibility herself; she was anxious to involve staff fully in decisions affecting the whole school and as part of this established a collaborative system involving three main stages:

(a) Issues were first considered in the *senior management team* (SMT) which met on Mondays to decide priorities before involving all the staff.
(b) Groups of teachers then met in *age-group phases* on Tuesdays, both to receive information from the SMT meeting about whole staff issues and discuss matters specific to their age-phase.
(c) On Wednesday evening, the *full staff meeting* allowed for feed-back into the main body and appropriate discussions and decisions.

In addition, *Year teams* met later in the week for detailed curriculum planning. This system ran reasonably smoothly for about two years, but over that time a number of fault-lines began to appear and threaten both the usefulness of the process and the whole collaborative enterprise:

• The demands upon both Mary and her staff to attend these regular meetings became excessive, especially in the light of the constant changes to national reforms such as National Curriculum attainment targets, assessment procedures and reporting to parents, which affected the intensity of their workload. In short, they became tired and close to exhaustion in trying to maintain the tight schedule of regular meetings while at the same time interpreting the implications of the reforms for their professional responsibilities.
• Some teachers felt that a decision-making structure in which the SMT decided which issues were relevant for the staff's consideration prevented the remainder of them from hearing a description of the particular issue

first-hand; instead, they were reliant upon the SMT representatives to interpret and convey the message.

- The idea of collaborative, collegial school management and curriculum
  development assumes that schools are strongly consensual organizations.
  However, in the case of this school there was sometimes a lack of consensus,
  and when this occurred, development was impeded. Consequently, the
  report-back during full staff meetings tended to be inconsistent, one phase
  having prepared their response carefully, the other having given relatively
  little thought to the issue.
- Staff absence (including the headteacher's) could seriously disrupt the
  programme.
- Many staff were worried that the amount of time spent on dealing with
  external demands created a squeeze on discussing immediate school concerns, notably agreed policy for behaviour and discipline.
- On occasions, *dissensus* (Pfeffer, 1978; Bennis, Benne and Chin, 1985; Beach,
  1989) created tensions that had not been foreseen and for which allowance
  had not been made in terms of time and opportunity to resolve issues. The
  structure was posited on the assumption that fuller collaboration would
  lead to a more clearly articulated common position. In practice, the teachers'
  differing philosophies, values and priorities sometimes acted against an
  agreed outcome.

Mary found herself in a dilemma. To deal with the plethora of information
and innovations that were hitting the school she wanted to involve staff more
closely, yet at the same time protect them from exposure to things which did
not directly impinge upon their daily working lives. It had not been her intention to hinder discussion of the pressing issues associated with internal school
affairs, but she found that external statutory pressures obliged her to meet
certain deadlines which allowed for little flexibility. In an attempt to resolve
the problems, yet continue to nurture a collaborative climate, she instigated
the following amendments:

- opening the SMT meeting to any member of staff who wished to
  attend;
- allowing an 'open agenda' time during the first part of the full staff
  meeting;
- reducing the size of the SMT, thus freeing curriculum co-ordinators
  from the burden of attending meetings;
- granting the phase groups more flexibility to meet as and when they
  thought necessary;
- making further efforts to enhance communication throughout the
  school.

As a result of these changes, staff concerns over receiving 'second-hand' information were ameliorated. Paradoxically, although the size of the SMT

shrank to three (the headteacher, deputy and a newly appointed 'third in charge'), staff seemed more settled. The busyness did not abate, but teachers were able to concentrate more closely on their own class affairs and curriculum responsibilities. The opening-up of the SMT meeting to anyone who wished to attend appeared to satisfy the teachers that nothing furtive was happening behind their backs (a particularly important fact in the light of the threat of redundancy which emerged during this period).

The open agenda time at the start of staff meetings was initially swamped by individuals and groups raising immediate or pressing concerns at the expense of the formal agenda; however, after a few weeks, the system settled into a routine and the main business proceeded more smoothly. Nevertheless, there were some anxious moments for Mary as she struck a balance between allocating time to the formal agenda and responding to the teachers' immediate concerns.

As a result of curriculum leaders finding more opportunity to concentrate on their particular area, the extent and quality of their involvement increased. The preparation of papers by co-ordinators for general discussion became more commonplace; Mary became more relaxed in her chairing as she allowed them to develop this role. Curriculum issues did not pass out of her hands though, for prior to the staff meetings she ensured that she had discussed the presentation with the particular co-ordinator to satisfy herself that all was in order. Co-ordinators seemed to welcome this process, reassured that they were conforming to the headteacher's expectations and could therefore proceed with confidence in front of their colleagues.

Lifting the insistence upon phase groups to meet regularly every week had an unexpected outcome. Initially, staff enjoyed the luxury of the extra 'free' time and confined their collaboration to Year team meetings for the purpose of fine-tuning the broader plans agreed at the phase meetings. After a few weeks, however, staff discovered that the effort required to meet to discuss age-phase issues informally or arrange a different time to meet each week exceeded that which was needed to meet weekly at a fixed time. By the end of the first half-term, both phases had reverted to their original pattern; the practicalities of communicating effectively necessitating this regular and fixed contact.

Mary also re-evaluated her own attitude towards the government reforms and began to take a more relaxed view of the situation. She learned who in the LEA could be trusted to share confidences and give advice and (with a number of changes on the governing body, including the resignation of the original Chair due to pressure of work) found that communication with governors became more open and rewarding (Golby, 1985). Mary persevered with closer involvement of governors in everyday school affairs and provided an 'open door' for them. She delegated to her staff as far as she felt able, sensitive to the fact that everyone was already burdened with work, and made opportunity for her deputy to enhance his own professional development through courses, leading staff discussions, and taking a central role in assisting other staff with their own development. The school's popularity with local teacher training institutions and the consequent volume of student-teachers who spent time on teaching practice led Mary to delegate the co-ordination of this aspect of school life to a senior member of staff.

Generally, Mary became more cautious in providing instant responses to every directive which came her way and more skilled in differentiating the essential from the second order management issues (Mortimore *et al.*, 1988). Although she often commented that the pace of life was hard to bear, she believed that she managed to keep the school on course despite many set-backs over resources and maintaining staff-pupil ratios. In the midst of her own problems, she considered active staff participation in school life to be axiomatic.

Maintaining Staff Enthusiasm for Involvement

Mary Tyler's determination to involve her staff more fully in the decision-making process was not, as we have seen, without its problems. She had to make a number of adjustments to structures and procedures to convince staff that the offer of participation was genuine and the effort they made, worthwhile. My own interviews with teachers helped to clarify some of the factors influencing their level of involvement and willingness to be participants in the process (Price and Reid, 1988; Campbell, 1985). An analysis of those interviews indicated that Mary needed to take a number of things into account as she worked to develop a collaborative climate:

The Teachers' Priority was for their own Class of Children

Whenever teachers met together informally, the conversation invariably centred upon the children. Many teachers referred to the importance of putting their own pupils' interests first. For example, one teacher claimed the right to modify original curriculum decisions with regard to the classroom context, adding that teachers needed to remain 'true to themselves' as professionals and as people:

> As a caring professional one has to modify what one does in the classroom to suit the environment in which we're teaching. If we were trying to work in a way which we simply couldn't because we didn't agree with the way in which we were being asked to work, bumbling ahead blindly, carrying out directives when your heart wasn't in it, this would clearly affect your teaching and lead to negativism coming back from the children.

The staff's determination to place the children's welfare ahead of other considerations was a regular and powerful factor in their attitude towards the development of school policy and their involvement in staff discussions. On every occasion that the needs of a particular child or group of children emerged during a meeting, there was, without exception, a surge of conversation and contributions from the teachers. Typically, from an experienced teacher:

> There are times when you have to prioritize whatever the issue is and live your life by the principles in which you believe. The one guiding principle I hold to be paramount over all else is: 'Are the children going to benefit from this?' . . . When it comes into the area of 'the children' or 'not the children', the children win out every time; then after that we fight for the scraps!

Some of their additional responsibilities as curriculum leaders or part of the management team which absorbed time were perceived as threatening this role:

> I'm anxious that the expectations of me as a 'management person' are growing. I didn't come into teaching for that! First and foremost I'm a class teacher. I came into teaching to teach and that's my prime motivation for being here.
> First and foremost I'm a teacher. I'd like to think that my class-room set-up is organized well enough to allow me access to go around and do whatever task might be needed . . . Yes, you do look to your class because you know them best and apply examples to your own class, your own children.

This reference to her class as *belonging* to her was one used by other teachers. The use of expressions such as *my kids* or *my children* and the desire to ensure that they were doing well was important to them both for the sake of the children and, it would appear, themselves. This may be one explanation for their level of anxiety about clarifying school policy for issues such as discipline and control. Uncertainty and insecurity in this area would leave them feeling vulnerable and threaten one of the major sources of their job satisfaction, namely, their ability to achieve success with children in the teaching-and-learning situation. Teachers' willingness to be involved in the decision-making process depended to a significant extent upon their view of their role as class teacher. If this was seen to be under threat or circumstances appeared likely to make their job more difficult, there was a strong move towards resolving such matters before concentrating upon other decisions.

For Mary, there was little choice but to respond to external directives, but she became increasingly aware of the impact that this was having upon teachers and sympathetic towards their love for classroom work. Indeed, she confessed on several occasions that the pressure of management tasks had made it difficult for her to carry out much teaching, a fact she very much regretted. For Mary, too, a great deal of her fulfilment lay through success in teaching. However, she also had to recognize that her attempts to enhance fuller participation were likely to suffer due to the teachers' tendency to value their classroom autonomy ahead of whole school curriculum policy. Mary's sympathy for the priority that teachers placed upon their teaching was tempered by the knowledge that she was accountable for monitoring National Curriculum continuity and progression across the school.

Staff were under Considerable Time Pressure

All primary school teachers reading this account will empathize with the severe time pressures that existed at Patter's School. Only alien beings can be unaware of the impact of recent legislation upon staff in maintained schools. For Patter's teachers this resulted in them monitoring their time usage closely and, in some cases, making specific decisions about priorities. There simply wasn't time to do everything, and decisions about the relative importance of any issue undoubtedly influenced the extent of their involvement. Typically:

> The time factor is a problem. We can't discuss things in enough detail. We need regular wide staff meetings, little and often. Sometimes it's a month before we have a real get-together. There's such a backlog of things to talk about, you can't cover it. Frustrations set in; decisions aren't made.
>
> The staff throw up their hands in horror saying: 'We can't possibly do twenty things in the first term; there isn't enough time!'

One senior teacher graphically described how difficult it had become to fit everything into a single week:

> There are the demands of midday meetings, senior management group, phase meetings, lunchtime clubs . . . they all eat into the time and make it impossible to discuss curriculum matters . . . then I get all sorts of things dumped in my pigeon hole that I don't know what to do with!

She later explained that these different responsibilities resulted in a tension between her differing roles, including her job as a class teacher:

> The conflct comes through time and things overlapping. If there are things to organize, or making contact with colleagues about certain things. It's a balance. For example, leaving the classroom to make contact with other colleagues about, say, an extra meeting, rapidly collecting information I need or leaving a message — and then back again.

Alutto and Belasco (1972) referred to the danger of staff becoming so closely involved in the decision-making process that they were unable to cope with all the differing demands for decisions ('decisional saturation'). They suggested that involvement in decision-making could, if excessive, result in agitation and stress for those members of staff and that more emphasis should be placed upon the *quality* rather than the number of decisions. At Patter's School, the rapid pace of change witnessed throughout the period of the research affected everybody on the school staff, sometimes leading to a sense of panic that the detail of proposals was insufficiently explicit. For example:

> There's so little time. I haven't seen the Humanities draft anyway . . . we've got the Science and Maths . . . but the Humanities is only going to be aims and purposes, and still won't be usable so that you can get your teeth 'into it. You know, we do this in the first year, then next year aim at this. Even the Science one is very, very broad aims and not actually the topic, and we're still doing our planning in phase groups.

One teacher explained how staff could become disgruntled when a policy document (in this case, Language) had to be restructured over a period of a year.

> For example, what are we going to do over the next three terms? And the volume of work to be covered, plus Language coming up again after spending the whole of the first term on it. It didn't go down too well. Everything became very repetitive and I was bored thinking this is quite a waste of time. From what I've heard, everyone feels the same way.

Similarly,

> A lot of issues are discussed that don't really have to be; they are just sidelines. For example, the English syllabus, digested and regurgitated several times, and still we have to do it next term, and everybody throws up their hands. Some of those meetings could be used to iron out things to do with the general running of the school, things which matter to the staff.

One result of the time pressures and the weight of externally imposed change was not only that policy decisions were hindered and important issues rushed through, but the implementation gap between initial presentation to staff and classroom practice was sometimes longer than had been anticipated when the original management plan had been drawn up. Problems experienced over deadlines and the length of time required for working parties to complete their assignments and disseminate the information to staff slowed the process. Concerns over meeting implementation dates were always apparent, though they were gradually overtaken by the practicalities of assessment procedures, appraisal, redundancy and record-keeping. In practice, these, and related issues, burdened the teachers far more than curriculum implementation, which was viewed as unrealistic. Mary was aware of the pressures upon her staff and anxious not to add to their burdens, but it took time before she recognized its full impact and, consequently, its effect upon the climate of collaboration.

They had to be sure that Involvement was Real

Around half the teachers interviewed stated that they felt that some matters had already been decided prior to the full meeting and that consultation was therefore contrived (Hargreaves, 1992). One teacher's perceptions were unusually firm.

> I feel that decisions are out of reach; they're made by senior management and the head . . . the decision's already been made, so what are we bothering for?

The majority were more temperate, recognizing the perceptions that existed among the staff about the decision-making process:

> It appears to some members of the school community that . . . decisions are made in smoke-filled rooms and we're simply told of things that may matter to us very much in our area of the school (or may not). Sometimes people feel that things are being imposed upon them rather than what they perceive should be happening in terms of them having an input towards a decision. We're sometimes faced with what appears to be a *fait accompli*.

Reference was also frequently made to the role of the headteacher and the power that accompanied her status; in particular, younger staff accepted that Mary's position and status gave her the right to exercise the final decision:

> Things are brought up at staff meetings; we say what we want; it goes to the head who has the final say on whether it's accepted or not . . . it's a bit more complicated than that; they have the management meetings; we're below the management, and ultimately it's the head's decision.

Another new teacher did not appear to find the idea of prior decisions unacceptable, but rather viewed the consultation process as a means of modifying a previously agreed decision rather than reaching a decision. 'Generally decisions are made beforehand and the talk is for understanding and modifying.'

In truth, interviews with the headteacher and deputy indicated that some issues *had* already been decided, but more often than not, the manoeuvrability available during whole staff consultation was severely limited by external requirements. It was often as a result of the directives and missives from external regulating bodies that the available options were restricted, rather than a deliberate manipulation by the headteacher to achieve her desired purpose (though Mary articulated her own position strongly when she felt it to be for the good of the school or in line with her own philosophy). However, teachers were not always clear about the different purposes of discussion. There was sometimes a need for Mary to explain to staff the different *status* of discussions:

- general debate about an issue for which there wasn't any obvious solution;
- deciding between a number of clearly defined options;
- confirming or giving moral support to a decision previously determined;
- contributing ideas, knowledge and expertise in pursuit of satisfactory implementation of an imposed decision.

Discussions which took place in which staff were under misapprehension about their purpose led to a mood of dissatisfaction or dismay. For example, if suggestions they made as part of a consultation exercise were subsequently rejected by the headteacher when they believed they were being involved in making a democratic decision, they felt slighted. It was therefore essential that Mary clarified the status of a particular consultation exercise, either with an individual or a group. If Mary's intention was to gauge opinion and gain perspectives prior to making the decision herself, she needed to explain this. If, on the other hand, it was to make a consensual decision, a similar explanation was necessary to avoid misunderstandings and subsequent chagrin.

Their Wish for Decisiveness

Mention has been made of the importance of convincing teachers that their involvement was valued, if they were to contribute actively and enthusiastically to discussion. For a few teachers, a further constraining influence upon their willingness to participate was a return to the same subject of discussion when they believed that it had already been dealt with. These teachers referred to the fact that time and effort spent in discussion and reflection, through age-phase meetings, full staff meetings and informal gatherings, yielded too little reward. For example, 'We spend a lot of time talking during staff meetings and too much is discussed repeatedly, just not getting anywhere.' Similarly, 'it seems that on occasions when we have actually prioritized an issue and used some time to discuss that issue, at the end of the meeting we are faced with a chance to make a decision which doesn't actually occur'.

From the staff's perspective, indecision was linked with the school's internal decision-making structure. They were initially convinced that the fixed procedures contributed to the repetition and resulted in a weariness with the topic that acted against decisiveness. In attempting to respond to this difficulty, the number of items included in the school's development plan under consideration during any period was reduced to allow a thorough, less protracted examination of fewer issues. This strategy, in conjunction with clarification about the purpose of different meetings and carefully recorded decisions, offset some of the staff concerns. It could not take account, however, of the continuing vacillation which characterized national policy-making at this time and often disrupted the best laid plans. For instance, the NCC's insistence on modifying the Attainment Targets for Science, new regulations for reporting to parents (which occurred at the very time the 'old' report forms were being filled in by staff) and the annual modifications to the composition of SATs, created extra work and increased the level of frustration among the staff. In the light of these circumstances, Mary could be forgiven for appearing a little bewildered and torn between different priorities.

The problem of indecisiveness, initially linked with the decision-making process existing *within* the school, was increasingly laid by teachers at the door of the government, the expression 'this lot' (i.e., government ministers) usually figuring somewhere in the complaint. Mary's attempts to develop a collegial system struggled with the reality of imposed directives which were sometimes difficult to interpret and implement, leading to delays and further meetings to clarify points which required time to ponder and master.

The Fluctuation of Staff Morale

Primary headteachers frequently express their gratitude for the hard work and perseverance of teachers in their school but have little way of knowing the extent to which their staff accept such accolades. At Patter's, many teachers referred to the way in which their state of morale affected motivation. One experienced teacher pointed to the critical tone of media coverage as proof that her status in the community was undervalued. Thus:

> Fundamentally, everyone wants to remain loyal to the school and do the best for the children; all the teachers are working jolly hard, but sometimes I feel that our efforts are not recognized; they are taken for granted. The government and press don't really appreciate what we do; your feeling of self-worth is undermined all along the line.

The rapid pace of change had caused more experienced staff (in particular) to feel that they were being swept along on a tide of legislation and statutory requirements which took insufficient account of their expertise and experience. The deputy was blunt in his condemnation of the tide of reforms:

> There's too much stuff from the DfE and LEA, in assessment for example; there's a need for continuity . . . There's still considerable

anger (among staff) about government policy. Most people accept the National Curriculum as good, but Potter's has been hit hard by LMS.

In addition to these external factors, some reasons were related to the way teachers' viewed their status *within* the school. For one experienced teacher, the belief that her efforts were being overlooked by governors was the main source of disillusionment:

> I feel rather undervalued; my expertise isn't being adequately used . . . Since my old Scale 2 was taken and absorbed into the new professional grade I've continued to do the tasks I did formerly, but I've never been considered for an extra allowance. I've reached the point where I'm easing upon the voluntary activities I once did.

Mary struggled to maintain morale and exercise decisive, upbeat leadership at a time of general depression about the state of education in the country. The staff's perceptions of her efforts were also significant. They perceived her as someone who worked very hard and was doing a difficult job under trying conditions. Generally, they were sympathetic about the demands placed upon her. However, they were also concerned about their *own* problems and expected Mary to demonstrate active and sincere concern for their position. During times of extra stress and worry, any failure on Mary's part to attend to personal detail affected morale and she had to learn to be 'as wise as a serpent and innocent as a dove' if misunderstandings were to be avoided. For instance, if Mary communicated something by letter to a member of staff when the teacher felt that it should have been by word of mouth, or if there was no expression of appreciation after a particular special effort made by the teacher, discontent soon surfaced. As such, Mary became a touchstone for staff satisfaction and security. Even her sorties out of school were received with a mixture of relief (the boss is away) and suspicion (why is she out again *this* time!). In a nutshell, teachers expected Mary to be both empathetic and sympathetic towards them and offer some quality time supporting their needs, aspirations, doubts and triumphs. They did not doubt her ability to manage school affairs, but they were looking for something beyond this 'ability to cope'. Above all, they wanted to be reassured that all was well, things were under control, and that under her leadership they could and would weather the storm.

The Difference made by the Headteacher's Presence

Mary didn't perceive herself as being a threat to her staff. She knew that her philosophy did not enjoy the full support of every teacher but was not prepared to compromise to the point where her own ideals were modified beyond recognition. However, she accepted that teachers would interpret decisions differently and was willing to allow variations in implementation, providing it accorded with general policy decisions. As such, Mary acknowledged the need to promote professional responsibility, but felt that it was part of her job to ensure that Patter's was (a) responding to statutory requirements, and (b) reflecting her own priorities for the image of the school. An important element of (b) was, of course, an increased level of collaboration at all levels. With this in mind, Mary needed to bear in mind that there were occasions when teachers hesitated to express their views publicly for fear of upsetting her. The reasons they gave for this hesitancy included:

- their desire for a quiet life which allowed them to interpret decisions loosely without undue negotiation;
- concerns that their career prospects might be damaged;
- worries that their remarks might betray their misgivings about school policy and be interpreted by the Head as disloyal;
- a belief that the headteacher was more likely to be correct and should not be challenged, frequently expressed through use of: 'She's the boss!'

The desire for 'a quiet life' was generally admitted by those staff who did not aspire to career advancement. They saw themselves remaining at Potter's for a long time and accepted that it was easier to accept a decision and interpret it loosely (especially in the teaching situation) to reflect their own priorities, than to publicly voice objections. Concerns over damaging career or enhancement prospects were uppermost for staff who admitted that they hoped to improve or alter their circumstances in the near future (Bottery, 1990). This issue proved more complex than it initially appeared, for the aspirations were not singular in character. There appeared to be three elements: those staff who were anxious to gain promotion elsewhere; those who wanted internal promotion; those who simply wanted to leave the school because they were dissatisfied and would accept a 'sideways' move. Two teachers at least, however, were scornful of the suggestion that they were reluctant to speak out, claiming that Mary knew that they were outspoken, but that it was always in the children's interest that they did so. Nevertheless, when Mary was present, contributions at formal and informal level were, for some staff, affected by thoughts of future prospects. 'After all, I shall need a good reference if I'm to get anywhere' was a comment mentioned by more than one teacher.

The belief that Mary had the right to act independently: (a) because of her status and (b) due to her superior knowledge and experience, was a surprisingly common reason offered by staff when interviewed. Despite any dissatisfaction with the methods of consultation and decision-making that may have been felt, including the forms of dialogue and level of involvement, there remained a deference to the headteacher as the appointed leader and authority figure; this appeared independent of the level of an individual member's respect for her as a person. The acknowledgment that care had to be exercised in expressing views publicly due to the headteacher's power to influence situations, was mirrored by a belief that she carried authority through her position.

Concerns over the headteacher's reactions were, therefore, highly significant in tempering the nature of participation. These concerns depended to a large extent on the type of issue under consideration; issues affecting teacher-autonomy or threatening their preferred method of teaching approach were most likely to cause an adverse reaction. Where staff perceived that Mary had made her mind up, come what may, objections to the proposed course of action were usually restrained. Public resistance to a proposal was more likely to take the form of indifference or unenthused restraint. The staff's desire for involvement had to be matched by their confidence about headteacher approval.

Mary grew to understand that she was a key player in shaping the nature of teacher participation. Her own approval or disapproval of a course of action or method of response affected the disposition of the staff and could create a climate of ease and trust or suspicion and defensiveness. Mary's support for collaboration as an appropriate vehicle for achieving goals and reaching decisions was a powerful factor in influencing teachers' willingness to accept the principle and respond positively.

Therefore . . .

The staff's response to the invitation to participate more fully in the decision-making process was subject to a number of constraints:

- teachers' insistence that the welfare of their classes came first;
- the severe time pressures under which they worked;
- doubts about the genuineness of their involvement;
- frustrations over indecision and delay;
- fluctuating morale;
- concerns over the headteacher's opinion.

These constraints did not prevent the collaborative process continuing and evolving, but they did affect Mary's plans for establishing a collaborative climate as she recognized that within the staff there were teachers whose response to the prospect of change varied between co-operation, resistance, retreat and manipulation (Osborn, 1992).

The show must go on

The case-study at Patter's Primary indicated that the headteacher's search for a collaborative climate as a suitable environment for effective school management and curriculum development required clarity of purpose and sensitivity to the demands upon the staff and their differing reactions to the opportunity to participate more fully in the process.

Life as the headteacher of Patter's Primary was complex and exhausting. The search for a collaborative climate sometimes seemed an impossible one as Mary responded to the ongoing demands of day-to-day school life and put in place the statutory requirements while coping with increasing responsibility due to local management and a delegated budget. The competing demands upon her own time and the concerns of teachers about their level of involvement strained her ingenuity to develop strategies which would involve staff, use their abilities and provide them with a sense of well-being and satisfaction. Mary also had her own battles to stay abreast of circumstances and provide positive leadership at a time when she herself felt vulnerable. Over time, as she grew in confidence and recognized the restrictions upon the development of a collaborative culture as well as the possibilities, she was able to restructure the management teams, respond to teachers' concerns, find time to gain wider perspectives and be reconciled to the changing nature of her role.

The Benefits and Costs of Collaboration

Mary came to appreciate that collaboration and the involvement of staff in whole-school issues provided for a variety of outcomes. First, involvement sometimes brought with it a *cost* to the teachers (Chapman, 1990; Campbell and Southworth, 1992) in terms of:

- the time spent on committee work, administration, consultation and liaison with colleagues;
- the fatigue and stress associated with these extra burdens which could lead to unwelcome consequences such as reduced classroom effectiveness, less tolerance, and impaired judgment;
- in the worst cases, ill-health and absenteeism.

There were also potential *advantages*:

- broader experience within school leading to greater professional fulfilment;
- the opportunity to exert greater influence upon whole-school policy;
- increased sensitivity to the broader issues affecting primary school management.

Second, the disposition of individuals or groups of teachers towards the opportunity for greater participation had more far-reaching implications. The involved teacher, through exerting influence and thereby affecting outcomes, might be expected to experience satisfaction with the direction of school policy and subsequently enjoy a deeper attachment to the decision-making process.

On the other hand, teachers who rejected the opportunity or were very tentative about involvement could find themselves alienated from the process, leading to disenchantment with outcomes and a decreasing commitment to future forms of collaboration.

Third, artificial forms of collaboration, in which there was a contrived collegiality operating were likely to damage working relationships rather than enhance them. The danger of this occurring will alert headteachers to the fact that although they may genuinely espouse the merits of whole staff involvement, they need to be careful that they are explicit about the nature of that involvement. Sometimes, Mary discovered that her willingness to *consult* with staff (intending to make the final decision herself) was misconstrued by teachers as the process of making the decision itself. Collaboration which is for the purpose of consultation and carries with it the notion of persuasion (Elliott-Kemp, 1982) must be clearly distinguished from that which is a consensual act in which an agreed outcome is implemented.

At its worst, collaboration could lead to a gradual polarization of staff, divided between those who perceived themselves as being 'part of the process' and those who perceived themselves as being external to it (Gaziel and Weiss, 1990). At best, it could help staff to feel fulfilled and use their expertise for the benefit of the whole school while enhancing their professional identity. Collaboration, therefore, had costs and benefits, and its place in the decision-making structure had to be evaluated with these points firmly in mind.

Implications for staff development

Closer collaboration and higher levels of staff involvement opened up opportunities for staff development that hierarchical models of management were unlikely to offer. First, there was the chance for all teachers to assume a leadership role, either formally through chairing working groups and committees, or informally through presenting carefully prepared arguments, offering expertise to colleagues or compiling papers as a contribution towards a debate. In these ways, talents and abilities which might have remained hidden behind classroom doors became publicly acknowledged.

Second, wider involvement in school-based decision-making offered staff the chance to experience aspects of school life which would otherwise have remained a mystery. As such, they become empowered to consider 'life beyond the classroom' and, we hope, use the vitality gained through these new experiences to enhance their teaching work. There was, however, a balance to be struck here, for an over-willingness to accept non-teaching commitments could, as we have seen, have detrimental effects. Nevertheless, for a teacher who was normally only engaged with a single curriculum responsibility, the benefits of involvement could be considerable as his or her horizons were extended.

Third, with the changes to the promotion structure in primary schools and the imposition of a single pay spine without designated posts of responsibility, the increasing number of teachers who were likely to stay at the same school for many years could not be allowed to become isolated or 'becalmed' in their work. Teachers committed a lot of time and emotional energy to school (Nias, 1989), and it was important that they had the opportunity to assume some ownership of the decisions by contributing to the process. It was also possible for teachers to become stale from working in a similar situation from year to year, and a healthy climate of collaboration allowed for stimulating interaction, change of direction and challenge.

The way ahead

We have seen that efforts to nurture a collaborative culture could lead to positive gains or harmful division. As headteachers and senior staff in school face this issue, they will need to be reconciled to the fact that there may be teachers who consciously opt for limited involvement in school wide issues. With the pressing need for a teaching staff to 'stand together' in the face of rapid change, there is an equally urgent requirement for senior staff to be clear about the collaborative climate they want for the school. Headteachers, in particular, if they are anxious to develop collegiality within their schools by means of enhanced collaboration, will benefit from re-appraising their decision-making structures and their understanding of the positions of individual members of staff to the process.

All staff must be comfortable with the place they occupy as a member of the school community. As headteachers exercise leadership within the school, they will need to ensure that the boundaries of responsibility and accountability are clear for every teacher. A sense of identity, security and belonging are necessary prerequisites of co-operation, utilization of potential, and whole-hearted allegiance to the collaborative process. Ideally, there should be a place for every teacher to feel valued and welcome. No headteacher, however skilled and committed, can be expected to spin all the plates all of the time.

References

ALUTTO, J.A. and BELASCO, J.A. (1972) 'A typology for participation in organisational decision-making', *Administrative Science Quarterly*, **17**, pp. 117–25.

BALL, S.J. (1987) *The Micro-Politics of the School*, London, Methuen.

BEACH, R.H. (1989) 'Rationality and planning', *Planning and Change*, **20**, 2, pp. 67–75.

BENNIS, W.G., BENNE, K.D. and CHIN, R (1985) *The Planning of Change*, New York, Holt, Rinehart and Winston.

BLEASE, D. and LEVER, D. (1992) 'What do primary headteachers really do?', *Educational Studies*, **18**, 2, pp. 185–99.

BOTTERY, M. (1990) 'The ethics of participation', *Curriculum*, **11**, 1, pp. 42–52.

CAMPBELL, R.J. (1985) *Developing the Primary School Curriculum*, London, Holt, Rinehart and Winston.

CAMPBELL, P. and SOUTHWORTH, G.W. (1992) 'Rethinking collegiality: Teachers' views', in BENNETT, N., CRAWFORD, M. and RICHES, C. (1992) *Managing Change in Education*, London, Paul Chapman Publishing.

CHAPMAN, J.D. (Ed) (1990) *School-Based Decision-making and Management*, London, The Falmer Press.

ELLIOTT-KEMP, J. (1982) *Managing Organizational Change*, Sheffield City Polytechnic, PAVIC Publications.

FULLAN, M.G. and HARGREAVES, A. (1992) *What's Worth Fighting For In Your School?* Milton Keynes, Open University Press.

GAZIEL, H.H. and WEISS, I. (1990) 'School bureaucratic structure, locus of control and alienation among primary schoolteachers', *Research in Education*, **44**, November, pp. 55–66.

GOLBY, M. (1985) *Caught in the Act: Teachers and Governors After 1980*, Exeter, University of Exeter School of Education.

HARGREAVES, A. (1992) 'Contrived collegiality: The micropolitics of teacher collaboration', in BENNETT, N., CRAWFORD, M. and RICHES, C. *Managing Change in Education*, London, Paul Chapman in association with the Open University.

HARGREAVES, D.H. and HOPKINS, D. (1991) *The Empowered School: The Management and Practice of Development Planning*, London, Cassell.

KIRKPATRICK, G. (1990) 'LMS: Preparing for practice; is a head a teacher who manages or a manager who teaches?', *Head Teachers' Review*, Spring, pp. 12–14, 16.

LAWS, J. and DENNISON, W.F. (1991) 'The use of headteachers' time: Leading professional or chief executive?', *Education 3–13*, **19**, 2, pp. 47–57.

MORTIMORE, P., SAMMONS, P., STOLL, L., LEWIS, D. and ECOB, R. (1988) *School Matters*, Wells, Open Books.

NIAS, D.J. (1989) *Primary Teachers Talking: A Study of Teaching As Work*, London, Routledge.

NIAS, D.J., SOUTHWORTH, G.W. and YEOMANS, R. (1989) *Staff Relationships in the Primary School: A Study of School Cultures*, London, Cassell.

OSBORN, M. (1992) 'The impact of current changes in English primary schools', *Teachers College Record*, **94**, 1, pp. 138–51.

PFEFFER, J. (1978) 'The micropolitics of organisations' in MEYER, M.W., FREEMAN, J.H., HANNON, M.T., OUCHI, W.G., PFEFFER, J. and SCOTT, W.R. (Eds) *Environments and Organisations*, San Francisco, Jossey-Bass.

PRICE, M.D. and REID, K. (1988) 'Differences between headteachers' and teachers' views on aspects of decision-making in primary schools', *Research in Education*, **39**, May, pp. 83–105.

STONE, C. (1989) 'All that remains is ambivalence: A headteachers' reflections', *Education 3–13*, **17**, 3, pp. 4–9.

SULLIVAN, M. (1990) 'A headteacher's battle with aims', in PROCTOR, N. *The Aims of Primary Education and the National Curriculum*, London, Falmer Press.

Chapter 5

Manageability and Control of the Primary Curriculum

Jim Campbell

Introduction

To those responsible for the management of the primary school curriculum, 1993 was a watershed year. Following the earlier acknowledgment by its chairman (Pascall, 1992) that the 'collective weight' of the statutory curriculum was too great, the agency responsible for the National Curriculum advised the Government that the statutory curriculum would have to be slimmed down (NCC, 1993a); the agency responsible for the national inspection arrangements reported that those schools that had nearly covered the statutory curriculum had done so only by encouraging superficial learning in their pupils (OFSTED, 1993). After reporting annually (Campbell and Neill, 1990; 1992; 1993; Campbell *et al.*, 1991) research findings that the 'balanced and broadly-based' curriculum of the Education Reform Act 1988 was structurally unmanageable, I welcomed official recognition of the problem. I had some doubts, however, whether attempts at its resolution would be based on an understanding of the real problems confronting classroom teachers, heads and governing bodies. When the official review process was set in train under Dearing, the interim and final reports (NCC/SEAC, 1993; SCAA, 1993) confirmed my fears that the main function of the Dearing review might be to save the Government's face and John Patten's neck, but not the curriculum. The real manageability problems confronting class teachers, heads and governing bodies had been avoided. The purpose of this chapter is to analyse these problems and explore ways forward in the mid- to late-1990s.

Background

One of the paradoxes was that there would have been no manageability problem without the principles embodied in the curriculum required by the 1988 Act. These principles were that pupils were entitled to a broad and balanced curriculum of nine (ten in Wales) foundation subjects, Religious Education and Other Teaching; that expectations for pupils' attainment should be raised and embodied in nationally agreed criteria; that the curriculum should be modernized to include Science and Technology; and that assessment should serve formative purposes. It was because these principles had attracted wide-spread professional commitment (Campbell *et al.*, 1991; Muschamp *et al.*, 1991) that schools faced an unmanageable curriculum. Without them teachers could have continued their previous practice of attending to the basics of literacy and numeracy, of giving token time and status to other subjects and restricting assessment to norm-referenced tests in reading comprehension and number (Gipps, 1988). The problems of curriculum manageability arose from both the legal force of, and the professional support for, the principles underlying the Government's reform of the curriculum.

None of the above is to deny that, for teachers, manageability problems were aggravated by mismanagement of the implementation of the reforms. The changes occurred too quickly, the curriculum and assessment orders were constantly revised and, in particular, there developed an unfortunate and ill-conceived language for the discourse of reform. *Level* was about the most inappropriate term for what statements of attainment represented. They stood for, according to the Task Group on Assessment and Testing Report (TGAT) (DES, 1988), about two years' progress for a typical pupil — that is to say, they represented gradients not levels. The courtroom and the tax office were summoned up by requiring teachers to provide *evidence* and engage in *audits*. *Delivery* was seen as a mechanistic term (invoking the post office or weapons systems) for the delicate interchanges thought to characterize teaching and learning (see Desforges, 1993), although I think we could reclaim the meta-phor's value by invoking the maternity hospital. Most importantly, with the exception of Coopers and Lybrand Deloitte (1991), no-one took into account the time which it would take teachers to prepare, implement and assess the statutory curriculum. Irritating, dispiriting and demoralizing as these were, they were mechanical matters, the consequence of generally-accepted princi-ples being inexpertly operationalized and poorly managed by quangos (NCC and SEAC, 1993), aggravated by direct and illicit interference by Ministers (Graham and Tytler, 1993). The real manageability issues were more deep seated, embedded in an anachronistic system, relying almost exclusively on the generalist class teacher. As Alexander expressed it, 'the late-twentieth-century visions of primary education and the late-nineteenth-century structure for delivering them have become increasingly incongruent', (1992: 194).

Three Problems

The problems that arose for those charged with managing the curriculum at the school level can be analysed in three discrete categories: curriculum time allocation, teacher expertise, and resources in primary schools.

The first reason for unmanageability is the apparently simple matter of *time allocation*; how much time is needed for each subject and for the whole curriculum. The problem has been commonly represented as the quart of the statutory orders and the pint pot of the teaching week (or year). I say 'apparently simple' because, if you are sitting on a national committee inventing or revising the statutory curriculum, it must appear merely a mechanical matter. Reduce the content until the whole curriculum matches, or is slightly less than, the time available.

The second reason concerns the *task demands on class teachers* attempting to deliver the whole curriculum — most obviously the range and level of subject knowledge required, the pedagogical skills necessary, including differentiation, the sheer detail and number of Statements of Attainment, and techniques necessary for reliable assessment. These have now been seen as unrealistic demands to make upon normal classroom teachers by all save the dismal succession of Ministers of State parading before us to assert that primary teaching, especially at Key Stage 1, is not a particularly demanding job, needing for its successful performance neither graduate knowledge nor long training.

The third reason concerns *resources*. As Alexander *et al.* (1992) pointed out, primary schools are staffed less favourably than secondary schools, even when the comparison is based on only Key Stage 3, yet the range and demand of their educational activities, and therefore their staffing needs, are almost identical. When Kelly (1991) ran a computer model of Stockport's curriculum-led staffing, she found that it led to staffing needs that were more-or-less identical across the five to sixteen age range.

Curriculum Time Allocation

The first difficulty faced by teachers was simple; there was too much curriculum for the time available. One reason commonly given for this was that the statutory curriculum had been invented by means of committees of subject enthusiasts who were unable to consider how their subject had to fit into the whole curriculum. As Graham, the chairman and chief executive of the National Curriculum Council at the time, noted in what might be thought of as a Pilate-like distancing commentary:

> Eventual reform of the curriculum was inevitable the moment it was decided to introduce it subject by subject. The appointment of individual subject working groups guaranteed that zealots outnumbered cynics — always a dangerous thing — that no subject would be knowingly undersold. When the full enormity of the consequences became clear, complexity and over prescription became the cry of those who caused it . . . Nonetheless, if one had to err, it was a magnificent aberration.
>
> (Graham and Tytler, 1992: 118)

There was some truth in at least the first two of these sentences, but the extent of policy error was substantially greater than Graham and Tytler allow. First,

Table 1: *National time allocation to the primary curriculum*

SUBJECT	Per cent	Hrs: KS1	Hrs: KS2
Mathematics	20	4.2	4.7
English	20	4.2	4.7
Science and Technology	12.5	2.6	2.9
History	7.5–10	1.6–2.1	2.4 (10 per cent)
Geography	7.5–10	1.6–2.1	2.4 (10 per cent)
Art	7.5	1.6	1.4
Music	5	1.1	1.2
Physical Education	5	1.1	1.2
Religious Education	5	1.1	1.2
Other Teaching	5–10	1.1–2.1	1.4 (6 per cent)
ALL	100	21	23.5

Adapted from *Education*, 3 April 1992.

at an early stage Ministers had worked on a broad view that the Education Reform Act would create a curricular framework in which the national prescription should cover substantially less than the whole curriculum. This was because Religious Education and other important curricular areas such as health education and moral development were conceived of as lying beyond national prescription. The consultative document (DES, 1987a) suggested that in schools where there was 'good practice' the National Curriculum subjects would occupy 70–80 per cent of curriculum time. Angela Rumbold was quoted in Hansard (17 December 1987: 209) as follows:

> As the legislation tries to set out the content of the curriculum . . .
> it is logical to suggest a time allocation for [the] subjects within the
> school week or term. During the consultation period we discussed
> how to achieve what is required in the core and foundation subjects
> within a given time and whether the time allocated to them should be
> 60 per cent during the primary years.

It is uncertain how the discussions referred to by Mrs. Rumbold progressed, but they appear to have been short-lived. For in the event, the working groups were given notional time allocations for their subjects, as shown in Table 1.

Three implications arose for curriculum management from the notional time allocations in this table. The most important is that they represented an error that was to have disastrous effects as the curriculum was implemented. The notional time for English and Mathematics (the two basics) combined, was dramatically lower than was conventionally provided by primary teachers, according to every study that had examined time allocations in the post-war period (see Bassey, 1977; Bennett, *et al.*, 1980; Galton and Simon, 1980; DES, 1987b; Tizard, *et al.*, 1988; Alexander, 1992). A summary covering much of the relevant research in the last fifteen years (see Campbell, 1994) showed that

50 per cent of time was typically given to English (30 per cent) and Mathematics (20 per cent), excluding their application to other subjects.

Empirically, the phenomenon of 50 per cent of time on these two subjects — what we might call the 'basic instinct' in the primary curriculum — is firmly established. Indeed, a study by Meyer *et al.* (1992) which is an examination of official elementary and primary curricula world-wide across this century until the late 1980s, argues that the phenomenon has been a global constant — irrespective of region, political economy or state of development. They show that the national language takes one-third and Mathematics one-sixth of official curricula: one-tenth of time is allocated to each of Science, Social Studies, Aesthetic Subjects, Physical Education and to Moral/Social/Religious Development. In the primary curriculum the basic instinct rules, OK?

The second point refers to the time available for the whole curriculum. It relates to 'evaporated time', a term coined in a professional development programme (ILEA, 1988) and used by Campbell and Neill (1994) to indicate time technically available for teaching but used for non-cognitive purposes such as supervising children changing for PE, moving them from one location in the school to another, lining up and clearing away. It is important because it is assumed to be available for teaching, but the studies referred to above that took account of this time by excluding it from teaching time, showed that something between 22 per cent and 6 per cent of teaching time evaporates in this way, the amount depending upon the age of the pupils and the physical layout and size of the school and the methodology of time analysis. In general, younger pupils and those in open-plan settings experience more evaporated time. It occurs in small units of time in any one day, but in Campbell and Neill's (1994) research, based on time logs of over 3000 days from over 300 primary teachers, the average evaporated time per week was calculated at nearly two hours per week, equivalent to nearly 10 per cent of the teaching time available and equal to the notional time allocated for at least one of the non-basic subjects, in the National Curriculum.

Thomas (1993) argues sharply that the view I have just outlined represents a top-down 'university' view of subjects and that the activities involved in evaporated time could be used for cognitive goals: getting a sense of place, number bonding, etc., as well as important social goals such as tying shoe laces, learning social rules, etc. This is true but it is empirically unlikely that this is how the teachers generally use or plan to use such time.

A third point, made in the classroom observational studies is that subjects given large amounts of time are the ones in which lowest proportions of pupil time on task were observed. For example, Alexander's (1992) study showed pupils distracted for 21 per cent of time on average in all curriculum areas, with 26 per cent and 23 per cent of time spent in English and Mathematics respectively distracted, but only 13 per cent and 10 per cent distraction in Music and PE respectively. We cannot translate time formally allocated, directly into time spent by pupils on learning the subject. Moreover, as in all human activities, with the possible exception of sexual intercourse, the time spent does not necessarily reflect quality. Long hours spent on repetitive computation exercises do not necessarily mean challenging learning for bright pupils any more than do long hours spent by low-attaining pupils on tasks too difficult for them.

Nonetheless, the conclusion from the research findings on time showed no general problem in primary classrooms about the adequacy of time being spent on teaching and learning the two basic subjects. Evidence after the introduction of the National Curriculum suggested that little had changed, with Campbell and Neill (1994) showing 51 per cent (Key Stage 1) and 49 per cent (Key Stage 2) of time devoted to the basics.

The reasons for this state of affairs are three well-known ones. First, as Ashton's (1975) research showed, drawing on a national sample of 1500 primary teachers in the early 1970s (i.e., just after the infamous 1960s), the highest curricular priority was given to the basic skills of Reading, Oracy, Mathematics and Writing. Art, PE, Music, Sex Education, Science and Technology and a second language were given low priority. A follow-up study by Ashton, (1981) with a less representative sample at the end of the 1970s, showed, if anything, higher priority placed on Mathematics and formal language competence. Thus, commitment to the basics has always been at a premium in the professional culture. Second, parents and governors place highest curricular priority on the basics also, as Thomas's (1986) investigation of London schools showed, and the Government has required greater teacher accountability to parents and governors. Third, there has been a long tradition, stretching way back before 1988, of formal testing focused on Reading Comprehension and Mathematics, (see Gipps 1988 for a detailed analysis of the scope and focus of LEA testing programmes), a tradition reinforced by National Curriculum assessment arrangements, though it is now slightly broadened by the inclusion of Science in the core. Such testing washes back into curriculum priorities. The basic instinct is sustained and reinforced by the workplace culture in primary schools.

Thus it becomes startlingly clear that the National Curriculum in primary schools, introduced by a series of Secretaries of State who had constantly banged on about the need to get back to basics and to raise standards of literacy and numeracy, put in place policy guidance designed to reduce the time typically spent by primary teachers on the basics, and especially on English, where the astonishing reduction of about one-third of existing time was proposed. With respect to time allocations, the policy guidance outstripped the practice in the schools for liberality and breadth. It offered a fundamentally different concept and ideology of curriculum balance.

Let me make the point most sharply. The guidance given to the working group devising the English curriculum was such as to encourage infant teachers to reduce the time they typically spent teaching children to read and write from about seven hours to little over four hours a week. No wonder there was widespread stress at Key Stage 1 with infant teachers accurately reporting that (Evans *et al.*, 1994), against their own professional judgment, they were having to reduce the time on hearing children read in order to fit in everything else.

As if to confirm this interpretation of the general policy, the National Curriculum Council (NCC) issued guidance on planning the Key Stage 2 curriculum (NCC, 1993b) in which three presumably recommended case studies of school planning were provided: two of them (Year 6 and 5 classes) suggested that the basics should be planned to occupy 41 per cent and 37.5 per cent of curriculum time respectively. The Year 5 class plan was developed into a yearly programme in which Mathematics and English occupy 316 out of the 846 hours available, some 37 per cent of curriculum time in their terms. Schools are urged by the NCC to review the exercise, including reviewing whether the time allocations are appropriate. In this context, it is interesting, but confusing, to see that in the summer (1993) *Update* from the NCC, the curriculum planning in a Coventry primary school was celebrated; it initially used a plan which involved only 40 per cent of time on basics, but after trialling, it changed to 50 per cent.

There was thus built into the curriculum at national level a four-pronged problem for every primary school: too much planned prescription overall (90–95 per cent of time was planned); too much content in the statutory orders for each subject; not enough flexibility to allow for evaporated time; a pretence or assumption that there would be more time available for the non-basics than there was in actuality.

Task Demands on Teachers

The task demands placed on class teachers by the National Curriculum have been analysed by Thomas (1993), who shows that in the slimmed down (but pre-Dearing) curriculum, teachers at Key Stage 2 had to be familiar with about 500 statements of attainment, detailed and confusingly presented programmes of study, poorly defined cross-curricular themes and religious education. In addition they would have to possess subject knowledge in the ten subjects up to about Level 6, or to be able to differentiate the planning, teaching and assessment across at least 4 levels (= eight years' progress) of the curriculum in each subject. To achieve all this they would need to be the curricular school equivalent of Albert Einstein, Marie Curie and Linford Christie rolled into one. The evidence about subject expertise sometimes takes a narrow view of the concept (see Richards, 1994 for an extended analysis of it) but the review of research by Bennett and Summers (1994) suggests that there are serious deficiencies in individual primary teachers' understandings, especially but not exclusively in the science and technology areas. Graduate students training for primary teaching provide no greater reasons for being sanguine, if those studied by Bennett and Carré (1993) are typical. They brought with them to their PGCE courses misunderstandings of everyday phenomena, such as the energy in a sledge moving down a hill, the explanations for night and day, and basic arithmetic competencies such as expressing £18 as a percentage of £120. Bennett and Carré's research used tests in Mathematics, English and Science based on National Curriculum levels 4, 5 and 6, and Assessment of Performance Unit (APU) tests. In some of these latter, the top 20 per cent of primary pupils scored higher than the average of the PGCE students. Technically, of course, the curriculum demands are placed on the whole school rather than the individual teacher, but in practice for the medium term future, most teachers will remain responsible for teaching most of the curriculum for the pupils in their class. Given the research findings, Alexander, Rose and Woodhead's (1992) assertion that, 'Teachers must possess the subject knowledge which the statutory orders require' (para. 120) sounds like a plea of desperation. A major management issue therefore becomes how the specialist expertise in the whole staff group can be deployed to extend the work of class teachers, with the overarching purpose that, as Richards (1986) argued, such deployment should 'support not undermine' the class teacher's role.

The Resourcing of Primary Schools

The previous two problems for manageability apply to all schools irrespective of location, size or other factors. Resource issues affect schools differentially, depending upon funding formulae, school size or pupil characteristics. There is however one key resource issue — the level of staffing. The disadvantage for primary schools of historic staffing allocations has been acknowledged for almost a decade (White Paper, 1985; House of Commons, 1986; Simpson, 1990), although the difficulty of translating the acknowledgment into staffing resources has been enormous, particularly since the acknowledgment occurred in a period of public expenditure restraint. Nonetheless, if primary schools are to develop more specialist approaches to the curriculum, if class size should rarely exceed 30, and if teachers are to have some time free of class teaching in the school day; if, in short, the schools are to be enabled to implement the National Curriculum without stress and overload remaining a chronic feature of teachers' work (see Campbell and Neill, 1994, Evans *et al.*, 1994), some improvement in the resourcing of schools is required. Acknowledgment (as in Alexander *et al.*, 1992) is no longer enough. The funding formulae at local level and the approval of schemes of devolved management at national level will need to be based on realistic assessment of the work activities now required of teachers in modern primary schools (Simpson, 1988; 1990). Without the development of such national or local policies there will remain constraints on the extent to which the curriculum reform policy can succeed.

The Dearing Review

For the management of primary schools, the Dearing review's interim report (NCC/SEAC, 1993) appeared to hold out seductive promises to make the curriculum manageable by slimming it down.

Table 2: *Hours (annual) allocated to subjects by the Dearing review*

	KS1 per cent		KS2 per cent	
	HOURS PER YEAR			
English directly	180	29	162	24
(through other subjects)	(36)		(18)	
Maths	126	21	126	19
Science	54	9	72	11
IT (through other subjects)	(27)		(36)	
Foundation subjects (x6)	36	6	45	7
RE	36	6	45	7

TES January 21, 1994.

In terms of the analysis provided so far, however, it was limited to the issue of time allocations, and my evaluation of Dearing starts from this recognition; the review had nothing to say about subject expertise or resourcing, perhaps more fundamental problems than time allocation. Even the restricted problem-solving of the final report (SCAA, 1994) is a sleight of hand in respect of the 'curricular arithmetic' of time allocations, according to Alexander and Campbell (1994). Dearing's approach was to allocate 20 per cent of curriculum time for discretionary use by the school and to free two weeks of the school from any curricular prescription, and then to offer guidance on time allocation (in para. 4.20 of the report) for the remaining time, viz for 80 per cent of thirty-six weeks. In discussing his own arithmetic, Dearing acknowledged that it was difficult to apply it to primary schools: 'Specific time will have to be set aside for work in English, but the full 30 per cent (KS1) and 25 per cent (KS2) does not have to be found in addition to time given to other subjects.' Perhaps too defensively Dearing added, 'This is not sleight of hand; it is a statement of fact based on the realities of teaching . . . expressed by teachers' (para. 4.19). His own arithmetic was presented in a table in para. 4.20. I give it above, in Table 2 with the bracketed figures referring to cross-curricular application, and therefore not counted in the total. I have added percentages based on the total annual hours of 612 and 675 (KS1 and KS2 respectively) for which national prescription was envisaged (i.e. 80 per cent of thirty-six weeks of 21 and 23.5 hours), and these percentages appeared to reflect the historic practices of teachers, at least at KS1, with about 50 per cent given over to the basics. There was however an assumed reduction in the proportion given to English at KS2. Alexander and Campbell however provide an alternative arithmetic, based on the overall time, not just the 80 per cent. Their arithmetic is given in Table 3.

Expressed this way, Dearing appears to have rendered almost a quarter of the school curriculum year discretionary, and therefore to have solved the

Table 3: *Hours (annual) in Table 2 expressed as a percentage of annual hours available for teaching*

	KS1 per cent	KS2 per cent
English directly	22.5	18
Maths	16	14
Science	7	8
Foundation subjects (x6)	4.5	5
RE	4.5	5
TOTAL	**77 per cent**	**75 per cent**

TES January 21, 1994.

manageability problem. However, as Alexander and Campbell show, there are five reasons why this has not really happened. First, the percentages for English and Mathematics are dramatically lower then previous or current practice, and time will have to be taken from the allegedly discretionary time to restore the basic instinct of 50 per cent time on them. Second, there is no educational or research-based justification for Dearing's assertion that as primary children become older they need less time on English. The DES (1987b) Primary Staffing Survey found 27 per cent allocated to English in the junior stage, and while it is obvious that the nature of English at KS1 is different from that at KS2, it is not clear why it should take less time. Nor has it done so in practice (DES, 1987b; Campbell and Neill, 1994). Third, time on Science has been reduced from what was previously proposed as necessary (see Table 1, p. 92) and the 10–15 per cent of time that was actually needed for the science curriculum (Campbell and Neill, 1994). Fourth, national testing remains focused on the core subjects, pressing in on school management to ensure that teachers give priority to them in time allocation. Allowing for evaporated time, Alexander and Campbell calculated that all discretionary time would have to go to the core. Fifth, the time remaining for the other subjects will be inadequate, especially for those that are time consuming, such as PE, Music, Art and Technology. Sixth, without good reason, excessive time has been set aside for RE. As a consequence, the only way the curriculum will become manageable is if it is recognized for what it is, underneath the Dearing rhetoric — a return to the elementary curriculum of the basics and RE updated with some Science and Information Technology. But manageability will have been gained at the expense of breadth and balance. As Alexander and Campbell comment: 'The elementary school curriculum is alive and well and living in Dearing.' Thus Dearing's solution to the curriculum manageability problem was to draw on a mechanistic arithmetic which enabled him to pretend to a retained commitment to the broad and balanced curriculum, while leaving in place all the old pressures in the primary school culture to concentrate on the basics at the expense of other subjects. As I argued above, the issue of time allocation is only one part of the problem, but even this aspect has been mishandled. What are the implications for the management of schools?

Management Implications

This stage of the argument is based on two assumptions about the relationship between a national quango (in this case the School Curriculum and Assessment Authority) and individual schools. National quangos are not good at details, and have little competence in respect of the curriculum organization of individual schools. For example, within the space of nine months the National Curriculum Council (NCC, 1993b) and the School Curriculum and Assessment Authority (SCAA, 1994) could not even agree on the simple technical matter of how many hours per year should be considered as available for instruction. Second, as Thomas pointed out, the National Curriculum was established by reference to the best practice in each subject. To be 'best' or even good at everything is not common in individual human beings or their institutions so that there was and is a certainty that virtually all schools would, to some degree, fail to meet the statutory requirements. He added that 'Schools in other countries commonly fail to meet the requirements of their national curricula' (1993: 6).

If these two assumptions are confirmed, the first lessons for school management are that it is in the individual school, not a national agency, that will create a curriculum that can be made to work for the school concerned; and that concern to cover the whole curriculum will have to be tempered by consideration of quality and standards in pupils' learning. This latter goal might be more readily arrived at by the school establishing its curricular priorities than by attempting to deliver every statutory prescription equally well. It was, after all, the quango charged with the inspection of schools that first made clear that coverage had been achieved only at the cost of depth in pupil learning (OFSTED, 1993). To restore confidence in their own professional judgment, it may first be necessary for teachers to lose faith in the ability of the national agencies to manage the curriculum implementation process sensibly. Dependency on external forces is as counter productive for the whole school staff as it is for the head (Fullan, 1992; Fullan and Hargreaves, 1992) and is likely to reduce rather than increase empowerment and accountability. On this basis six possible ways forward may be identified, though each will be contested by some teachers because of the value assumptions it contains.

Time Allocation

First, in respect of time allocation, there is the possibility that much more of the teaching of English and Mathematics than currently might be planned, delivered and assessed through their application to other subjects. This is a position advocated for at least fifteen years by HMI (see DES, 1978), but has been found problematic in practice. The problem is not helped by the framing of the curriculum in single subjects, nor by the tendency for mathematics and English schemes to be subject-specific. It is a good example of how a staff would have to have confidence as HMI had (DES, 1978), that standards in the basics would improve by their being applied to other subjects. Unfortunately, it may be easier for staff in schools where pupils already have high achievement to develop such confidence than for staff where pupils appear to need substantial amounts of time on basic skills.

Second, schools might consider the use of homework as part of their overall policy, especially perhaps at KS2. If there is shortage of time for English, part of the solution might be to cease to consider the pupils' curriculum time as synonymous with the timetabled school day. Successful experience at KS1 with parental partnerships (see Tizard *et al.*, 1988) provides exemplars for developing similar approaches at KS2. Some opposition might be raised by those who would see such a systematic approach to homework as increasing the disadvantages of pupils who live in unsupportive families or physical conditions unconducive to doing homework. School-based provision for facilities for doing homework, while a contradiction in terms, might go some way to mitigating the difficulties, though at a cost in staff supervision time.

A third solution to the problem of curriculum time might be to extend the school day, week or year. This is clearly sensible for those schools who currently spend less than the minimum expected weekly hours on instruction. It will be opposed on grounds of workload (either for pupils or teachers or both) and of inappropriateness in rural areas where pupils have to travel long distances (NCC, 1993a). It might also be surmised that while the current assessment and testing policy remains in place, any extra time would be devoted to the core and thus not release time for the non-core, which is the problem.

Subject Expertise

It has been suggested (Bennett and Summers, 1994) that a solution to teachers' lack of confidence and competence in subject expertise could be remedied by a greatly expanded In-service training programme along lines similar to the DES twenty-day courses. This is obviously true, assuming that the courses are effective, and that their effects are long-lived, an assumption that Bennett and Summer's review of research questions in part. However, the problem for primary schools is that extensions of In-service training programmes are also extensions of the times when teachers have to be away from school and their class, so that a substantial programme of In-service Training in the school day may have disadvantages for pupil learning where schools do not have access to good quality supply cover.

A second possibility lies in suggestions (see Campbell, 1985; House of Commons, 1986; Alexander *et al.*, 1992) that schools should deploy their staff in ways that enable their subject expertise to be exploited more effectively to the benefit of the school as a whole, whether as specialists, semi-specialists or as coordinators. Again, within limits, this might offer gains to some schools, especially those with staffing allocations that permit some flexibility of deployment. For most schools, however, there is almost no flexibility, and, as school size reduces, the range of subjects in which there is staff expertise also reduces.

A third possibility is that more use should be made of class texts (taken to mean learning materials of all kinds, not just textbooks) in which the teachers can have confidence that the intellectual content is reliable, freeing them to concentrate more upon planning for how pupils may learn more effectively from the texts. There may be some reluctance in the profession to the purchase of texts for whole classes, since it is seen as at odds with concepts of good practice which stress learning from first hand experience, building on pupils' interests, and practical investigations. While recognizing that purchasing class texts will not solve all problems, I detect a note of educational political correctness in such opposition, perhaps influenced by past images of whole classes sitting reading class textbooks at the same pace, each pupil being asked to read aloud with the rest of the class following. The way texts are used with primary classes is obviously an important matter, but the adoption of good quality class texts would be the quickest way of helping class teachers cope with both the cognitive demands of the whole curriculum and the time demands of preparing all learning materials for their pupils. There is something puritanical in a professional culture which implies that the virtuous teacher is the one who prepares every worksheet herself. I would even go further and suggest that one of the few ways that a national quango could make itself useful to teachers would be to issue 'kitemarks' to texts to indicate that the statutory orders were accurately and adequately covered by them and that there were useful assessment activities integrated into them. This is, politically speaking, quite different from requiring that schools use one particular prescribed text.

Resources

Little useful can be added about the formulae by which, externally, resources are allocated to schools, beyond what has been argued earlier (p. 96). On the internal allocation of the resources when allocated, one further point needs to be raised. In most primary schools lack of time, especially lack of time in the school day, has been a major obstacle to effective delivery of the curriculum. (See Campbell and Neill, 1994). Yet Campbell and Neill showed that teachers spent about eighteen hours a week teaching, and between five and six hours a week on low level routines, such as mounting displays, supervision, moving pupils round the school, registration, and collecting dinner money, etc. Where teachers had more time with a non-teaching assistant, they tended to spend more, not less, time on such routines, probably because of the 'collaborative cultures' (Nias *et al.*, 1989) operating in them. Yet there is something unsettling about the picture of teachers naming lack of time as the main obstacle to achieving the cognitive objectives of the curriculum while spending so much time on non-cognitive routines. Given that teacher time is the most valuable and most expensive resource available to a school, it is worth the management of the school exploring the advantages of re-thinking the use of time of all adults on the staff of the school, to see whether the non-teaching assistants' time might be used imaginatively to free up teachers' time. On a more radical analysis, the automatic replacement of a departing teacher by another one rather than by a part-time teacher with more extensive non-teaching support, may need exploration.

Conclusion

In conclusion, however, none of the arguments proposed above constitute even the beginning of solutions without the kind of framework of curriculum priorities and professional self-confidence outlined at the beginning of this section. A National Curriculum is, almost by definition, not absolutely realizable by any one school. Indeed, the virtues of unmanageability need to be recognized. At the sixth annual conference of the Association for the Study of the Curriculum at York and Ripon St. John College in September 1993, a headteacher complained in the plenary that the papers presented (Alexander, 1994; Campbell, 1994; Weston, 1994) assumed manageability was a desirable objective. While the curriculum was recognized — pre-Dearing — as unmanageable, he argued, he could not be held accountable for all of it. He therefore could develop his school's whole curriculum to reflect, within limits, his and her staff's values, preferences and priorities. As soon as the whole curriculum was rendered officially manageable, he would lose such exercise of professional choice. For school management, the important goal in the next five years is to have priorities for the curriculum agreed by the governing body, the head and the staff, so as to incorporate the possibilities for raised standards and a broad curriculum that lie within the national curricular framework. If this means that pupils cover somewhat less content, but in greater depth, such priorities will be justifiable to parents, and even to OFSTED inspectors, than the rushed scampering across the surface of the statutory orders that has characterized attempts to meet all the statutory requirements of the pre-Dearing overweight curriculum, and will continue to characterize attempts to cover the post-Dearing allegedly slimmed down one.

References

ALEXANDER, R. (1992) *Policy and Practice in Primary Education*, London, Routledge.
ALEXANDER, R. (1994) 'What primary curriculum? Dearing and beyond', *Education 3–13*, **22**, 1, pp. 24–35.

ALEXANDER, R., ROSE, J. and WOODHEAD, C. (1992) *Curriculum Organisation and Classroom Practice in Primary Schools: A Discussion Paper*, London, DES.

ALEXANDER, R. and CAMPBELL, J. (1994) 'Beware Dearing's time warp', *Times Educational Supplement*, 21 January.

ASHTON, P. (1975) *The Aims of Primary Education*, London, Macmillan.

ASHTON, P. (1981) 'Primary teachers' aims: A follow-up study', in LOFTHOUSE, B. (Ed) *The Study of Primary Education*, **3**, London, Falmer Press.

BASSEY, M. (1977) *Nine Hundred Primary School Teachers*, Nottingham, Trent Polytechnic.

BENNETT, N. and CARRÉ, C. (1993) (Eds) *Learning to Teach*, London, Routledge.

BENNETT, N. and SUMMERS, M. (1994) 'Subject knowledge for teaching and learning' in POLLARD, A. (Ed) *Look Before You Leap*, London, Tufnell Press.

BENNETT, N., ANDREA, J., HEGARTY, P. and WADE, B. (1980) *Open Plan Schools*, Windsor, NFER.

CAMPBELL, R.J. (1985) *Developing the Primary Curriculum*, London, Cassell.

CAMPBELL, R.J. (Ed) (1993) *Breadth and Balance in the Primary Curriculum*, London, Falmer Press.

CAMPBELL, R.J. (1994) 'Managing the primary curriculum: The issue of time allocation', *Education 3–13*, **21**, 1, pp. 3–13.

CAMPBELL, R.J. and NEILL, S.R. (1990) *1330 Days*, London, Assistant Masters and Mistresses Association.

CAMPBELL, R.J. and NEILL, S.R. (1992) *Teacher Time and Curriculum Manageability*, London, Assistant Masters and Mistresses Association.

CAMPBELL, R.J. and NEILL S.R. (1993) *Four Years On: Teacher Commitment and Policy Practice*, London, Association of Teachers and Lecturers.

CAMPBELL, R.J. and NEILL, S.R. (1994) *Primary Teachers at Work*, London, Routledge.

CAMPBELL, R.J., EVANS, L., NEILL, S.R. and PACKWOOD, S. (1991) *Workloads, Achievement and Stress*, London, Assistant Master and Mistresses Association.

COOPERS and LYBRAND DELOITTE (1991) *Costs of the National Curriculum in Primary Schools*, London, NUT.

DES (1978) *Primary Education in England: A Survey by HMI*, London, HMSO.

DES (1987a) *The National Curriculum: A Consultative Document*, London, HMSO.

DES (1987b) *Primary Staffing Survey*, London, HMSO.

DES (1988) *Task Group on Assessment and Testing: A Report*, London, HMSO.

DESFORGES, C. (1993) 'Children's Learning: Has it improved?' *Education 3–13*, 3, pp. 3–10.

EVANS, L., PACKWOOD, A., NEILL, S.R. and CAMPBELL, R.J. (1994) *The Meaning of Infant Teachers' Work*, London, Routledge.

FULLAN, M. (1992) *The New Meaning of Educational Change*, London, Falmer.

FULLAN, M. and HARGREAVES, A. (1992) *What's Worth Fighting for in Your School?*, Milton Keynes, Open University Press.

GALTON, M. and SIMON, B. (1980) *Inside the Primary Classroom*, London, Routledge and Kegan Paul.

GIPPS, C. (1988) 'The debate over standards and the uses of testing', *British Journal of Educational Studies*, XXXVI, 1, pp. 21–37.

GRAHAM, D. and TYTLER, D. (1993) *A Lesson for Us All*, London, Routledge.

HOUSE OF COMMONS (1986) *ESAC 3rd Report: Achievement in Primary Schools*, **1**, London, HMSO.

ILEA (1988) *Planning the National Curriculum*, London, ILEA.

KELLY, A. (1991) 'Towards objective funding: An activity-led model of teacher staffing in primary and secondary schools', *Annual Conference of BERA*, Nottingham University.

MEYER, J.W., KAMENS, D.H. and BENAVOT, A. (1992) *School Knowledge for the Masses*, London, Falmer Press.

MUSCHAMP, Y., POLLARD, A. and SHARPE, R. (1991) 'Curriculum Management in Primary Schools', Bristol Polytechnic, School of Education.

NATIONAL CURRICULUM COUNCIL (NCC) (1993a) *The National Curriculum at Key Stages 1 and 2: Advice to the Secretary of State*, January.

NATIONAL CURRICULUM COUNCIL (1993b) *Planning the Curriculum at Key Stage 2*, York, NCC.

NCC/SEAC (1993) *The National Curriculum and its Assessment: An Interim Report by Sir Ron Dearing*, London, HMSO.

NIAS, J., SOUTHWORTH, G., and YEOMANS, R. (1989) *Staff Relationships in the Primary School*, London, Cassell.

OFSTED (1993) *Curriculum Organisation and Classroom Practice: A Follow-up*, London, HMSO.

PASCALL, D. (1992) 'In search of excellence' Speech Cambridgeshire LEA, Headteachers Conference, Leicester University.

RICHARDS, C. (1986) 'The Curriculum from 5–15: Some emerging issues' SCAA (1993) *The National Curriculum and its Assessment*, Final Report, Sir Ron Dearing.

RICHARDS, C. (1994) 'Subject expertize and its deployment in primary schools: A discussion paper' *Education 3–13*, **22**, 1, pp. 40–3.

SIMPSON, E. (1988) *Review of Curriculum-led Staffing*, EMIE, Windsor, NFER.

SIMPSON, E. (1990) 'The Stubborn Statistic', *Education*, 21 April.

THOMAS, N. (1986) *Improving Primary Schools*, London, ILEA.

THOMAS, N. (1993) 'Breadth and balance and the National Curriculum', in CAMPBELL, R.J. (Ed) *Breadth and Balance in the Primary Curriculum*, London, Falmer Press.

TIZARD, B., BLATCHFORD, P., BURKE, J., FARGUHAR, C. and PLEWIS, I. (1988) *Young Children at School in the Inner City*, London, Lawrence Erlbaum.

WESTON, P. (1994) 'Managing coherence: A letter to Sir Ron', *Education 3–13*, **22**, 1, pp. 14–23.

WHITE PAPER (1985) *Better Schools*, London, HMSO.

Managing Assessment: Have we Learned any Lessons from the Experience of National Curriculum Assessment?

Colin Conner

It is certainly the case that the last few years have been both dramatic and traumatic for primary teachers as far as assessment is concerned, culminating in the Dearing reviews (1993 and 1994), and what a number of opposition politicians described as 'the latest and greatest government U turn'. (Ann Taylor, the Labour Party's education spokeswoman, reported in *The Independant* 6 January 94. p. 1) The most recent and final Dearing report has been hailed as representing common sense and as an acceptance of the advice and suggestions offered by the profession. At the press conference when the report was introduced, Sir Ron Dearing commented, 'I hope teachers will see this as an honest and constructive response to their concerns. I think they will welcome very much the trust these proposals place in schools and teachers' (Judd, 1994).

The changes that he has proposed are significant. As paragraph 2.7 of the report indicates,

> The opportunity should . . . be taken to reduce the present number of attainment targets and statements of attainment. The scope for reducing the number of attainment targets is greatest at the lowest levels. The aim in reducing the number of statements of attainment should be to produce a definition of what is expected at each level which is sufficiently clear and rigorous to be of use to teachers, but which avoids the excessive detail of the current approach.
>
> (Dearing, 1994: 8)

Reference to the current situation is also made in paragraph 7.25 of the report, which suggests that,

> we have created an over-elaborate system which distorts the nature of the different subjects, which serves to fragment teaching and learning in that teachers are planning work from the statements of attainment,

and which has at times reduced the assessment process to a meaning-
less ticking of myriad boxes.

(Dearing, 1994: 61)

If implemented, the proposals Dearing offers should reduce considerably
the assessment demands that primary teachers have had to cope with since the
introduction of statutory assessment and they reassert the proposals of the
Task Group on Assessment and Testing (TGAT) (1988), that teacher assessment should have equal status to standard assessment. As Whalley argued in
1988,

If assessment lies at the heart of the learning process, then teacher
assessment lies at the centre of any system. The assessments made by
teachers are based on numerous different samplings over a long period. The assessment is made in the knowledge of the context in
which learning takes place.

(Whalley, 1989: p. 10)

As a result of the changes that have been proposed, it would be very easy
to assume that assessment will now take a back seat, because of the considerable reduction, especially of statutory assessment through the use of Standard Assessment Tasks (SATs). During the last five years, however, it is
important to recognize the significant gains that have been made as a result of
the assessment expertise developed in primary education, particularly in the
early years at Key Stage One. In the effort to make assessment more manageable
we need to be wary that we do not lose a lot of those hard earned benefits,
increased knowledge and expertise, by naively assuming that there is to be a
similar reduction in teacher assessment. What has to be recognized is that
teacher assessment is now the major element in the assessment of children's
achievements, because the SATs focus on such a narrow range of competence,
and as a result it is important that we continue to work to improve the
quality, reliability and validity of these assessments.

For the last four years, local authorities in the eastern region of England
have participated in three linked evaluation and research projects carried out
by Mary James and me at the University of Cambridge Institute of Education.
The first study was an evaluation of Key Stage One assessment training in
Bedfordshire Local Education authority during 1990/91, during the suppos-
edly 'unreported' initial run of National Curriculum assessment in the core
subjects of English, Mathematics and Science. This project involved observation of assessment training and the implementation of assessment in schools
during 1991 and interviews with teachers, headteachers, moderators and LEA
advisers. The findings of this study were presented in a report to the LEA
(Conner and James, 1991) and subsequently shared with the other LEAs in the
region. This stimulated a second study, funded by four LEAs (Essex, Hertfordshire, Norfolk and Suffolk), which focused on the moderation process

and the obligation placed upon LEAs in 1991/2 by the Schools Examination and Assessment Council (SEAC), 'to promote consistent standards of assessment within and across Local Authorities'. Moderators were observed while being trained, during training sessions that they organized for their schools and during the process of moderation visits to schools. These visits also provided the opportunity for discussion with teachers, headteachers and the moderators. The outcomes of this study resulted in another report for the LEAs (James and Conner, 1992) and an article in the Curriculum Journal (James and Conner, 1993). A third study continued this research, monitoring assessment practice, and was extended to include six LEAs (Bedfordshire, Cambridgeshire, Essex, Hertfordshire, Norfolk and Suffolk), and as a result of the Assessment Order for Key Stage One for 1992/3 directed the focus upon case studies of schools, two or three in each authority. This was a response to the requirement introduced by the DFE in Circular 12/92 which gave headteachers and governors statutory responsibility for consistent assessment in their schools and ensuring that their school's assessment standards conformed to national standards. The results of this study were presented to the LEAs in September 1993 (Conner and James, 1993). The project is continuing in 1994, again funded by the six East Anglian LEAs, and will focus upon LEA policy and the structures and procedures that have been developed within the region to assure intra- and inter-LEA consistency. Taken together, we believe that these four research projects provide a useful multi-faceted, longitudinal study into the ways schools and LEAs have tackled their responsibilities for assessment. What they also serve to demonstrate is the effort that has been expended on assessment and the expertise that has been developed. As one of the headteachers who was involved commented,

> If I compare the comments that my staff make now about their children with the kind of things that we were saying a few years ago, there is no comparison. What we offer now is quality and detail. Our reports and discussions with parents are informed, and the parents respect that. More than that, the information we generate is useful. It helps us to plan where we go next.

It is important to recognize however, that not all schools are at the same point in their development and that it is wrong to assume that because one teacher or a group of teachers in one school are both committed to and understand the demands of assessment, that this necessarily applies to all colleagues on a staff. Differences between schools and between the practice of individual teachers within a school in terms of their application of assessment procedures and processes should not be taken as a means of differentiating between schools and teachers or their effectiveness. Over the last few years, as a direct result of the never-ending stream of demands from central government, schools have had to face competing priorities, only one of which has been concerned with establishing effective and efficient assessment systems. In the final report on the 1993 project, described above, we commented.

- schools are at very different stages in understanding and practice depending on development priorities within the schools and the commitment to assessment by senior managers.

(James and Conner, 1993, p. 5)

This point was illustrated by a number of comments from participants in the project. One headteacher suggested that,

Assessment isn't really happening here, not in the way it is intended. You could probably say that we are in the dark ages as far as assessment is concerned.

This headteacher went on to explain that there had been a series of staff changes over the previous few years which had seriously undermined attempts at the development of consistent whole school policies. In other schools, where there was strong commitment of the headteacher and an established staff, assessment was regarded as the fundamental basis of curriculum planning and was, 'on the agenda the whole time'. Several headteachers questioned how far this might continue however. As one of them suggested,

Assessment has been a major priority in the school development plan for the last two years. It has to give way to other priorities next year; yet I know we've only just started to get it right.

The two case studies that follow are drawn from the most recently completed project and are offered as illustrations of the ways in which schools are working at developing and improving their practice of assessment. The two studies offer examples of schools at very different stages in their thinking about assessment, but each of them provides evidence of the professional commitment of the teachers involved.

Case Study 1: The Domino Primary School

Introduction

This study illustrates a number of important issues related to the development of a school assessment policy. In particular, it reinforces the effect of the existing school culture and previous experience in the development of whole school policies. Further, it reminds us of the nature of the change process and the effect of a school context on the speed at which change takes place and finally, it emphasizes the importance of the role of the moderator as a catalyst and supporter of the change process.

Background

The Domino Primary school is a school of 202 children and 9.2 staff (including the non-teaching headteacher), in a well established suburban area. The school has a very pleasant site which provides the children with plenty of opportunity for using the school grounds, which at the time of visits were well-endowed with flowers. In 1993 there were twenty-five children in Year Two, taught by an experienced Year Two teacher for whom this was the third year of involvement in SATs.

At this primary school, the headteacher opened the conversation at the first interview with the comment that the story of assessment in this school, 'will not take very long'. It was explained, that there was no structured whole school policy and assessment was seen primarily as the individual responsibility of each teacher. As the headteacher commented, 'It is something that we all do and that we are doing all of the time, we do it intuitively. It's a natural part of being a teacher'.

The head teacher went on to describe the kinds of assessment practice that existed in the school and in doing so offered evidence of a lot of appropriate and purposeful assessment, based on a strongly held philosophy that placed the children at the centre of the process. It was immediately accepted that the major weakness was that this set of practices were somewhat idiosyncratic, with each teacher tending to 'do their own thing', and that there was a need for practice and thinking to be refined into a formal policy which, 'influenced practice consistently across the school'.

School development and support

The headteacher suggested that the most rigorous assessment was taking place in the classroom of the Year Two teacher, who had developed a variety of procedures which included children's portfolios with annotated examples of children's work to illustrate the varying levels of achievement that could be seen in her classroom. The rest of the staff had shown little interest in this material, had limited contact or experience of the procedures involved in National Curriculum Assessment and as yet did not really see it as part of their responsibility. At the time of the first interview there had been no use of SAT materials by other members of staff and the headteacher admitted to being '. . . reticent, holding back to see what future changes were likely to occur'.

As far as Key Stage 2 was concerned, the deputy headteacher had participated in a range of LEA in-service courses on assessment, but had only adopted the ideas that had been proposed in the training to a limited extent, awaiting further information on the likely organization and structure of assessment at Key Stage 2.

During the first interview, the headteacher explained that the LEA audit moderator had agreed to join the staff for a series of three after-school discussion sessions with a view to 'developing our own assessment system. We want to develop something that is ours, that supports the way we work here.'

Moderation

The moderator opened the first of these sessions by suggesting that the series of meetings should be seen as an opportunity to introduce coherence into the school's system of assessment and record keeping and to draw together the successful practices of each teacher for the benefit of the school as a whole. Each teacher took it in turn to describe how they assessed in their classroom and this quickly illustrated the similarities and differences that existed in their practice. It also provided examples of the variety of procedures employed as well as leading to questioning of each other to justify the procedures used. The moderator then invited them to consider how they might rationalize the variations in their practice and suggested that an appropriate starting point might be to consider the central question: WHY? Why are we assessing? Addressing this question was then used to lead the discussion on to consideration of what is the most useful procedure for this purpose? This was suggested as a useful way of reducing the wide range of different procedures that were being employed and as a way of making assessment more manageable and consistent.

Three main answers emerged to the question of *Why we are assessing*, primarily as a result of prompting and guidance by the moderator. These were, that we undertake assessment:

- To celebrate children's achievements;
- To corroborate our judgments;
- To meet legal obligations.

The moderator suggested that each of these needed to be addressed separately.

The Local Authority had advocated the use of a Record of Achievement as a way of fulfilling these requirements. It was suggested that celebration of children's individual achievement was best satisfied in a portfolio of evidence, where the emphasis was on achievement not just attainment in National Curriculum terms. Achievement for some children, in some contexts, it was argued, might appear limited when compared to National Curriculum Attainment targets, but of considerable significance to the child's progress. A record of achievement celebrated such significant gains. The moderator went on to describe some of the features of the child's portfolio. It was suggested that the involvement of the learner should be a central feature of the process of deciding what might be included, that it should be a dynamic process which meant that as one piece of illustrative evidence was added, something had to be removed from the portfolio. Again, it was an important learning experience for children to engage in such decision making. The portfolio should contain no more than 8–10 pieces of evidence at any one time and what was included would vary for each child and therefore did not necessarily have to reflect the whole curriculum. It was also suggested that the processes involved were likely to be more successful if the procedures adopted were common throughout the school.

Not surprisingly, each of these suggestions stimulated a lot of discussion, especially related to practical issues of implementation. Weren't they likely to be time consuming? Were they really necessary? A particular concern related to who controlled the process. Some were in favour of the teacher making most of the decisions to ensure that an appropriate range of work was represented in the portfolio. Others were more in favour of the responsibility being primarily that of the child. One further point which emerged from the discussion was a recognition of the importance of annotation, to ensure that anyone else seeing the portfolio could understand what the elements included were illustrating. This concern naturally led the discussion on to the second purpose previously identified, that of corroboration of judgments.

To satisfy this second purpose, the development of a school portfolio had been advocated by the LEA. In introducing this idea, the moderator explained that the generation of a sample of work for each level, initially in the core subjects, which had been discussed and agreed by the staff as a whole, would demonstrate the application of rigorous and consistent standards across the school. This could then be used by moderators, inspectors and other schools to corroborate judgments. Working together as a staff on such an activity it was suggested, leads to internal agreement on interpretation of attainment targets and statements of attainment. All of this, it was advocated, provided evidence to satisfy the third purpose of fulfilling legal expectations.

As might be expected, this also stimulated considerable debate amongst the teachers. The feasibility of what was involved seemed daunting to those with no experience of National Curriculum Assessment training and reservations on the part of some of those who had experience. Questions were raised about the problems of agreeing about what it meant to say a particular statement of attainment had been achieved. Reference was made to differences of opinion at previous agreement trials that had been attended, where even though agreement appeared to have been achieved, some teachers were not prepared to accept the conclusion reached. One teacher of Y4 made reference to a child who had been assessed as achieving a particular attainment target in the SATs at Key Stage 1 but who was no longer able to satisfy the requirements. There was a suggestion that 'a level 2 in the Infants is not the same as a level 2 in the Juniors'. As a result of this discussion, however, the staff themselves came to realize that the only way in which such uncertainty can be removed is by continuing to talk together, that it was in everybody's interests to work towards the development of consistency in assessment and that the best way to do this was through the development of a school policy. Many of these issues were revisited at the second discussion session, but the final session moved the process forward as they attempted to engage in the process of producing a school assessment policy.

In preparation for the session which focused on the school policy, the moderator met with the headteacher during the afternoon before the third meeting, to discuss the most appropriate way of moving forward. The headteacher had produced a draft policy as the basis for discussion during the evening. The moderator's initial reaction was that it did not include any statements which clarified the purposes of assessment, beyond the need to satisfy current legal requirements, and which might have drawn upon the discussions that the staff had been engaged in. Nor was there any attempt to relate the proposals for assessment to the school's own philosophy about what influenced effective learning. The headteacher accepted these concerns and commented that in producing the document, his main concern had been to 'steer a path which supports the differences of opinion which exists amongst the staff'. In effect, it could be argued, that the headteacher was indicating his knowledge of the prevailing culture. In order to move staff thinking on in a difficult context he had to attempt to keep channels of communication open. Preparing the ground for the evening discussion was a way of doing that, as was attempting to avoid anything that might be seen as controversial.

The moderator suggested that perhaps the best way forward would be for the head to use the document that had been prepared as an *aide-mémoire* for the meeting and to invite the staff to offer suggestions about the purposes of assessment that should underpin *their* policy and to use *their* words in any policy that was produced. During this preparatory session questions were asked of the moderator about the nature of policy documents. Were they to be presented as 'a set of useful hints for teachers' or should they be 'a set of clearly espoused principles which enshrined what a school was about?' It was agreed that any principles should be seen to be translatable into practice and that any proposals should not be set in stone. Regular evaluation of their effectiveness and appropriateness should also be an important part of staff deliberation.

The headteacher opened the staff meeting by reminding colleagues that the purpose of the meeting was to begin to put the ideas discussed over the previous weeks onto paper. It was natural, it was suggested, to see the demands for assessment in purely bureaucratic terms but it was important for them to base their ideas on principles that were educationally justifiable and which reflected the values that were held within the school. The staff were invited to offer reasons as to why assessment might be important in their school. This stimulated some thoughtful and perceptive comment which illustrated the developments in staff thinking that had taken place as a result of the discussions led by the moderator. A variety of justifications were offered that included:

- To find out where the child is;
- To suggest where we [the teacher] should go next;
- For diagnostic purposes;
- To satisfy the demands of the range of ability in each class;
- As a means of ensuring continuity and progression;
- To contribute to our end of year record of achievement;

Discussion then moved on to a consideration of *how* assessment was to be undertaken and how this was to be described in the policy. Variation in opinion re-surfaced when discussion focused upon the children's portfolios. Is the teacher in control, is the child in control or should it be seen as a joint responsibility? The moderator offered a detailed justification for it being seen as a joint enterprise, and one where the children knew what was expected of them and why pieces were to be included in the portfolio. This, it was argued, contributed to the development of children's understanding and it was emphasized that the portfolio should be seen as 'the culmination of current work of quality and an indication of significant progress'.

The explanation for the inclusion of any item had to be more than, 'because I like it!'. The reasons have to be explained, and through experience of the process children get better at doing it. There was further discussion on what records should be kept and how this might be described in the policy. The headteacher then provided a summary of agreements that had been reached during the discussion and agreed to put these together in a draft policy document for staff consideration and concluded by saying, 'Assessment must not dominate our lives. It must back up our judgments and inform our next moves.'

Case Study Two: Field Gate Lower School

Introduction

This case study illustrates the importance of the role of the headteacher in promoting assessment as a fundamental responsibility of the whole school. It also reinforces the necessity of seeing the development of thinking and understanding about assessment as a long term process and that progress towards shared agreement takes time. Much of the discussion about assessment that was observed took place in relation to science, which had been identified as a priority in the school development plan. The creation of an environment in which disagreement can be seen as a positive feature of debate and not something that is necessarily negative also emerges as a feature of this particular case.

Background

Field Gate Lower school is a well established school on the edge of a large city centre. At present, there are 360 children at the school and sixteen teachers, including the headteacher and two part-time members of staff. There are three experienced Year Two teachers at the school, all of whom have had previous experience of SATs. They work closely together as a year team and they have strong views on the kind of assessment that is appropriate for young children.

According to the headteacher, assessment is now a central element of the planning of this first school. It has been a major focus of the school development plan for the last two years and its importance has been reinforced by the fact that the headteacher has taken the main responsibility for co-ordination and development of the system of assessment adopted throughout the school. The head has extensive knowledge of the school and the staff, having joined the school as a probationer, gaining promotion to deputy head-ship and more recently to the headship of the school. The rest of the staff are well established, many of them having been at the school for a number of years. They are thoughtful and perceptive and there is a strong commitment to the development of whole school policies which emerge after lengthy debate, in which all members of staff participate. The school is thought of highly in the local authority and has recently become involved in the Articled Teacher scheme, training future teachers in the school context.

School development and support

In the early days of their discussions about assessment, the headteacher recog-nized that there was considerable hostility amongst a number of the staff, who felt that many of the demands were totally unnecessary. In fact, it was commented that 'initially assessment was rejected and the first run through of SATs was a disastrous experience'. This led to a recognition that assessment had to be debated and planned for. 'Now assessment is on the agenda all of the time.'

There are regular internal agreement trials across the whole school, the staff are working together towards the development of a school portfolio and there have been attempts at moderation between classes via various internal release procedures. For example, the technology co-ordinator has been released to 'audit' judgments and to offer advice to colleagues on progression in tech-nology and the presence of an articled teacher has created some space to allow the mathematics co-ordinator to visit other classrooms to offer advice on assessment in mathematics.

The headteacher felt confident that common standards of interpretation and assessment were being established between colleagues at the school but was less certain about the extent to which this was happening beyond the school and nationally.

> It is very easy for schools to be generous in their assessments. We already have experience of that. We tend to prefer to be cautious. We are not doing the children any good if we overestimate their achievements.

It was further suggested that,

> Liaison with other schools is not really beneficial until we are clear in our own minds about what a level means. We are working on that at present.

Experience of agreement trials with other first schools and with the local middle school had not been particularly successful, which led the headteacher to suggest that, 'agreement trialling with other schools is very low on our agenda at the moment.'

To date, the three Key Stage 1 teachers had attended agreement trials organized by their Local Education Authority assessment team and that while impressed with the commitment of the advisory teachers for assessment, felt that they had not gained very much from the experience. They all commented that the level of debate in the school was better than that experienced at these sessions. As a result, they were reluctant to attend future meetings, although it was accepted that participation in these sessions was necessary for the purposes of endorsement. As a further contribution to checking the consistency of judgments within the school the headteacher took advantage of opportunities to meet with other headteachers in the authority. This allowed for the sharing of successful experience, practice and materials. It was also seen as an important forum to 'represent the views of the staff'. This was also true of the area assessment meetings which were contributing to understanding and the development of consistency of interpretation, especially in the core subjects.

Despite these varied opportunities for debate, the current demands of the National Curriculum, coupled with the responsibilities involved in running a school, created considerable difficulties for this to happen sufficiently regularly. As the headteacher forcefully commented, 'We're so buried in what we are doing here. I don't *really* know what's going on in other schools.'

Liaison with the local middle school has been variable. This year, attempts have been made in relation to physical education, mathematics for Years 4/5 and discussions are proceeding with regard to what information and documentation should go with children as they move from the first to the middle school. A bridging topic started by the children in the latter stages of the first school and continued into the early weeks of the middle school had been proposed but there were problems of commitment from some of the other feeder first schools.

Entry to school and the monitoring of progress is being carefully considered and criteria have been developed for a pre-school skills checklist for use with parents on home visits and during the early weeks in the reception class. This, it was felt, provided an indication of the value that has been added by the school as the children moved into Key Stage 1 of the National Curriculum.

One major issue that had been identified in the school development plan as a focus for the year was the development of the school policy for science. During the debates that had taken place earlier in the year common uncertainty had emerged regarding attainment in Science Attainment Target One (Sc1). An in-service day was organized at the beginning of the summer term to focus on this. The very effective way in which this was organized satisfied a number of important purposes. It contributed to further clarifying common understanding of the various strands and statements of attainment in Sc1. It offered illustrations of the way in which Sc1 was tackled throughout the school and thereby contributed to progression and continuity of experience. It provided a variety of examples of how other colleagues were attempting to assess in this area and finally it resulted in the production of annotated materials, moderated by the staff as a whole, for inclusion in the School Assessment Portfolio which illustrated attainment at Levels 1 to 4.

In preparation for the session, each teacher had been invited to bring an example of an activity from their current practice which they felt illustrated some element of achievement in Sc1. Each teacher took it in turns, in chronological order of the age of the children they taught, to describe their activity and the context in which it had taken place. They also provided examples of children's work to illustrate the task in action and then offered their assessment of what had been achieved by these children. The judgments offered were debated by the whole staff and an agreed conclusion produced. Finally, these materials, appropriately annotated, were presented to the headteacher for lamination and inclusion in the School Portfolio.

During these discussions, which were searching and forthright, the role of the headteacher was of considerable importance. Asking appropriate questions to further understanding, reminding colleagues of earlier agreements, making reference to advice from the LEA or SEAC, and generally moving the discussion forwards towards clarification and justification of their judgments. The staff were reminded that ultimately,

> Making a judgment on any of the strands has to be based upon sustained knowledge generated over time and that the material offered is *illustrative* of a level, it is not *the* evidence. A teacher's knowledge of the child will always provide additional information.

As the session continued, knowledge and understanding of what was involved in Sc1 was increased and it was suggested that this debate might be carried on at a future meeting where they could all work on the development of a bank of open-ended tasks with clear specification of each activity, the associated strand(s) and statement(s) of attainment it was intending to address and what the children needed to do to demonstrate achievement. It was proposed that this set of material would be available to the whole school and that information would be provided of the requirements of the tasks for all of the levels dealt with in the school. The intention was to generate a set of materials that could be trialled and modified in the light of experience.

The group met together on a closure day in May to continue their deliberations and to begin the process of developing the set of open-ended tasks as agreed at the previous staff development day. The session opened with a final discussion on the science policy. The science co-ordinator provided individual copies of the policy at its current draft stage and proceeded to read slowly through the document, breaking whenever anyone felt that there was a need for further debate or clarification. The policy included the following comments on assessment: 'Individual assessment is used to help with future planning, to ensure differentiation, progression and continuity for all pupils.'

A bank of Assessment checksheets and activities have been devised and agreed by all the staff for ATs 2, 3 and 4. These are kept on completion in the child's profile. Agreement trials have been held to moderate AT 1 assessments. Selective examples of AT 1 achievement are also retained in the child's profile. Moderated and annotated examples will be kept in the School Portfolio for reference purposes. Regular opportunities are provided for open-ended investigations to be carried out for the assessment of AT 1. Day-to-day records are kept by teachers using grids related to specific activities and notes as appropriate. Evidence of pupil's achievements and levels of attainment is gathered by a variety of methods, for example, teachers' recording of observations of activities, pupil presentations, questioning, listening, discussion, written, pictorial, and graphical work, and through the use of relevant matrices and structured written answers.

Formative records are updated termly in Key Stage 1 and half-termly in Key Stage 2. Ongoing evidence of achievement is provided by the children's current work, in their topic folders, which are retained in school for one term after completion. Summative assessment sheets are completed annually in accordance with county policy. Pupils are prepared for their end of Key Stage assessments by being provided with similar activities throughout their course.

Conclusions

Over the three years covered by these studies, we have witnessed a change in emphasis in many schools from an almost exclusive concern with the mechanisms of administering the SATs and recording results towards wider and more professional concerns for teacher assessment, the collection of evidence, the sharing of judgments and the development of whole school policies in which there is full staff participation. There is evidence of increasing confidence and competence in undertaking useful and pertinent assessment which is less intrusive and makes more effective use of time. It would be wrong to suggest that development is uniform across all schools and as was suggested earlier, our evidence indicates that schools are at different stages in understanding and practice depending on development priorities within the school and commitment to assessment by those with power and influence. However, in the East Anglian region, consistent development appears to be taking place, encouraged by the LEAs and supported by the training and support they offer. A number of common features are becoming evident.

First, there is a recognition of the need to provide evidence to support judgments about children's achievements. The tick lists of statements of attainments that were so common in the early days of National Curriculum assessment are being slowly replaced by portfolios of individual children's work. There is still anxiety about how much evidence is necessary, but in general, the recommendation is to retain a limited amount of information, which has been carefully annotated to illustrate that the processes of assessment have been professionally undertaken and to provide material for the discussion of judgments during moderation and agreement trials. In addition to the development of individual portfolios, schools are being encouraged by LEAs to develop school portfolios of evidence of children's work agreed by the whole staff for the various levels of the National Curriculum. These were similar to those developed by SEAC in their series of *Children's Work Assessed* and equivalent to collections that many of the LEAs were also producing. It is also the case that advisory teachers in the region are meeting regularly to engage in their own agreement trialing with the intention of producing an Eastern Region Portfolio. Materials of this kind serve as a reference for teachers and as a very useful way of communicating standards to parents. By comparing their own child's work with that included in the school portfolio, parents are able to draw their own conclusions about their child's progress. Many teachers felt that this kind of information was much more meaningful than the tables of national comparisons proposed by central government.

Second, there is increasing evidence that internal discussions about assessment are taking place as well as occasions when schools of the same phase and from different phases meet to compare and contrast their interpretations. In a paper presented to the British Educational Research Association, my colleague Mary James (1993) commented,

> Despite growing familiarity with this kind of procedure teachers nevertheless experienced difficulty in challenging the judgments of others. In giving an account of such a meeting, one teacher said: 'Nobody wanted to say that they disagreed, especially when they thought that one of their colleagues has assessed too lightly. Teachers aren't like that are they?' The reasons for the difficulty therefore appear to be cultural. Teachers are easily threatened, especially at the present moment in history, and avoid situations that make them vulnerable. Acceptance of the need for critical examination of judgment in a public forum will entail a certain amount of cultural change which inevitably takes time.
>
> (James, 1993, p. 21)

Despite these concerns, many of the teachers commented that agreement trials were essential and needed to happen regularly if consistent judgments were to be developed. It was important to recognize however that such consistency did not emerge immediately.

A third common feature that is beginning to emerge in the assessment practice of teachers in the Eastern region is the recognition that some of the better SATs could be used across the school to develop consistency in judgment and that the structure of the SATs provided a model for the construction of school-produced tasks, with clearly defined criteria and evidence requirements. These could be included as a normal part of teaching and could be used to establish more reliable and consistent teacher assessment.

The final element relating to the development of consistent practice concerns the support available from the LEAs themselves. Throughout the project, the importance of the support provided through training and moderation visits should not be under-estimated. The most effective assessment practice is dependent on partnership at all levels within the system.

Many of the suggestions presented here are reflected in evaluations of the developing practice of assessment which have been undertaken by OFSTED (1991; 1992). The management of effective assessment is dependent upon the support and commitment of the headteacher and the development of a clear and agreed set of principles, a policy for assessment, which is regularly evaluated and modified in the light of experience. There should be regular opportunities for debate about assessment which should be based upon real classroom instances. Agreement trials have been an excellent professional development opportunity when organized properly. Successful debates about assessment have generated appropriate materials for inclusion in school portfolios which illustrate 'how we do assessment here'. They cannot be produced overnight, but take time. The effort invested is worthwhile. Finally, it is essential to recognize the importance of involving the learner in the process — after all, whose learning is it that is being assessed?

Note

1 The arguments presented in this chapter are the author's and do not necessarily represent the views of the participating Local Authorities.

References

CONNER, C. and JAMES, M. (1991) *Bedfordshire Assessment Training, 1991: An Independent Evaluation*, Cambridge, Cambridge Institute of Education (mimeograph).

CONNER, C. and JAMES, M. (1993) *Assuring Quality in Assessments in Schools in Six LEAs, 1993: Report of an Independent Study funded by Bedfordshire, Cambridgeshire, Essex, Hertfordshire, Norfolk and Suffolk LEAs*, Cambridge, University of Cambridge Institute of Education (mimeograph).

DEARING, R. (1994) *The National Curriculum and its Assessment: Final Report*, London, SCAA.

JAMES, M. (1993) *Everything in Moderation: Experience of Quality Assurance at Key Stage One*, paper presented at the BERA annual conference, Liverpool University 10–13 September.

JAMES, M. and CONNER, C. (1992) *Moderation at Key Stage One across four LEAs, 1992*, Cambridge, University of Cambridge Institute of Education (mimeograph).

JAMES, M. and CONNER, C. (1993) 'Are reliability and validity achievable in National Curriculum assessment? Some observations on moderation at Key stage One in 1992', *The Curriculum Journal*, 4, 1, pp. 5–19.

JUDD, J. (1994) 'National Curriculum is torn up', *The Independent*, 6 January.

Colin Conner

OFSTED (1993) *Assessment, Recording and Reporting 1991–1992*, HMSO.
SEAC (1991) *National Curriculum Assessment: Assessment Arrangements for Core and Other Foundation Subjects, A Moderator's Handbook 1991/92*, London, SEAC.
TGAT (1988) *Task Group on Assessment and Testing: A Report*, London, DES.
WHALLEY, D. (1989) 'TGAT is torn apart', *The Times Educational Supplement*, 25 August.

Part III

Development

Becoming Someone Other: Teacher Professional Development and the Management of Change through INSET

Marion Dadds

Introduction

Carol is the heroine of this story. As Deputy Head of a large urban Primary school, she attended a sixty-hour course on assessment, recording and reporting at the University of Cambridge Institution of Higher Education. This course was one of three which were included in some small-scale research I undertook. The research was exploring the effects of award-bearing in-service teacher education (INSET) projects on classrooms and schools. The INSET project was an important part of each course. It gave course members the chance to focus upon an issue or area of development of interest to themselves. The project was a means of developing this interest. It was also a chance to link study from the course to practical development work in schools. Carol's story emerged from this research. The story became interesting for the insights it raised into the variety and complexity of learning which the INSET project demanded of her.

Many of the INSET teachers chose to pursue projects which were directly related to some area of practical need in their schools. In that sense, the projects could be seen as school development activities which were stimulated, advanced or sustained by the teachers' contact with the INSET course. Carol's project was of this kind. Her story was, thus, also interesting for what it showed of the preliminary school-based history of the project, demonstrating how it emerged from a complex set of changing circumstances within the school. These circumstances had been evolving for some two years before Carol eventually took the initiative and turned an evolving idea into a practical whole school innovation. The story shows the part which the INSET course played in the development of this innovation. It also shows the demands which leadership of the innovation imposed on Carol. It shows her multiple learning and growth as she prepared for and managed the innovation in its early stages. It shows how, in this process of managing institutional change (a new professional challenge for her) she, herself, underwent change, becoming someone other than the person she was.

Carol was willing and interested for me to follow her and her project after the sixty-hour course had ended. The story is re-constructed from interviews with Carol and two of her school colleagues. Data were also used from Carol's written course report of her project. The research initially covered the period of a year, during which time Carol attended the course, took ideas back to her colleagues, worked with them on the innovation and prepared for work to start in classrooms. Longer term interviews were conducted with children after a year. These gave insights into some of the preliminary effects of the innovation on children's experiences. The data from these are not discussed here as they lie outside the focus of this chapter but have been written about elsewhere (Dadds, in progress).

The Growing Development Climate in Carol's School

Carol chose to develop the use of pupil profiling and pupil self-assessment in her school for her INSET project. With this she carried a school development mission to her course. As such, she had a school mandate for her project 'as assessment was an area given high priority in the school's development plan'. This mission and mandate had emerged from the increasing interest and attention which had been given to assessment in her school for almost two years prior to the course.

Several features of the school context had been enriching the soil for the sowing of the project. '[There were] a lot of threads that were being discussed and had been ongoing in the two years that I had been here.' In taking the initiative to attend the course, Carol also took the initiative, on behalf of her colleagues, for bringing these threads together. She was also lucky in having the full support of her newly appointed Head. She was certainly not working in a climate of disinterest or apathy as other INSET teachers often are (Dadds, 1991; Dadds, 1994).

One significant factor in Carol's first year at the school, two years before she attended the course, had been 'an appraisal by the Inspectorate to see how we assessed the wide range of curriculum to our special needs pupils.' The school had a relatively high proportion of children with special needs for whom pupil profiling was already well developed. The local inspectors liked this work and said so as a result of their appraisal. Out of this good assessment and recording practice, the inspectors saw further potential for development, saying that 'it was a pity that [this] kind of pattern wasn't repeated for the rest of the children.' They concluded that this 'was an area that [the school] needs to address'. This advice contributed to the school development climate in which the project started to grow. 'So there was, that lying around,' Carol said.

Parallel to this were other discussions which were feeding the development climate. The teachers had 'talked around [issues] in assessing, recording and reporting', as a result of national arrangements imposed by the government. The head in post at that time had been involved in moderation of Key Stage 1 SATs for the Local Education Authority. This work had influenced the attention given by the Head to assessment in her own school. It had clearly impacted on the staff and had raised awareness of pupil assessment throughout the school as a result. Talk was being translated into individual, if fragmented, practice. 'A lot of experimentation has been done within individual classrooms about doing specific pieces of work with specific targets to assess them against National Curriculum criteria.' People were also beginning to consider ways of embedding assessment within teaching, 'and there had been a lot of thought about planning on-going assessment targets into topic work.'

An ideological commitment became explicitly challenged, however, as the teachers trialled National Curriculum record keeping materials. These materials seemed to offend the teachers' beliefs about assessment and recording as they offered only limited and narrow perspectives on children. In contrast, Carol's colleagues wanted approaches that gave a broader view of children's learning and achievements. The narrower National trial materials were inconsistent with this. Carol expressed this lucidly in her written project report.

> As we struggled to come to terms with three national curriculum record-keeping grids (for maths, science and language) which were being trialled by all of the primary schools within our cluster, we felt that we needed to fight hard to keep a firmly held belief that a child's achievement in any area, not necessarily the purely academic, was valuable, positive and needed to be recorded.

Although the development climate was ripening in these ways, it was not quite ready. 'We seemed to have been talking around and not getting anywhere for a long time.' Ideas, interest and commitments needed drawing together, coordinating and developing by someone, but the most fruitful management context was lacking. The reason seemed clear and valid. The head at that time was approaching early retirement and she obviously did not want to determine the development agenda too rigidly ahead of her in-coming colleague, preferring to leave it, perhaps, in a state of readiness for a new direction and vision. 'The project was, therefore, put on ice, but not forgotten.'

Carol, then, was waiting her time in a ready and positively expectant state of commitment, a time which came with the advertising publicity for the sixty-hour course on assessment, a time which also came with the new, supportive, encouraging headteacher. Events and commitments were coming together in a productive way. Carol applied for the course. The pupil profiling project received the green light from head and staff and initiation was firmly under way. Colleagues were providing the interest and enthusiasm. Carol could provide the leadership.

> obviously at the . . . point the course was advertised it seemed quite
> a good jumping off point with a new head. And [I thought] if I got
> on this course we could get the whole thing together as a staff. We
> talked it through and [the head] thought it was a very good idea.

Carol was, thus, already looking ahead; imagining whole school possibilities;
hoping, and perhaps expecting, that some realization of her project was possible.

Carol's Substantive Learning from the Course

Carol saw the course as a chance to think through the broad range of related
assessment issues and implications for her project, to take stock of her own
understanding, to develop it. Her own development would then provide a
firmer basis for school and staff development, the one being a necessary fore-
runner of the other.

> It seemed like a good idea for me to actually use the course as a time
> for me to go and discuss and think and clarify my thoughts, and then
> use that as a jumping off board, perhaps illustrating some kind of
> procedure for the staff which I did.

This basic plan for her own development seemed wise. Other INSET
teachers have borne witness to the increased self-confidence which comes
with their developed professional knowledge resulting from INSET (Dadds,
1991; Kinder and Harland, 1991). This improved knowledge and confidence
can become a valuable resource subsequently, for leading curriculum change
and for supporting colleagues through their associated professional development (Dadds, 1991). Carol predicted early in the course that her professional
learning would provide a store from which she could draw on, supporting her
colleagues' learning, 'to have some of the answers, if you like, or some kind
of solutions or materials to bring . . . to staff.'

The time it afforded her was time for quality reflection. Such time, she
suggested, one rarely has or makes, in school.

> What I was getting from the course was the . . . philosophy . . . the
> thinking behind [assessment] . . . the course was helping me there . . .
> giving me time and opportunity to think these sorts of issues through,
> because in all honesty . . . anybody (who is) practically involved in
> the day-to-day routine of teaching has got very little time to think
> about deeper issues. We ought not to be, but practically you're doing
> things on the hoof and catching problems as they arise.

Quality time for reflection was complemented by access to two of the INSET
tutors, 'the expertise from the tutors' as well as some freedom on the course

to pursue independent study, 'the opportunity to go into the library to pull out the philosophy . . . the free study time was quite useful, because obviously I was able to go into the library and read around as much material as I could.'

This development space helped Carol to clarify and confirm her beliefs in a broader approach to assessment through pupil profiles and self-assessment. It also helped her to realize that, despite innovation overload in school, this self-chosen approach was a matter of ideological priority. Her beliefs seemed to have been confirmed through formal and informal discussion with course colleagues and tutors. Here value congruence (Kinder and Harland, 1991) between the student and the INSET provision seems to have occurred spontaneously. It also helped Carol to strengthen her confidence in her beliefs.

> What did come out of this collaboration and discussion with colleagues on the course was confirmation in my belief that this was the way in which to go. There's so much to worry about, how we're going to record the National Curriculum levels, which I think is important, I'm not denying that, and . . . obviously . . . SATs . . . we can't ignore . . . it's needing to be done . . . but I felt that talking with people, realizing how bogged down they were with that, and how worried they were about that, is confirmation in my belief that we need to do the pupil profiling, as a balancing act, if you like.

Carol saw the introduction of pupil profiling as her 'professional answer' to the limitations of government Imposed Standard Assessment Tasks. Five interrelated processes can be identified in Carol's learning as she clarified her beliefs and tried to create, and extract meaning from, the course. First, she tried in the early stages to absorb as much as she could of the new ideas she encountered, 'like a sponge trying to soak it all up.' Second, as the course moved on, she engaged in more focused selection of course content and input. 'After the second or third week, particularly once we got the programme and we knew what the focus for each week was going to be, then it became easier.' In this she focused upon experiences that linked directly to her school development project. 'So then it was easier to actually take in the things that were pertinent to (my project).' Third, from these processes of absorbing and focusing she began to construct her own meanings around the project. 'There was a clarification process going on of my own sort.'

Fourth, Carol was spontaneously applying her course experience to the intellectualization of her school development project. She realized that there was no singular universal approach that she could adopt unreflectively, despite her wish that it were otherwise. In this, we see that in the process of applying her learning, Carol was also adapting her understandings to the particularities of her situation.

> I suppose I was looking for practical answers in lots of ways. It would have been nice to come and have a blue-print, and this is how you do

it, this is how you get pupil profiles going, this is the sort of area you need to be looking at, these are the dangers. But I should have known better.

The blue-print approach was neither her preferred approach to professional development, nor that of the INSET providers. She had the intellectual capability to construct her own meanings and subsequent action and actively enjoyed doing so. She continued,

> Because one of the reasons I enjoy the Institute courses is that they don't give you the answers pat because there isn't a pat answer, it depends on the school and the body of people you work with.

In adapting her learning, Carol realized that processes of implementation had to be constructed by her in relation to the unique context of her school. Here are the early signs of her situational understanding (Elliott, 1991), realizing that what works in one situation may not work in another and that adaptation may be the key to successful adoption of innovation. This seems to have been a significant aspect of her INSET learning. She explained,

> One of the learning things for me has been to realize that when we get a system going for this school, something that is appropriate for here and for this staff, that doesn't mean to say that if I move on anywhere else that's going to be a blueprint I can use . . . I would probably have to go through the same sort of processes and come out with a different result in the end.

In addition to these processes of absorbing, focusing, constructing, applying and adapting, Carol seems to have been storing some learning as potential capital for future unknowns, 'a whole bank of seeds that have been sown that will probably come to fruition later on.' This storing process was familiar to Carol from her previous and more extended Advanced Diploma course which she had completed successfully some three years earlier. Material was stored and then recalled, retrieved and applied at later relevant moments.

> I found that with the Advanced Diploma [there were] things that were not immediately relevant or interesting; [for example] I've got lots of notes and bits of reading [and] there have been two or three occasions where I've suddenly thought, now we did something about that on the Diploma [and I've been able to refer back to the notes and reading]. So although things are not immediately useful . . . there is a kind of subconscious retention there that helps you to know where you've filed things for later reference.

While her beliefs and her 'professional answer' were being shaped through the course processes, she also realized that the development of practice in her particular and unique school was a major challenge. To this end she began to identify and articulate the practical implications for her school colleagues during her ten weeks on the course. She employed practical dissemination strategies in school from the start. She kept communication going with her school colleagues through feedback meetings, steadily building bridges between her INSET and their perceptions; she tried to alleviate any professional suspicion or jealousy there may have been, 'because people thought I was on a little away-day every Wednesday, so in a sense I had to justify my going'; she tried to capitalize, in these early stages of development, on the genuine staff interest there was, because 'there is quite a body of staff here who are really interested in what is going on, and one or two people would say, what did you do, have you got any interesting print-out or pieces that we can read?'; she brought this interest into a collective forum rather than leaving it individualized and uncoordinated, 'so rather than do that on an individual basis, once a month we had a slot within the staff meetings where I gave a quick up-date.'

Carol also recognized that there had to be forward movement from these early initiatives that would need conscious organization if colleagues were to be helped in developing their own thinking. 'And by about the first month into the course it became apparent that we were really going to need a training day to look at it as a whole staff.' Here, perhaps, we can see the features of collectivism that provided the context within which the INSET project could grow. Carol's commitment, drive and willingness to communicate kept the project alive in the minds of colleagues at the beginning of a much longer journey to institutional adoption. Interest from the majority of colleagues provided healthy conditions for the project's early growth. The support and backing of the head added status and credibility which, possibly, gave Carol confidence and purpose. The energy from the course added to this. Given these enabling features of collectivism, the balance seemed tipped well in favour of the development culture at this stage.

Losing Confidence

As Carol focused more closely on her project several weeks into the course, she began to wonder and worry about the size, scope and demands of the challenges she had brought upon herself. The initial enthusiasm and excitement which may have been necessary to thrust the project into its early beings (the falling-in-love stage, perhaps) was soon to be replaced by uncertainty, doubt, apprehension and a crisis of self-confidence. First the ecstasy and then the agony, for as Carol began to think and plan, to map out the intellectual and practical territory of her project, she was confronted with a challenge more complex, more demanding, more threatening and more difficult to manage than she had first imagined. Her original conceptualization, perhaps romanticized by her ideological commitment, was seen to be naive and over-simplified. The comfortable and seemingly manageable boundaries of the project became illusory. They quickly disappeared from Carol's grasp.

> When I started off, I was thinking that it is all going to be very neat and tidily parcelled, and that parcel split open fairly suddenly and I thought, 'Oh, I can't do this, this is too big a can of worms to open because there will be lots of issues that I think I haven't really thought through.'

There was the challenge of involving reticent parents; preserving children's confidentiality in pupil profiling; the existing overload on the staff from the Educational Reform Act; doubts about her own interpersonal and management skills to manage the innovation. Just as she had been able to visualize positive possibilities at the outset, she was now projecting imaginatively into many potential difficulties and pitfalls.

> I think at that time I could see all the negative things. I could see the staff thinking it was extra work load. I could see difficulties [with] how . . . we involve parents . . . who's going to have access to [pupils' profiles] . . . and if you're saying to the child this is your book and what you say is valued . . . there are going to be things in [that the child] is not happy for mum or dad to see.

Carol's close imaginery encounters with some of these impending practicalities made her feel that she had bitten off more than she could chew.

> So there were a whole lot of issues that suddenly exploded and the boundaries disintegrated and I was wallowing around quite a bit.

She began to doubt whether this was the right time, 'Have we got too much on, did we ought to be seeing some of the other things through?' And she doubted that she was the right person, 'I don't think I've got the skills to enable the staff to work through this.' She felt de-skilled and temporarily deflated, 'and basically some of my own confidence went.'

To have a supportive and encouraging friend or colleague at such critical times can, we know, make all the difference to the direction of professional development (Dadds, 1993). Carol was fortunate. Rather than being left to struggle alone with these doubts and feelings of inadequacy, she was offered positive encouragement by her new Headteacher. Carol had the good sense to seek this out and to discover 'whether [the Head] was going to feel I was capable of doing it.' The ensuing discussions gave rise to an analytical re-appraisal of the scope and worthwhileness of the project. Together, Carol and the head confirmed that this was not just a personal 'hobby-horse' of Carol's, the aberrations of a heroine innovator. Together they agreed that the school did need to do it and that 'it needed to be quite a long process.'

Just as important as the Head's support and confidence at this crucial time was a visit Carol made to two feeder secondary schools. This opportunity of a school visit of the student's choice arose from the structure of the INSET course. The timing was fortuitous. In her role as Key Stage 2–3 coordinator, Carol had already participated in substantial liaison with the two secondary schools, so friendly professional relationships were already well established. One secondary school in particular was in the process of evaluating 'and thinking through what they were doing' with their systems which had been established for several years. So Carol talked specifically with colleagues there about pupil profiling and the coordination of record keeping systems on the INSET visit day.

The lack of certainty which her opposite secondary colleague was experiencing in this review must have comforted Carol enormously. Like Carol, he was not exempt from the difficult and disorientating feelings which come with managing significant change (Schon, 1971; Morris, 1974). They had much in common, much to discuss, much to share. The meeting was a success, a comfort and a boost to Carol's morale. 'The [colleague] who was in charge of that and I had a super morning and chatted and I realized he was just as much in a turmoil as I was.' She seemed re-assured by finding someone else who had also lost his bearings in the unknown territories of the change process. Her experience was neither unique nor abnormal.

She then had a discussion with the Head of the secondary school. This lady 'who was very dynamic, very positive', and 'who had taken on an enormous amount of problems there', showered Carol with enthusiasm and energy. 'She was very very positive', offering a sense of purpose into the bargain, suggesting that Carol should 'go for it'. 'Let's liaise, let's see if we can work through commonly something that is going to be of value to you and us', this dynamic secondary head suggested, 'and that will give us a really good picture of the child at transfer . . . rather than just the national curriculum'.

Just as Carol had found value congruence (Kinder and Harland, 1991) with the INSET course, she found it, too, with her secondary colleagues. This added to the boost of confidence which her own head had tried to inject into the disintegrating situation. It helped Carol to re-establish a positive self-identity within a supportive if scattered, professional reference group. She no longer felt alone, no longer bereft of her mission, no longer depressed about her professional capabilities.

> And I suddenly felt that the three things really, talking to my head, getting more in touch with the course and then suddenly realizing that I wasn't alone here and doing it. There was a group of us actually looking at it. This made me think, alright, I can do it. We have managed this and I am not on my own. There are lots of shared expertises and experiences that I can have.

The power generated by these multiple sources of support and interest gave her a new lease of professional energy. She was not a lone traveller, reliant totally on her own resources. She was a member now of a group with common interests, common purposes, common values. This provided another positive professional climate for Carol's development and, relatedly, for that of her project. There were collaborative resources (Winter, 1989) upon which she could draw. And she had the wit and wisdom to do that. Her written INSET project report claimed, at this point, that she had felt 'excited at the opportunities offered for the future'. This positive affirmation of self had brought a positive up-turn in Carol's emotional state.

Carol's ability to re-construct her confidence in this way with the help of significant colleagues was, clearly, vital to the future of the project. It was still only Autumn and the suggested staff development day was a long way on the horizon at the end of the next Spring term. But a decision had been made to boost the growth of the project through this whole school event and Carol would be key organizer and leader. Her reconstructed self-confidence was vital to her effectiveness in this. The success of the staff development day depended upon it.

Moving as a Team

The head's restated confidence in Carol was well founded and by the early spring term this new, confident Carol had made some fairly detailed and positive plans. These were underpinned by five key aims which circumscribed the redefined scope of her project. She aimed to bring together all preceding and related assessment discussions; to review existing record-keeping practices; to write an assessment policy; to share work with secondary colleagues with a view to discovering a mutually useful system; to begin trialling pupil profiling the following Autumn. Her common sense understanding of the nature of change helped her to realise that 'this is not obviously going to be achieved at once and so the main initial thrust will be towards the pupil profiles.'

The staff development day was to be an important contributor to this, drawing upon some of the ideas and activities from Carol's course, a not uncommon strategy for linking external INSET to school development (Dadds, 1991). Carol would 'share some of the issues raised during the course' during the first part of the day. Then there would be 'a practical session', where colleagues 'will be asked to engage in a game aimed at prioritizing statements in relation to a policy document.' Teaching teams would then brainstorm the practicalities of pupil profiles, 'the what, how, when and where'. These ideas would be processed after the staff development day, by a volunteer small working group. This small group would, hopefully, be 'a representative cross-section of the school, whose later brief will be to collate ideas from the staff development day into a workable format for later presentation to the whole staff.' Carol had hopes that some of the school's INSET budget would fund staff release for members of the working group to do their job, 'so that a draft lay-out would be available for discussion at a staff meeting, possibly early in

June.' She also hoped for INSET budget money to release teachers for liaison with secondary colleagues.

Her plans showed a regard for full staff participation in policy-making and in conceptualizing the practice of pupil profiling. At the same time she recognized the need to create and support the new structure of the proposed working group, given that 'time constraints are a major consideration'. Full staff participation in all these processes may have been desirable but may well have worked against these time constraints. Hence, the need for a smaller working group to carry developments forward on behalf of all colleagues. There was much work to be done if profiles were to be trialled the following autumn. Release from teaching for the working group should 'allow sufficient time for ordering any resources or printed materials.' Carol, it seems, wanted to be getting on with things. She felt that all the preliminary stages of discussion were passing and 'that we can only move forward in the same way as that in which we encourage much of our children's learning — it's time for us to have a go.'

Even so, there was still work to be done in persuading staff that developing the pupil profiles would be an evolutionary process. Feasibility depended upon their cooperation in this, and practical plans were needed to help build their confidence, 'particularly so if staff can be re-assured that we cannot expect to get it right at the first go.' So 'constant monitoring and evaluation, probably over the next two or three years, should play a part in the whole process until staff have a workable document that is easily maintained, but will play a vital part in the education of the whole child.'

Carol seemed to have the ability to read her colleagues' uncertainties in this way. The careful plans and insights into future processes which she provided may have been vital in helping colleagues to step out with some reassurance into the unknown territory of innovation. Here, Carol needed to be receptive to others' feelings and experiences of change and to account for them in the process of managing the project's development.

The staff development day came and went successfully at the end of the spring term aided by Carol's sensitive reading of the climate and her colleagues' needs. The timing of the event had not been ideal in the busy school calendar but had been almost forced upon them by other time constraints. So Carol had 'tried to make the day meaningful but fairly light.' She was all too aware of colleagues' tiredness, so she treated them well and carefully. 'We had some caterers in to give everybody a good lunch, and I tried to make the activities fairly easy.' She felt that people had been able to relax and enjoy the day, so that as a result her purposes had been achieved.

'It has fired everybody's enthusiasms', claimed Yvonne, a teacher colleague. Along with others, Yvonne willingly volunteered to be a member of the working group as a result of the impact of the day on her developing understanding of profiling. Of particular interest to Yvonne was 'to have a whole school approach . . . so that everyone knew that we were together to [work on the profiles].'

The effectiveness of this day was in Yvonne's view largely due to Carol's commitment, her drive, her belief in the future, 'the fact that she wanted it to happen . . . the fact that she was enthusiastic about what she was talking about . . . enthusiastic about the course she had done and was able to come back and say, I think it is going to work and it's going to be valuable.' Carol's hopes and expectations were high. Some colleagues had been able to draw from these high hopes to fund their own attitudes and actions.

Sure enough, the next autumn and the new school year saw these plans materialize into practice. The small working group, which included Carol and four colleagues, had done their homework in release time. There had been no shortage of volunteers on the staff development day to join this group. 'In fact,' Carol reflected, 'it is a pity . . . that we couldn't have done it as a whole staff, because I think there was enough interest.'

By September, the working group had a draft policy document and 'a whole collection of (pupil profile) sheets' for trialling across the school. Information flow and communication had been good 'and members of the working group have reported back to their teaching teams, so there has been constant feedback all the time.' The existing structures in the school helped enormously in the flow of information, and Carol knew how to use them to aid the pupil profile innovation. Teams of teachers and their support assistants were already established for planning, evaluating and teaching. These teams met regularly, as 'they have release time timetabled within the working day to get together as a team.' The path of the pupil profile innovation was, thus, clearly helped by these existing structures.

Coping with the Hardships

Lest we develop a false and rosy whole-school picture from the story so far, however, it is well to acknowledge that the path of the project's development was neither smooth nor easy, despite the generally positive all-round support it was receiving. It was hard work and there were difficulties to overcome. In addition to Carol's early crisis of self-confidence, for example, there was the inevitable resistant colleague whose strategies for side-stepping change challenged Carol's interpersonal skills. The colleague's resistance was 'part and parcel of a pattern of things that she actually says yes to, and then does something differently.' The colleague also seemed quite skilled, albeit unconsciously perhaps, at managing Carol's feelings and responses to advantage. 'She's very clever at catching you when you are in the middle of thirty-six thousand jobs and says, ever so sympathetically, "Oh you know I couldn't do this because it's been absolutely dreadful and the children are far too young."' Perhaps she relied on Carol being spontaneously sympathetic and that may well have been the case, for Carol admitted, 'and your heart goes out to her and you think poor soul.'

Sympathetic though Carol was, however, she felt that she had to learn to deal with the problem of resistance. She adopted a new response that was a judicious blend of empathy combined with determination. She replied courteously to her colleague, 'I have taken on board what you said but I am ever so busy. Can I come and see you and let's talk it through.' She seemed determined to analyse the problem face-to-face as a basis for understanding its nature.

Carol made reference many times to her awareness of overload on colleagues but she seems to have decided, too, that this should not block development of the project which had, after all, been agreed collectively. She was sympathetic towards her resistant colleague and more than willing to offer practical help and support, such as release of time to 'give her some time actually to do it'. She doubted, however, that the solution would be that easy. She felt that the problem was 'more a question of won't than can't'.

If the support strategies failed, which Carol suspected they might, she would have to think of something else. And since managing change at this level was, for Carol, a new experience, she would be extending her own learning in this, 'because I have never been into that sort of thing before, but that will be a learning process for me, won't it'. Coping with others' perceptions of her had also been something of a challenge. Carol felt that she was perceived as 'a bit of a bossy boots', which used to 'really, really bother me', she admitted, even though she felt she was also perceived to be enthusiastic, a good organizer and a positive, supportive colleague.

In general, too, Carol felt that her role as deputy head and now as change agent had caused her to become other than the person she had wanted to be, the person who 'went out of [her way] to try to become a listening ear and everything to all people'. It was not possible, she felt, to be all things to all people, 'that you can't do that and do your job properly'. In particular, it seems that Carol had come to understand that the change agent needed to employ judgment and decisiveness in following an agreed course of action despite the inevitable imperfections in agreed plans and despite people's doubts and uncertainties.

Carol's colleague Barry confirmed that Carol had, indeed, been able to employ these qualities of judgment and decisiveness. It would, he felt, have been all too easy to lose the initiative at one stage. 'There was one particular session,' he judged, 'where it could quite easily not have started', where some people would have been willing to 'stall' a little longer, seeking the promise of ideal outcomes before first committing themselves to action, worrying about the workload with an attitude of 'I don't really want to be involved in this. There was a steamroller needed.' Carol supplied this valuable piece of management equipment with persuasive, if decisive words, according to Barry. 'I know its not perfect,' he recalls Carol saying, 'I know it's not exactly what we want, but this is what we have got and we will give this a shot, or words to that effect', Barry concluded.

This is not to suggest that Carol's own brand of steamrollering and bossiness would have worked anywhere. They were, however, acceptable in general to this particular group of people at this particular time. 'It has to be done in a certain way', Barry felt. Carol's particular way was supported by her qualities of empathy and patience which we saw with the resistant colleague. 'She doesn't overreact', Barry said. 'She does listen to all the sides of the argument. She does give time as well.' This style was helpful in this situation. Carol's calm, control, fairness and patience were important for stimulating and supporting others' change.

This was only part of the explanation of the project's movement and development for the collective ethos seems to have eased Carol's management task significantly. Carol was able to steamroller the project into being at this stage only because colleagues, on balance, wanted it, and allowed it to happen. 'I am not sure she would always get away with it,' Barry hypothesized, 'but I think fifty per cent of it was the fact that the staff really wanted it to happen.'

It was her role and duty too, Carol felt, to try to counteract the professional negativity towards change that surfaced as a consequence of colleagues' tiredness on certain occasions. This negativity was more likely to manifest itself at the end of the school year, a time which, unfortunately, was crucial for the development of the pupil profiling project. A July meeting had been necessary to clarify developments for the following September and to move ideas from the successful Spring staff development day into practice for the new school year. This was the meeting at which the problems of negativity were encountered and at which Barry judged that a steamroller was appropriate. Even though Carol said that she 'could understand and sympathize' with colleagues' seeming reluctance, a reluctance which probably marked professional exhaustion, she did not find the situation easy to handle. She had found the negative turn of events depressing herself and had needed to separate her personal feelings from her professional thinking in order to manage the event. 'There were some fairly negative waves coming over, which I found on a personal level quite depressing, but on a professional level I can rationalize why.' Colleagues had advanced arguments and obstacles which Carol felt were red herrings and which were probably indicative of the general professional exhaustion accruing from the almost impossible demands of the summer term. Carol had read the situation with empathy and humaneness again. 'They are tired. They are really tired. They have just gone through the report phase. They are doing records. They are sorting out [other things].' In response to this, she had adapted her approach. 'And I can understand that having someone bouncing different ideas [around] . . . is a bit irritating, so I do try to tone it down a bit.'

Carol was thus struggling with her own fragile and dark feelings at this meeting, as well as understanding, and being responsive to, those of her colleagues. She had to overcome the one of the *self* in order to support the other of the *group*. She knew her colleagues to be a generally positive group of professionals and she used that knowledge to judge that it was appropriate to carry on with the project.

They are a very cooperative [group] of people. They will probably grumble. There will probably be one or two grumbles in one or two areas more than others, but basically I know them well enough to be confident. . . . that they will give it their best in September, that they will come back . . . and say, well alright we will have a go at this.

Carol was taking a calculated risk with the steamroller. But with the confidence she had in her own understanding of her colleagues in the situation, she probably felt that the risk was low, even though the stakes were high. Her reasonably sound situational understanding provided a good foundation for employing 'situational action' (Dadds, 1991).

This end of year exhaustion could have deterred the more faint-hearted. As Barry had said, 'Carol was able to steamroller the project through this July minefield because of who she was and because of what her colleagues wanted. Carol perhaps knew this too'. Time proved them both right in their judgments.

Climbing the Learning Curves and Becoming Someone Other

There is a sense, then, in which Carol was becoming someone other than the person she used to be, in order to cope with the demands and challenges of being an agent of innovation and change in her school. She still displayed strong qualities of empathy and understanding of others, 'in their shoes I am sure I [would] be feeling exactly the same', she admitted. This sensitivity towards others' feelings may have been vital in helping her colleagues to handle their own learning and change processes (Saltzberger-Wittenberg *et al.*, 1983). But now it seemed essential for her to worry less about others' views of her, because she realized that she could not be sweetness and light to everyone in all events. She was having to learn to cope with resistance, with others' tiredness, negativity and manipulations. She was having to learn to manage those alongside her determination to see the project come alive in school practices. If she could not manage these difficulties she could not, probably, manage the project nor bring it further to fruition.

Managing general morale and her own had become part of her role in managing this particular change. There was much to learn in this. She had to struggle with, and master, her own difficult feelings, as she managed sensitive and controversial situations, not letting these critical incidents pull her down into defeatism or laissez-faire. She had constantly to read and understand the social and professional context in which the project was growing. She tried to identify where other professional strengths lie, 'I often have to rely on others for really creative ideas', she declared. She needed to recognize that moods and commitment change with the nature of the school year. 'I am really confident that they will come up with a super year's work but now is not really the right time to be confronted with it, which is why the negative waves are there', she judged. She had to invest faith and regard in her colleagues' professional commitment to matters that improve provision for their children.

It is clear, too, that she had to have faith in herself and in the validity of the project which she had initiated, for at these early, tender stages, there would probably have been no development without Carol as the co-ordinator and flag-bearer of this collectively desired innovation. If Carol were to have had public doubts at this point, who knows what effect that would have on developments.

Through the difficulties which the project encountered Carol recognized that she was undergoing significant change and that she was now on at least her second learning curve since she took that decision to attend the INSET course. The first learning curve, as we have seen, represented the development of her own knowledge and understanding of the substantive assessment issues. This carried her through the preliminary phases before implementation, through the staff meetings, the staff development day and up to the tricky July meeting. The INSET course acted as 'the kick-off point for all of us really' in providing the substantive background. And even beyond that phase, she was still drawing on the substantive stimulus of the course, going back through course notes and reading lists, for example, 'where various teams have [asked questions] about particular issues'. She was also continuing to use her own knowledge and confidence as a resource for others' learning, acting 'as a sounding board for other people's thinking, in the way that the course acted as a sounding board for mine'.

From this crucial point in July, the conscious focus of Carol's learning shifted onto the understanding and practice of change management. She was beginning to imagine others' experiences of the change; the difficulties; the multiple perspectives of the staff group. She realized that individuals can and do have vastly different experiences of and responses to a common innovation. 'Some staff have been more comfortable than others, so there is not an overall pattern.' She realized too, that uncertainty and apprehension may be common feelings, 'and . . . those that have been a little bit reticent about it weren't quite sure what would come up'. This makes change far from straight-forward and certainly not a simple linear process, she realized. People and their personal responses needed managing if change is to be managed. The innovator and change agent needs wisdom and judgment in these matters.

This second learning curve seemed steep for Carol.

Up to July . . . was a lot of new learning about the actual process of assessing, recording, what was actually involved in doing the pupil profiles. What I have learned from July, I think, has been how much it demands of staff to do it properly. I have gone to that extra stage, to be able to have more of an overview of what it is taking out of the staff to do it properly, of how difficult it is, how people view it in different ways, how what one person takes on as a challenge becomes a direct threat to somebody else; how you think you have decided something as a group, you think you have sorted through and come to a common understanding, but in practice there still remains tremendous discrepancies of understanding. So for me it has been a learning process about how staff actually cope with change and innovation, and . . . even having discussed it and gone through all the initial processes, it is still not a straightforward process that you think it should be, because there are a lot of issues about personnel management and judgment in it.

It is doubtful that a co-ordinator and change agent could develop whole school practice very far without evolving a personal theory of change in this way. Carol is developing general insights into the nature and management of change, based upon her evolving 'theories of people' (Dadds, 1991) and upon her reflections and analysis of first hand experience. To understand change, she needs to understand relevant others in the situation, what motivates them, how they feel, how they perceive the innovation. She also needs to stand back from her experience, look at it, try to make sense of it and theorize it.

Theories of others, however, were not enough, for it seemed important for Carol to understand herself and her influence on the situation, just as well as she understood others. There was evidence that Carol was evolving what we might see as 'theories of oneself' to complement her theories of others; developing insight into her own change processes; beginning to reflect upon the impact of her self on others and on the development of the project.

Personal conviction was important, she felt, to 'have definite views of your own . . . to know where you stand about it'. But lest this conviction solidify into dogma, Carol felt it needed to be complemented by 'open-mindedness about it' so that she could be responsive to other opinions and points of view, 'because I have to realize that other members of staff may feel very differently about it and I need to be able to take that on'. Flexibility was, thus, a necessary associated personal quality, she believed, if her own convictions were to be tested, developed, trialled and meshed with others' ideas. So Carol felt that she needed 'to know that there isn't one definite way of doing it'.

Maintaining the Self

This developing situational understanding had to be converted into situational judgment and action. There had to be strong links between thinking and doing, reflection and action, theory and practice. For example, Carol realized that maintenance of a positive sense of self was necessary in order to foster a good climate for change.

Against the background of innovation overload and political negativity which primary teachers were suffering during this project, Carol felt that she had to aspire constantly to being positive. There was, she felt, a battle to fight against these negative political influences that were seeping into school. 'There are so many negative influences that we've got to fight very hard.' The fight demanded that she focus on and celebrate the positive successes and achievements. 'There are a lot of positive things to be said . . . about teachers and schools, and . . . we need to be over-emphasizing that to balance all the negative things.'

Trying to foster and maintain a positive climate against which planned change could happen was, as we have seen earlier, not always an easy matter. It demanded personal resources which Carol seemed to have most of the time but which sometimes evaded her as she struggled under the psychological and emotional weight of the macro-climate outside school. 'I recognize that it's very hard (to be positive) when you're tired and you're getting a bad press and you're loaded with paperwork. I find it hard to do and there are days when [I feel I don't succeed].'

There is, thus, a further self-management challenge for the coordinator and change agent. Strength has to come from somewhere in order to provide positive, active leadership for others. Earlier we saw Carol drawing upon the strengths and resources of her head and her secondary colleagues. She also knew how to stay personally buoyant in dangerous times, focusing positively on other areas of her work. She looked for celebrations in teaching and learning, in her exchanges with colleagues, in the appreciation of parents. Never a day seemed to go by when she didn't encounter something to celebrate, something that reminded her of the educative heart and purpose of her work. She seemed to have a vital capacity to draw upon these celebrations, to feed upon them and to gain strength from them.

'There's nearly always something that happens in school every day. Sometimes it's children, sometimes it's staff, sometimes it's a parent unexpectedly coming in and saying, "I'm ever so pleased this has happened".' She emphasized the strength which could be drawn from seeing children progress through their own challenges. This after all was the heart of the matter. 'But it's nearly always the children, I think. You go in and you think, I can't face this, and something happens and you think, even though my role is becoming more of an administrator, . . . you've got to remember that that's what we're about.'

She gave an illustration.

A little lad in my class, [was] writing his report for himself, and he said he'd had a bit of trouble in school with friendships. He's a bit of an aggressive lad and he tends to fight with his fists. If he is angry his fists go out. And people have tended to isolate him a bit. This year he has managed to control his temper a bit and he has had quite a few social successes. So he has written in his report, 'still find it difficult to keep my temper but I do try and when I have got older friends my work went off a bit'.

The relationship between her endeavours and children's successes was symbiotic. The rewards were mutual. Without Carol's developing interest in pupil self-assessment this learning process may not have happened for this child. Nor would Carol have been able to derive pleasure and satisfaction from it. 'So this is what the job's about. This is what the positive side is.'

These daily celebrations seemed to contribute positively to Carol's emotional resources, resources which were consequently used to feed school change and development, resources upon which her colleagues could in turn draw. So it seemed important that Carol allow the just rewards to flow back from the children, the pupils, colleagues and to feed her own spirit in this way. This seemed to be one of Carol's main battle strategies in fighting the ravages of negativism; a way of contributing to the development climate in which her project could grow; another of her professional answers.

Adding up the Learning

The project moved successfully into classroom practice in the following school term under Carol's management and agency. But we will leave the story at this point in order to summarize and reflect upon the range and complexity of learning which development of this INSET project has demanded of Carol.

Along this development road have been two broad and complex areas of understanding which Carol needed to evolve. First, the development of Carol's substantive understanding of assessment and pupil profiling was necessary in order to establish an appropriate theoretical basis for the project. The store of substantive knowledge and understanding provided a resource from which Carol's beliefs were clarified. Knowledge, understanding and clarification of beliefs led to increased confidence for Carol in the early stages. They also provided the basis upon which Carol made judgments about the practices in pupil profiling and self-assessment that would be appropriate to foster. All these qualities then became resources upon which school colleagues drew for their own learning and development.

Second, a range of situational understandings was required of Carol in order that she put her substantive learning to good use in the school and that she make the links between her INSET learning and school development. She needed good understanding of how the school as an organization worked; the structures, processes and roles that could facilitate change; the different channels of communication through which the business could be done — the existing team structures and meetings, the role of whole staff meetings, the use of staff development days, the informal one-to-one heart-to-heart talk, the power of the Head supporting and endorsing change. She also needed to develop her understanding of people within the organization. This was accompanied by some growing self understanding. This understanding of self and others enabled her to develop insights into the nature of organizational change. She developed a clearer understanding of ways in which people's feelings, ideas, beliefs, attitudes need accounting for and handling if one is to take an innovation forward.

Broad and demanding though these developing understandings were, however, they were not enough to bring about change through the INSET project. Substantive and situational understanding needed to be translated into situational judgment and action. Knowing had to be turned into doing. For this, Carol required many and varied qualities. The ability to plan, and follow through, an agreed course of action seemed necessary. Organizational skills played an important part and we saw these in operation as Carol programmed meetings, set targets and time lines, timetabled and resourced staff release, provided a challenging, supportive and relaxing staff development day, and created the new organizational structure of the working group. In addition, Carol also needed many of the qualities of the independent learner: taking initiatives, finding support resources when her self-confidence and development were endangered, and managing her own emotional life through the more difficult periods. Employing positive personal and interpersonal qualities was also vital: knowing what to say at the appropriate moment, to whom and in what kind of way; knowing when to apply a little pressure and when to avoid it; having a sense of how others might be thinking and feeling, where their commitments and energies lay; where trust and faith could be employed; where coercion was advisable. Perhaps more than anything, Carol needed fortitude and a good deal of emotional stamina for the project to continue. To this end, she seemed to understand the need for constant self-renewal. She allowed herself to enjoy and find reward in her work with children, parents and colleagues as a basis for keeping active, optimistic and committed. These qualities and attitudes helped her to present a positive face to her colleagues in a potentially debilitating political climate.

This analysis of the demands on and the development of Carol as an agent of change in her school, defies the simple cascade and delivery models of professional development through INSET. The analysis shows implementation from INSET to school development through the medium of the project to be a complex process. It shows that implementation of INSET is not simply a matter of taking substantive theory from the course and applying it to a practical school situation. Rather, it suggests that applying substantive understanding to the school context is itself a theoretical enterprise, demanding the development of understanding at several levels. Carol evolved theories of the organization, of other people and of her self during this complex process of applying her learning about assessment to the practical development of the school project. In this, she implicitly evolved a personal theory of change management and organizational development.

The INSET change agent is not, thus, a fully developed professional who simply needs to add to his or her substantive understanding through a structured course. Fostering school development through the INSET project is a learning experience in itself. And it is likely that members of an INSET course will be at different stages of development in their understanding of this complex challenge. Carol admitted that, in the management of change, she was at the beginning, novice stage. The case shows her moving further along the long and complex road towards greater expertise in this, as well as in her grasp of the pupil assessment issues. She learnt more about the management of change by doing it and reflecting upon the experience. In this process, she had to accept the need to shed a skin or two, to leave some parts of her old self behind in order to adopt new aspects of self which the challenge demanded of her. To act in ways which she felt were appropriate, she had, in part, to become someone else. This may, indeed, be inevitable for many INSET teachers who find themselves managing school change through their INSET development project.

It is also clear that help, support, encouragement and critical friendship may be beneficial, if not vital, for the learning processes which the change agent will encounter (Dadds, 1991). Without these, the learning may founder and the project may go down with it (Dadds, 1994; Dadds, in progress). In this, the learning needs of the INSET change agent may be no different from any other learner (Dadds, 1991) and may require just as serious consideration by INSET providers and other professional colleagues.

References

DADDS, M. (1991) 'Validity and award bearing teacher action research', unpublished Ph.D thesis, Norwich, University of East Anglia.

DADDS, M. (1994) 'Bridging the gap: Using the school based project to link award-bearing INSET to school development', in BRADLEY, H., CONNER, C. and SOUTHWORTH, G.W. (Eds) (1994) *Making INSET Effective*, London, Fulton.

DADDS, M. (in progress) 'The nature and use of the personal project on UCIE sixty-hour award-bearing courses', research report, Cambridge, University of Cambridge Institute of Education.

DADDS, M. (1993) 'The feeling of thinking in professional self-study', in ELLIOTT, J. (Ed) (1993) *Reconstructing Teacher Professional Development*, London, Falmer Press.

ELLIOTT, J. (1991) *Action Research for Educational Change*, Milton Keynes, Open University Press.

KINDER, K. and HARLAND, J. (1991) *The Impact of School-focussed INSET on Classroom Practice*, Slough, NFER.

MORRIS, P. (1974) *Loss and Change*, London, RKP.

SALZBERGER-WITTENBERG, I. *et al.*, (1983) *The Emotional Experience of Learning and Teaching*, London, RKP.

SCHON, D. (1971) *Beyond the Stable State*, New York, Norton and Co.

WINTER, R. (1989) *Learning from Experience*, Lewes, Falmer.

School Development: Lessons from Effective Schools and School Improvement Studies

Dick Weindling

Introduction

This chapter provides an overview of the research on school effectiveness and the attempts in the US to utilize the information in school improvement programmes. Other sections describe some of the approaches which have been tried in the UK, and the last section draws together the lessons which have been learned and the implications for schools.

There is considerable concern about educational standards, particularly in inner-city schools in both the UK and elsewhere. Research over many years has shown a high correlation between social class and educational achievement, and many inner cities have areas of considerable poverty and large numbers of disadvantaged families.

In the US various attempts have been made to provide additional help for at-risk children, such as Head Start which began in 1964–65 as a comprehensive intervention strategy for preschool children aged 3–6, and Follow Through which began in 1967 as a scheme for school age children to follow on from Head Start. The major support for at-risk children is now provided by federal money under Title I (previously called Chapter 1) funding. In 1987 about 1 in every 9 children was receiving support from Chapter 1 resources in over 90 per cent of the school districts. The 1992–93 budget was more than 6 billion dollars.

School Improvement should be seen as a systematic attempt to improve teaching and learning which has as its focus the classroom and school. It must not be taken in a negative way as an indictment of a school — any school can improve no matter how well it is doing. The roots of school improvement can be seen historically to have had two distinct threads of research: the first, and more recent, involves the study of effective schools; while the second, spanning many years, is concerned with educational innovation and the management of change.

School Effectiveness

Considerable problems arise if attempts are made to compare schools on various performance indicators without taking into account the obvious fact that their intakes, as well as other factors, differ. The current DFE league tables have caused concern among heads and staff because the data does not take the context of the school into account. The term *school effectiveness* is used to describe studies which do try to measure and relate intake, process and outcome variables. In this country a more recent term is 'value-added' which in essence can be taken as 'what do schools add to what children bring with them'.

The early work began in the US and consisted of large-scale input-output studies of student achievement, such as that by Coleman *et al.* (1966) and Jenks *et al.* (1972). The depressing conclusion which was drawn from this work was that schools made little, or no difference. Home background, IQ and rather surprisingly, luck, were found to be the main variables determining student achievement. However, Coleman has repeatedly claimed that his findings were misinterpreted and the following quote from the original report suggests that this may have been the case:

> the achievement of minority pupils depends more on the schools they attend than does the achievement of majority pupils. This indicates that it is for the most disadvantaged children that improvements in school quality will make the most differences in achievement.
>
> (Coleman *et al.*, 1966: 22)

But this statement was lost in the general conclusion which many people made — schools make no difference. Thankfully, some researchers refused to believe this and began to search for effective schools. An essential technique was to disaggregate the student achievement data so that it became possible to compare various groups of children on, for example, gender, socioeconomic status (SES) and race. It was also important to look inside the 'black-box' and find out what schools actually did.

An early example of this approach was George Weber who, after numerous enquiries, found four inner-city elementary schools which seemed to be particularly successful in helping students to read. He visited the schools and found a number of factors which were not usually found in unsuccessful urban schools. The most vocal and influential advocate of the effective schools movement was a black superintendent and researcher, Ronald Edmonds who died in 1983. He defined an effective school as one that 'brings the children of the poor to those minimal masteries of basic school skills that now describe minimally successful pupil performance for the children of the middle class'. An effective school 'must bring an equal percentage of the highest and lowest social class of students to minimum mastery' (Edmonds, 1979).

This means that there are two issues in school effectiveness: *Quality*, an improvement in overall student performance, and *equity*, in which the data have to be disaggregated to examine whether each of the groups (in terms of gender, race and SES) are achieving minimum mastery. Lezotte, who worked with Edmonds, suggested that when a school achieves a criteria of 95 per cent of all groups of students reaching mastery of basic skills, and maintains this over three years, it can be called an effective school.

From his work in Detroit and New York Edmonds identified a number of 'correlates' which were associated with effective schools, and this became known as the Five Factor model:

- Strong leadership;
- High expectations for children's achievement;
- An orderly atmosphere conducive to learning;
- An emphasis on basic skill acquisition;
- Frequent monitoring of student progress which is used as feedback.

Critics pointed out that the main focus of effective schools was too narrow and that schools had other aims as well as academic achievement. Methodological concerns were also raised about the small numbers of schools and the fact that the US research was largely based on urban elementary schools serving disadvantaged children.

In the UK, in contrast to the US emphasis on elementary schools, most of the studies (apart from Mortimore *et al.*, 1988) have looked at secondary schools using 16+ exam results as outcome variables rather than standardized tests of reading and maths. The main studies which have looked at school effectiveness in this country are:

- Reynolds *et al.* (1976) — four Welsh secondary schools;
- Rutter *et al.* (1979) — twelve London secondaries;
- Smith and Tomlinson (1989) — eighteen urban multicultural secondaries;
- Mortimore *et al.* (1988) — fifty London junior schools.

A more recent piece of research for the Department for Education (DfE) and School Management Task Force (SMTF) has looked at the related area of heads and teachers perceptions of effective management (Bolam, McMahon, Pocklington and Weindling, 1993). It is not possible to go into detail about the various projects in this chapter, but the important point to note is that most of the findings from these studies have produced results similar to the US research.

The general outcomes of the effective schools research seem to have reached DfE/Government level and it is interesting that the 1992 White Paper, in the section on tackling failing schools, says:

> The failure is usually one of leadership and management at school level. It has been shown that, with strong leadership and effective management, schools in disadvantaged areas can flourish. The Government

applauds the achievements of the head teachers and staffs of these schools; failing schools should learn from them. The key conditions for success in a school are:

- a high level of parental and community support;
- clear and widely understood objectives;
- consistently high expectations of pupils;
- thorough monitoring and review of performance.

(DfE, 1992)

Despite the methodological criticisms mentioned earlier, the various studies in different countries have reached remarkably similar conclusions. I have synthesized the findings from the UK and US research under eight broad headings. These are not in order of magnitude (as this is not known) and they almost certainly interact. There is now a consensus that more effective, or high attaining schools tend to be characterized by some or all of the following factors or correlates:

- Emphasis on Learning
  A curriculum which has relevance for all students. Heads and teachers need to carefully consider how the National Curriculum can be made relevant for *all*. The key term is, of course, differentiation, but this is very difficult to put into practice.

  Teachers have high expectations, a belief that all children can learn, given the right conditions.

  Related to this is another important factor, *efficacy*, which is used to define the extent to which teachers believe that they can make a difference to children's learning.

  Regular setting and marking of homework — which in primary schools would include sending reading books home, etc.

  Visible rewards for academic excellence and improvement.

- Classroom Management
  A high proportion of time is spent on the subject matter of the lesson (as distinct from setting up equipment, dealing with disciplinary matters etc.).

  A high proportion of teacher time is spent interacting with the class as a whole, as opposed to individuals. But the teaching style must be appropriate to the type of lesson, for example, some things are best taught whole-class, others in small groups.

  Lessons beginning and ending on time.

  Clear and unambiguous feedback to students on their performance and what is expected of them.

Ample praise for good performance — celebrate success.

* Discipline and School Climate
Keep good order and promote a safe and orderly climate that is not oppressive and is conducive to teaching and learning.

Buildings kept in good order, repair and decoration.

* School Management
Positive leadership by the head and other senior staff is necessary to both initiate and maintain school improvement.

A management style which encourages collegial work and shared decision-making.

The head and senior staff are skilled and knowledgeable about the management of change and the application of strategic planning.

* Vision and Monitoring
A shared vision is needed by the governors and all the staff. Clear, achievable goals for school improvement must be established.

Regular monitoring of students' progress is necessary to determine whether the goals are being realized. This information should be used as feedback to inform decision-making.

* Staff Development
To influence the whole school, staff development has to be school-wide, rather than specific to individual teacher's needs, and closely related to the curriculum.

An effective school development plan is needed which integrates staff development, institutional development and curriculum development.

Staff development activities need to be phased throughout the improvement process, and not just used at the pre-implementation stage.

* Parental Involvement
Parents are viewed and valued as full partners in the learning process.

Staff work to achieve positive home-school relations in which parents actively support the school.

The school reaches out to the community and encourages them to play an active role in the learning process.

* LEA and Outside Support
Fundamental changes require support from the LEA and few of the variables listed are likely to be realized without this support.

Consultants can provide valuable information and training and facilitate the school improvement process.

Research on the management of change shows powerful effects when a blend of inside and outside assistance is used. School improvement requires both pressure and support.

Reynolds (1992) reviewed and summarized the work on effective schools and pointed out that while schools do make a difference, the home background and individual capability are still the major factors in childrens' achievement — perhaps about 15–20 per cent of the variance is due to school. Also the classroom and school factors interact, and school performance varies over time — in other words, a school does not necessarily remain effective from year to year.

School Improvement

Although we now know a lot about the factors associated with effective schools, we do not know how these particular schools became effective, or a simple way of how to help a school become more effective. In 1984, when many states in the US were rushing to apply the effective schools research, Cuban provided the following warning:

> Unlike the way things happen in fairy tales, school reforms require more than a kiss to convert a frog into a shining prince. Furthermore, productive schooling entails more than raising test scores. No one knows how to grow effective schools. Road signs exist, but no maps are yet for sale.

School improvement is the planned and deliberate attempt to help schools move forward. One of the first projects began when the New York City district asked Ron Edmonds to put his ideas into effect in the New York School Improvement Program which started in 1979. A group of facilitators was trained to conduct a needs assessment and to support the development of schools. This project was very influential and other districts sent people to New York to see how the programme worked, and soon several Schools Improvement Projects (SIPs) were operating. The fact that programmes such as those in NYC and Milwaukee (Project RISE) showed dramatic improvements in student achievements on standardized tests of reading and maths, received good publicity and many districts and states began to take notice in the early 1980s.

The numerous US school improvement projects which were set up throughout the 1980s operate at district, state and federal levels. It is now estimated that over half the 16,000 school districts are operating some form of school improvement project. Although these vary in their approach, most make use of the research on effective schools and effective teaching, combined with what we know about the management of change — which is the other major strand in school improvement.

A typical US School Improvement project proceeds through the following phases:

1   Orientation and Preparation Phase

- Establish a planning team;
- Use a consultant to introduce the effective schools research to the planning team and the whole staff;
- Vision building — the team and the whole staff work to produce a shared vision.

2   Needs Assessment and the Formulation of the School Improvement Plan

- Collect school data on the effective school correlates;
- Review the disaggregated student data;
- The team formulates a school improvement action plan, including: priorities; time sequence; and resources;
- The plan is discussed and agreed by all staff.

3   Implementation Phase

- Implement the school improvement plan;
- Pilot and trial;
- Staff development is used throughout programme not just at the beginning;
- Monitor and discuss continually;
- Evaluate progress, for example, collect, analyse and review student data;
- Revise and modify the plan in the light of the feedback.

4   Incorporation Phase

- Build resources into base budget;
- Induct all new staff;
- Maintain number of key people, such as, when some leave replace them.

An important question for UK schools is what role should the governors play in the process? It could be argued that they should be part of the planning team as they already contain parent and employer representatives. If existing relations with the governing body are positive it makes a lot of sense to ensure that they play an active role in the school improvement process.

US School Improvement Initiatives

In this section I describe two models which have gained particular support: the first focuses on parental involvement, while the second attempts to integrate a number of components found to be successful from a review of the literature on teaching at-risk children.

School Development Programme — James Comer

James Comer is a psychiatrist at Yale Medical School and the Child Study Centre at the University. He grew up in a poor black family in Indiana, yet his mother, who was a maid, put all five children through college. Comer began to wonder why he and his brothers and sisters had succeeded while most of his friends were either dead or in jail. In 1960 he decided not to become a doctor but to work on the education of at-risk children.

The Comer approach begins with the notion that as he and his family demonstrated, humans thrive in a supportive environment, but these have decreased in recent years. In 1968, with backing from the Ford Foundation, he worked with two schools in New Haven, Connecticut, which were at the bottom of the list in terms of student achievement, to bolster the social and psychological needs of disadvantaged children as a precondition to effective learning. The key to the Comer model is what he calls the 'conspiracy of the whole community', to work together for the student. Three teams are established: the first step brings parents into a School Planning and Management team for the school, alongside teachers and others, and this is led by the principal.

The second step is to bring parents actively into the life of the school and create a shared sense of purpose between parents and staff through the Parents' Programme. Parents work in classrooms and in social events. The third step is to make the partnership more knowledgeable and effective by establishing a Mental Health team to assist the management group. This consists of psychologists, nurses, special education teachers, social workers, etc., which meets regularly to discuss the developmental needs of individual children and how to combat problems through services to the child and family.

The Management Group addresses three major issues which are considered critical to changing schools:

1   The school climate
2   The academic programme
3   Staff development

They look at student data and make a plan for the year. Resources are mobilized to carry out the plan and evaluate the outcomes.

The New Haven school system was very impressed with the improvements at the pilot schools and extended the scheme to all forty-two schools. Information about the success of the programme spread, and in 1981 a federal judge ordered schools in Benton Harbor, Michigan, to adopt the Comer programme as a way of saving the rapidly disintegrating and racially troubled district. This resulted in a significant improvement in student performance and behaviour. By 1990 there were over 100 Comer schools operating in eight states, and the Rockefeller Foundation agreed to provide eight million dollars over the next five years to help schools implement the Comer approach.

In 1993 Comer and his team were invited to a school improvement conference at the London Institute. A team from Halton, Ontario, also outlined their approach and both models raised considerable interest with the participants. (For details see the series of articles in *Managing Schools Today*, 1993.)

Success for All — Bob Slavin

This is a comprehensive programme for elementary schools based on a review of what works for children at-risk. It was piloted at a school in Baltimore, Maryland, in 1987, and has now been used in many other schools across the US. Evaluations of the programme have shown significant student improvements in comparison to control groups (Slavin *et al.*, 1993). The main organizing principle is that no child is permitted to fall behind in basic skills. Resources are concentrated in the early grades to attempt to ensure that every child is successful. Three essential ideas inform the design of the programme:

1   The best place to work on ensuring success for all is in the classroom and its instructional programme.
2   There must be a responsiveness to students' needs. When they experience difficulty they must be given specifically targeted assistance right away, not weeks or months later when small deficits will have accumulated into large ones.
3   There has to be flexible use of school resources, in particular time and personnel. In most schools, a set level of resources is provided for all students, and student success is allowed to vary. In Success for All, success is seen as an entitlement for all students, and it is the resources needed to ensure success that are allowed to vary.

Few if any students will be assigned to special education, and few if any will be retained in a grade. It is seen as the responsibility of the school to ensure that every child succeeds in the regular programme, no matter what their needs may be.

The programme has a number of key elements:

Reading tutors
Reading tutors are one of the most important elements of the programme. (This is similar to Reading Recovery.) They support students' success in reading and replace the special education teachers. The tutors work for twenty minutes on a one-to-one basis with students who are having difficulty with their reading. During the daily ninety-minute reading period for the whole

class, the tutors serve as additional reading teachers to reduce the class size. First graders receive preference as the primary function of the tutors is to help all students be successful in reading the first time, before they become remedial readers.

Programme facilitator
This person works at the school full time to oversee, with the principal, the operation of the programme. He or she helps the principal to plan the programme, oversees the tutor's work and offers suggestions, helps the teachers with any student behaviour problems, and coordinates the work of the family support team with that of the teaching staff.

Family support team
This consists of at least one social worker and one parent liaison person working full-time with the school. This team provides education for the parents and works to involve parents in supporting their children's success in school. They set up a home reading programme in which children read to their parents and establish opportunities for parents to work in the school.

Advisory committee
A steering committee composed of the principal, the programme facilitator, teacher representatives and university staff from John Hopkins meet weekly to review progress and solve any problems that arise.

Curriculum
In addition to the reading programme, there are also language/writing and maths components to Success for All.

Assessment
Every eight weeks the progress of each student is assessed and individual academic plans are produced to guide the work of the classroom teacher and the tutor. The results of the assessments are used to determine who is to have tutoring.

Preschool and kindergarten
This is the most expensive part of the programme, as the other costs are usually covered from Chapter 1 sources. The programme provides a half-day preschool for all eligible students in classes of fifteen children with one teacher and an assistant. The major emphasis is on language development.

The kindergarten uses a full-day programme in groups of twenty children with one teacher and an assistant. The curriculum provides a balance of academic readiness and music, art and movement. Continuing from the preschool, the emphasis is on language use and development.

Success for All is seen as one of the most effective programmes and by 1993 was being used in eighty schools in nineteen states across America.

School Improvement in the UK

In the UK we have not really attempted school improvement programmes directly based on the effective schools research. However, the following initiatives could be seen as attempts at various forms of improvement:

- GRIDS (Guidelines for Review and Internal Development) — McMahon and Bolam (1984)
- IBIS (Inspectors Based in Schools) — Hargreaves and ILEA (1984)
- School Development Plans (SDPs) — Hargreaves and Hopkins/DFE (1990s)

Until very recently the term *school improvement* was hardly used in this country, but now a number of new projects have begun which are quite explicit about their focus on school improvement. Brief details about some of these projects are given below.

One of the most established is Improving the Quality of Education for All (IQEA) — Hopkins and Ainscow (1993). A team from the University of Cambridge Institute of Education are working with several LEAs and twenty-six schools in south-east England and Yorkshire. The emphasis is on a collaborative approach and a contract is developed in each school among the staff, LEA representatives and the UCIE team. Each school designates a minimum of two people (one of whom is the head or a deputy) as project coordinators who attend ten days of training and support meetings. The group of coordinators form the *project cadre*. Various staff development activities are undertaken by the schools and participating teachers are released from teaching to participate in the classroom-based aspects of the project. (See Chapter 9 for further details).

The London Institute of Education are working with LEA staff and supporting projects in Haringey and Lewisham. Other LEA projects are taking place in Birmingham, Sheffield, Knowsley, Staffordshire and Hammersmith and Fulham. The project in Hammersmith and Fulham which is called Schools Make A Difference (SMAD), involves eight secondary schools and runs for about eighteen months. In a similar manner to the IQEA approach, the heads and coordinators, together with other members of the SMT were initially invited to a residential conference. Other sessions have been organized every 3–4 weeks on a range of topics, such as school effectiveness research, parental involvement, performance indicators and flexible learning. The project has a number of broad defining characteristics which are based on previous research; schools have submitted proposals on various approaches to improving teaching and learning. The schools were then allocated money for building modifications, such as learning resource centres, and for curriculum projects, like tutoring. (See Myers and Stoll, 1993 for a description of the various projects.)

Pocklington and Weindling of Create Consultants are currently working with five secondary schools. Westminster LEA have funded one of the projects and in Greenwich the work is co-funded uniquely by the Woolwich Building Society and South Thames TEC. The approach is similar to some of the US projects and uses a type of Organization Development (OD) which begins directly inside the school where the consultants interview a sample of staff and survey the opinions of all teachers using a diagnostic questionnaire. The results from this are feedback to all staff and a School Improvement Group (SIG) is formed to establish the priorities and implement strategies for improvement. The members of the SIG include the head and deputies, the chair of governors and a cross-section of staff (teaching and non-teaching) who are elected by their peers at each level, for example, the main scale teachers elect two representatives as do the A/Bs and C/Ds. The consultants chair and facilitate the group using the principle of *consensus decision-making* where everyone must be able to live with the decisions and fully support them outside the meeting. At one of the schools the main priorities have been consultation, communication and decision-making, and student under-achievement.

It is too early to report how successful the various school improvement projects have been as most have only just got under way. As the projects proceed it will be important to have evaluative data related to a number of levels such as: the school organization and processes; the perceptions of teachers, governors, parents and students; and ultimately, student outcomes.

Lessons from the Research

Levine and Lezotte (1990) provide an excellent review of the effective schools and school improvement literature and some of this section is drawn from their conclusions. They point out that the effective school movement has gone through a number of transformations. The first phase focused on the identification of effective schools. The second emphasized the description of the more effective school, while the third phase moved from description to the development of guidelines and approaches for school improvement. The fourth and current phase addresses the larger organizational context of the school — for example, the local, state and federal levels.

The number of US schools and districts that are implementing programmes of school improvement continues to increase, either through state mandates or local and individual initiatives. But whatever the origin, some underlying guidelines seem to be associated with successful change models.

First, the focus of change still needs to be on the single school. Creating more effective schools must occur school by school. But paradoxically, the school-by-school change process is most likely to succeed if the larger organizational context (for example, the LEA) supports the goals and strategies. A second observation is that the head, the SMT and the rest of the staff must be involved in a collaborative and collegial process designed to empower the change process. Too often principals try to do it alone.

One of the important new insights that emerges from the research is that success comes when innovations are broad-based and comprehensive. The school improvement strategies which were first used to implement the effective schools research often focused largely on the technical aspects. So, for example, to improve leadership the principal tried to 'walk the halls'. But, while this may be important behaviour for the principal, it does not by itself contribute to the change process. Technical changes have to be linked with both political and cultural changes in the school. The way to accomplish this is to address straight away the fundamental beliefs and values that define the culture of the school. When this linkage occurs, change is more likely to follow, and most importantly, more likely to be sustained. Schools will not become more effective through the efforts of bureaucrats who think that they can mandate change through technical rules and regulations that direct schools to improve. As McLaughlin (1990) points out, 'you cannot mandate what matters, but what you mandate matters'.

Levine and Lezotte provide the following guidance:

1   The effective schools correlates or factors should be viewed more as prerequisites for attaining high and equitable levels of student achievement than as any kind of guarantee that such a school will be successful. Success in dealing with some of the correlates will not bring about improved student achievement in the absence of action dealing with other correlates.
2   The correlates represent issues and challenges that the staff must deal with to make their school effective. But they are not a recipe or detailed prescription, because no set of actions is right for every school.
3   Schools struggling to improve face profound dilemmas which are built into the reform process. In unusually effective schools heads and teachers identify and address the obstacles. Ignoring problems often wrecks a school improvement project.
4   Emphasis should be placed on both the effective schools and the effective teaching research as they are mutually reinforcing. Comprehensive programmes recognize the need for staff to have a common language about effectiveness to facilitate discourse on school improvement.

Bearing the above points in mind, some of the qualities found in effective schools are:

* *Insistence* — that all teachers, students and others in the school take responsibility for improvement and adhere to high standards in the face of difficulties.
* *Persistence* — to overcome the numerous roadblocks which occur in the improvement process.
* *Resiliency* — in the sense that staff do not allow occasional setbacks to thwart their plans for continuous improvement.
* *Consistency* — in devising and implementing coordinated curricula and teaching approaches that result in high achievement among all groups of students.

Although there is no single recipe or blueprint for school improvement we can use the knowledge about effective schools and the change process to help schools become more effective. The following draws together the points made earlier in the chapter and offers advice to heads, teachers, governors, LEAs and the DfE.

To begin the process of school improvement, heads and staff need to review the school's strengths and weaknesses on each of the school effectiveness factors in order to establish priorities for the school development plan. However, it is important to remember that over time all the factors must be addressed. It is essential to have an agreed and shared vision to guide the change process and release the potential for school improvement that exists within the school. (Barth, 1992)

You cannot get school improvement by simply trying to bolt on another initiative because schools are suffering from innovation overload. School culture is the critical factor. Changing schools means changing peoples' behaviours and attitudes as well as the school's organization and norms. Hence, Fullan's (1991) emphasis on the importance of the *meaning* of educational change — people need to construct their own understanding of what the change means for them. There has to be a sustained effort which changes the school culture. School improvement is *steady work* and cannot be achieved by means of a quick-fix solution.

The US research shows that improvement in student results tends to show first in elementary or primary schools, and it takes longer to see the effects in secondary schools. Generally at least three to five years are needed, so the advice is to look for small improvements annually.

While schools can do much for themselves, support from outside is also needed. In the current UK projects this is provided by LEA personnel and a range of different consultants. School improvement is not achieved by either top-down or bottom-up programmes, but through a combination of these. A blend of pressure and support is required, but different amounts of each are needed at different points in the school improvement process. Outside assistance is obviously very useful in providing support in terms of INSET and general facilitation, but pressure to sustain the project is also required as schools struggle to cope with the myriad of issues that confront them everyday.

The objective of developing effective schools can be approached in a number of different ways. But to achieve maximum impact, the following approaches should be integrated to provide a comprehensive strategy:

- Using the research findings on effective schools and effective teaching;
- Gathering school-specific information e.g. conducting a needs assessment, and analysing student performance data;
- Fostering staff development and collegiality, for example, through team teaching, peer coaching and Investors in People (IiP);
- Exploring a variety of instructional initiatives, such as the study of teaching skills, and strategies such as cooperative and flexible learning;

- Making effective use of curricular initiatives — whole curricular (the National Curriculum), TVEI and subject-specific;
- Improving relations with parents and employers, such as by introducing parental involvement programmes and Education Business Partnerships and Compacts.

Whenever we talk about an effective school we need to be prepared to ask and answer two questions: Effective at what, and effective for whom? In 1979 Ron Edmonds said we already know more than we need in order to successfully teach all students whose schooling is of interest to us. I wish to fully concur with Levine and Lezotte (1990) who end their review by saying that we are even more sure today than we were that Edmonds was correct in his assessment.

References

BARTH, R. (1992) *Improving Schools from Within*, San Francisco, CA, Jossey Bass.

BOLAM, R., McMAHON, A., POCKLINGTON, K. and WEINDLING, R. (1993) *Effective Management in Schools*, London, HMSO.

COLEMAN, J.S., CAMPELL, E., HOBSON C., McPARTLAND, J., MOOD, A., WEINFELD, F. and YORK, R. (1966) *Equality of Educational Opportunity*, Washington, NY, US Government Printing Office.

COMER, J., ANSON, A.R., COOK, T.D., HABIB, F., GRADY, M.K. and HAYNES, N. (1991) 'The Comer school development program', *Urban Education*, **26**, 1, pp. 56–82.

CUBAN, L. (1984) 'Transforming the frog into a prince', *Harvard Education Review*, **54**, 2, pp. 129–51.

DFE (1992) *Choice and Diversity*, London, HMSO.

EDMONDS, R. (1979) 'Effective schools for the urban poor', *Educational Leadership*, **37**, 1, pp. 15–24.

FULLAN, M. (1991) *The New Meaning of Educational Change*, London, Cassell.

HARGREAVES, D. and HOPKINS, D. (1992) *The Empowered School*, London, Cassell.

HOPKINS, D. and AINSCOW, M. (1993) *Making Sense of School Improvement: An Item Account of the IQEA Project*, Cambridge, Institute of Education, Mimeo.

JENKS, C., SMITH, M., ACLAND, H., BANE, M., COHEN, D., GINTIS, H., HEYNS, B. and MICHELSON, S. (1972) *Inequality: A Reassessment of the Effects of Family and Schooling in America*, New York, NY, Harper and Row.

LEVINE, D. and LEZOTTE, L. (1990) *Unusually Effective Schools*, Madison, WI, National Center for Effective Schools.

McLAUGHLIN, M. (1990) 'The Rand Change Agent Study Revisited', *Educational Researcher*, **19**, 9, pp. 11–16.

McMAHON, A. and BOLAM, R. (1984) *Guidelines for Review and Internal Development in Schools*, York, Longmans for Schools Council.

MORTIMORE, P., SAMMONS, P., STOLL, L., LEWIS, D. and ECOB, R. (1988) *School Matters*, Somerset, Open Books.

MYERS, K. and STOLL, L. (1993) 'Mapping the movement', *Education*, 16 July 1993, p. 51.

REYNOLDS, D., JONES, D. and LEGER ST, S. (1976) 'Schools do make a difference', *New Society*, **37**, pp. 223–5.

REYNOLDS, D. (1992) In Reynolds, D. and Cuttance, P. (Eds) *School Effectiveness*, London, Cassell.

RUTTER, M., MAUGHAN, B., MORTIMORE, P. and OUSTON, J. (1979) *Fifteen Thousand Hours*, London, Open Books.

School Improvement in Managing Schools Today (1993) Series of six papers by MORTIMORE, P. **2**, 5, pp. 10–13: STOLL, L. and FINK, **2**, 6, pp. 12–15: FITZ-HARRIS, B. **2**, 7, pp. 24–28: HINDS, C. **2**, 8, pp. 12–15: TAGGART, B. **2**, 9, pp. 12–15 and MORTIMORE, P. and TAGGART, B. **3**, 1, pp. 12–14.

SLAVIN, R., MADDEN, N., DOLAN, L. and WASIK, B. (1993) 'Whenever and wherever we choose — the replication of Success For All', paper for American Educational Research Association (AERA) Annual meeting Atlanta, GA, April 1993.

SMITH, D.J. and TOMLINSON, S. (1989) *The School Effect*, London, Policy Studies Institute.

Chapter 9

Understanding the Moving School

Mel Ainscow and *David Hopkins*

In recent years primary schools have faced an enormous range of demands for change. Despite these pressures some schools find opportunities for improvement in this new context. This chapter will describe a school improvement project that involves groups of schools collaborating to develop ways of working that enable the current reform agenda to be turned to advantage. Specifically the chapter will focus on developments going on in three primary schools that are participants in the project, drawing out some lessons that have emerged from an analysis of their activities.

Improving the Quality of Education for All

During the past three years or so we and a team of colleagues have been working closely with some thirty schools on a school improvement project known as Improving the Quality of Education for All (IQEA). This project has involved the schools and us in a collaborative enterprise designed to strengthen their ability to manage change, to enhance the work of teachers, and ultimately to improve the outcomes, however broadly defined, of pupils. At a time of great change in the educational system, the schools we are working with are using the impetus of external reform for internal purpose. In other words they are attempting to become what Susan Rosenholtz (1989) has called *moving schools*.

IQEA works from an assumption that schools are most likely to strengthen their ability to provide enhanced outcomes for all pupils when they adopt ways of working that are consistent with their own aspirations as well as the current reform agenda. This involves building confidence and capacity within the school, rather than reliance on externally produced packages — although good ideas from the outside are never rejected out of hand.

The project in each school is based upon a contract between the staff of the school, the local education authority and the Cambridge team. This contract is intended to clarify expectations and ensure the conditions necessary for success. For our part, we co-ordinate the project; provide training for the school co-ordinators and representatives; make regular school visits and contribute to staff training; provide staff development materials; and monitor the implementation of the project. For the schools on the other hand, involvement in the project requires the following commitments:

- The decision to participate in the project is made as a result of consultation amongst *all staff* in the school.
- Each school designates a minimum of two members of staff as project co-ordinators (one of whom is the headteacher or deputy head) who attend ten days of training and support meetings (the group of co-ordinators is known as the *project cadre*).
- At least 40 per cent of teachers (representing a cross-section of staff) take part in specified staff development activities in their own and each others' classrooms. Each participating teacher is regularly released from teaching in order to participate in these classroom based aspects of the project.
- Teachers are able to use their participation in the project as a basis for accrediting their professional development work.
- Each school participates in the evaluation of the project and shares findings with other participants in the project.
- The whole school allocates substantial staff development time to activities related to the project.

The style adopted in the project is to develop a strategy for improvement that allows each school considerable autonomy to determine its own priorities for development and, indeed, its own methods for achieving these priorities. In this sense we (all the partners in the project) are involved in one project within which individual schools devise their own projects.

Within IQEA we place considerable importance on the need for inquiry, reflection and evaluation. The collecting of school-based data of various kinds for purposes of informing planning and development is seen as a powerful element within each school's strategy. Consequently the schools are expected to collect data about progress in establishing conditions for improvement, and, of course, about student and teacher outcomes. Agreement that these data would be shared is one of the specifications of the project contract.

The journals kept by the project co-ordinators provide a common approach to recording relevant information. In general terms the journals provide a detailed account of events, decisions and processes that occur, as well as summaries of significant outcomes that are noted. Co-ordinators are also requested to write reflective comments, indicating their personal reactions to what occurs and map their involvement in the project over time. In this way individuals can monitor the progress of their school's project and, at the same time, record developments in their own thinking and practice.

Throughout the period of the project the project team make regular visits to each school to support co-ordinators in their work and, at the same time, to collect additional data. All these data are systematically processed on a continuous basis in order to build up a clearer picture of the activities going on in each school. These findings are also being fed back to the school in order to inform development processes. In this respect the project can correctly be characterized as a process of collaborative inquiry within which all partners are contributing to its evolution.

From data collected through these processes we are gradually gaining a greater understanding of what goes on in schools that are successful in managing change during a period of intensive innovation. In what follows we draw out some lessons from three primary schools that seem to us to have made significant progress in providing a quality education for all their children.

Establishing a Climate

Our experience has been that it is vital to establish a climate in a school that encourages all colleagues to participate in improvement activities. Ideally, the aim should be to create a feeling amongst staff that they can contribute to the leadership of such developments. A commitment to participate in the leadership process seems to grow from the headteacher's commitment to secure participation — once staff believe the invitation is authentic then the quality of individual involvement increases. However, the building of openness and trust hinges on the quality of communication which is established alongside and around the decentralization of decisions. This communication needs to flow upwards and sideways as well as down, and to be seen as an important part of the influence process — where information replaces authority as the basis for decision-making then additional information inevitably changes the equation and sometimes the decision. Nurturing such an influence pattern is difficult in the larger school, where groups and individuals do not always meet one another regularly; it may be even harder in the smaller school where staff see each other daily and patterns of headteacher patronage are well established.

Within the IQEA project we have observed a number of schools that have moved towards a much more participatory climate. One of these schools, we will call it Eastside, is a particularly good example in that it involved a newly appointed headteacher in transforming staff expectations of leader behaviour.

Eastside is a large junior school serving a working-class district on the outskirts of a large city. The headteacher, Christine Jones, joined the school about four years ago at the same time as a new deputy head who had been appointed by the previous headteacher. Christine's previous experience had been as a teaching head in a very small primary school where she had been used to a relaxed atmosphere within which it was a tradition for all staff to contribute to development activities. When Christine met the staff for the first time she began to realize how different this school was from her previous experience. She knew, for example, that previously staff had addressed the head by her full title and there were real expectations of a formal and hierarchical structure being maintained. At that stage, therefore, she decided that her chief aim must be to gain their trust and respect. She also felt that she would have to take time to appraise the school as well as support her staff. Like many new heads, therefore, she faced many dilemmas about how quickly to act in introducing proposed changes.

Christine found that the leadership pattern established in the school was of a pyramid type, with ideas and decisions passed to the staff via the deputy and senior management team. She also gradually found that there were a small number of very influential teachers (not necessarily members of the SMTF) but that the majority saw themselves as being powerless. Except in one particular year group team, planning was very much carried out by individuals for their own classes.

Early on Christine and her new deputy head colleague decided to adopt a different approach to staff meetings in order to make it possible for everyone to participate. Indeed, the first step was to establish a pattern of regular weekly staff meetings. Before the meetings, information was circulated so that everybody knew what was to be discussed, and Christine chaired the meetings in ways that attempted to avoid undue pressure.

After some time there was evidence of increased staff participation. Teachers with responsible posts were encouraged to take on non-specific management tasks and were given opportunities to decide on resources in their own areas. As the power of the majority of staff gradually increased, however, the small group of teachers who had previously been influential experienced some loss of status. Consequently a level of distrust and uncertainty continued.

At the start of her second year in the school Christine decided to emphasize the idea that planning should take place within year groups. About the same time she produced a draft school development plan and submitted it to the staff for comments. In addition, use was made of various LEA advisers as part of the school's staff development programme. The main aim was to enable class teachers to develop their expertise in the light of new curriculum requirements.

In the spring of that second year the whole staff set out their priorities for the development plan and a system of working groups was established. Time was also allocated in order that year group teams could meet to plan for the following term. At first the whole staff worked on the core subjects, English, Maths and Science, but then people began to feel that this was taking too long. Working groups or subject co-ordinators, with advice and help from the authority, now prepared policies and schemes of work, which were presented to the whole staff for discussion and adoption as working documents. Much was achieved in a relatively short time as staff worked to get the best for the children. The ethos gradually became one of commitment and enthusiasm although this also led to occasional periods of exhaustion.

As the staff became empowered it became necessary to respond to their requests knowing that any demands that were made were for the benefit of the children. Christine felt that the recognition that no one person had all of the answers, even if theoretically they had the power, changed the way decisions were made. The belief that a team committed to working together with the same aim has more to offer than an individual wielding power is a very basic belief. It is also very uncomfortable at times because the team can propose some things that the head does not totally agree with and yet the style of management means that it must be tried out.

This account of what happened at Eastside underlines the importance of relationship building. The mutual trust which is needed for genuine empowerment hinges on the quality of the relationship between head and staff. The account also shows how trust builds once relationships are right. Communication is clearly important here too: new opportunities were created for staff to meet and talk about what is happening — occasions when the formal communications hierarchy gave way to whole school meetings where horizontal, vertical and, most importantly, upward communication were possible. But, better quality communication does not mean universal agreement — indeed, it was very uncomfortable at times. What is important is that although certain issues or discussions create discomfort, the staff feel able to raise them. This leads to a much healthier environment for handling conflict (i.e. by acknowledging and exploring it) than is usually the case in leader-dependent cultures, where differences in view tend to be minimized or hidden, rather than viewed as opportunities for growth.

This account also demonstrates the motivational potential of shared leadership — the staff feel more enthusiasm and commitment to their jobs because they are actively involved in decisions about them, creating a strong sense of personal identification with organizational jobs. It also shows how school leaders can, by transforming their ways of working, encourage the creation of a culture that is, to some degree at least, shaped by the values and expectations of the teachers themselves. These transformations represent the first steps towards a more empowered and autonomous staff group.

Clearly, to devise management arrangements that empower is a challenging task. Yet this challenge is already being attended to in many schools, since the pressures for change are creating a strain on the existing arrangements, and are leading governors, heads and staff to review traditional ways of managing and leading the school. Governors in particular are looking for new ways of working with the head and staff which build upon the good relationships already established. Teachers are also realizing that the management of classrooms cannot be isolated from the management arrangements for the school as a whole. As budgets are delegated to schools, systems for managing finance and resources have to be created to complement or replace existing arrangements. The National Curriculum is leading to a new approach to the whole curriculum, to the deployment of teachers and to the organization of teaching, learning and assessment.

Schools that are more successful in coming to terms with change will clearly need more leadership. There will be visions to be identified, agendas to be built, new ways of working to be designed, and climates of problem-solving and learning to be nurtured — among the many other major tasks — but there will be a need for better management as well. The school will inevitably become a more complex organization. More day-to-day interventions will be needed to make sure that the relevant teams have the resources to function effectively. Although the roles of teachers may expand and develop considerably, the head's role will be no less central. It seems, therefore, that all heads need to become better versed in creating climates that support staff in the process of change.

Creating Development Structures

Day-to-day maintenance has to be the priority of any school. Organizing large groups of children and adults requires a set of structures that ensure that order is maintained and tasks completed. In times of massive innovation, however, it is also necessary to build in systems by which the school can allocate resources to support staff in responding to new requirements.

Within the IQEA project we have many excellent examples of schools that have been able to establish successful structures for supporting development activities. These often involve the creation of temporary systems, such as staff task groups to get things done. The success of such groups requires a degree of sophistication and an emphasis on co-ordination and communication. Riverside primary school is a good example of how this can be achieved.

The school has twenty-four teachers. The use of staff groups has developed as an effective way of enabling teachers to focus on planning and be engaged in the development of specific curriculum areas, while, at the same time, maintaining their involvement in the development of the whole curriculum and whole school issues. There are three parallel, mixed-ability classes in each year group. Each year team of teachers is released for one-half day towards the end of the summer term so that they can make an overall plan of work for the coming year. The school has an overall curriculum framework that outlines the content for their plans. The year team decide how to group the subjects effectively, making use of their expertise. They can also ask other subject co-ordinators for advice. At the end of each term they are also released to make detailed plans for the coming term. One hour per week is included in the time budget for Year Team meetings. This enables them to refine and adjust their plans as well as to discuss any problems. The strength of the Year Team is in mutual support and inspiration.

The time spent on planning is valued as enabling the more efficient use of time and resources during the term. It is also seen as helping to raise the standard of work produced in the classroom. Monday is the regular staff meeting time. There is a sequence of staff meetings, middle management meetings (year co-ordinators and senior staff), staff INSET and curriculum groups. All staff are members of curriculum groups. Each year co-ordinator is also a subject co-ordinator. These groups change according to the current priorities for development. The Mathematics, Science and Language co-ordinators continue to develop their subject areas and these curriculum groups are reconvened when necessary.

In the current climate of change, staff are working to implement and monitor National Curriculum requirements. The use of groups means that a few staff can concentrate on developing one subject area and construct policy statements and school guidelines to ensure continuity and progression. All policies and documents produced by any group must be discussed by the whole staff and amended if necessary before being passed to the Governors for approval.

Recently there was concern with the time gap which was occurring between groups producing draft policies or guidelines and staff meeting time for discussion. Also, with a large staff, there was a worry that all staff might not feel able to contribute to the discussion through pressure of time and items on the agenda. It was, therefore, decided to give draft copies of the policies to the year co-ordinator for discussion within their year team. Each team can then scribble their comments on the draft version, either during a team meeting or individually, at a convenient time.

This proved to be an effective way of getting useful responses from all members of staff. The revised draft is again given to year teams for comments. The senior staff approve the final version before submitting it to the governors. This process also emphasizes the management role of year co-ordinators and ensures that all staff are fully involved in the decision making process.

All staff are involved in producing the school development plan. The curriculum groups and subject co-ordinators produce their own plans for the coming year. Whole school issues can be raised by any member of staff. All staff discuss all aspects of the development plan. This is regarded as essential if all staff are going to be committed to implementing the plan. After the whole staff discussion, the plans are discussed by the senior management team and the middle management team so that the advantages and disadvantages of each element can be discussed and prioritized.

The school development plan is organized on a financial year basis as many aspects are dependent on an allocation of money. Each co-ordinator is then allocated a budget to support their subject area. The use of staff groups enables staff to work more efficiently and effectively, to maximize the expertise available within the school and to develop their own professional skills. This format is not static but developing. Each year refinements or changes are made, either in response to staff requests or in anticipation of future needs.

Riverside is an excellent example of a well thought through development structure. Particular features that should be noted are:

- the way in which groups are constructed to ensure that all staff are involved;

- the allocation of time to support staff as they take on additional responsibilities;
- accountability of individuals who are designated to take on co-ordination tasks;
- attention to ensuring good communication between the various groups.

Improving Classroom Practice

Our experience has been that the establishment of a participatory climate and development structures can make a significant impact upon the quality of work going on in a school. However, this is only part of the story. A much greater impact can be achieved if these overall improvements can be made to influence what happens in the classrooms. Ultimately it is the interactions between pupils and teachers that have the greatest effect upon learning outcomes. Consequently real movement towards quality will only be achieved where there is attention to the improvement of classroom practice.

We could quote many examples of schools that have used staff development as a central strategy for supporting teachers as they have attempted to engage in improvement activities. All of them work from an assumption that attention to teacher learning is likely to have direct spin-offs in terms of pupil learning. All of them demonstrate the pay-off of investment of time and resources in teacher development.

An excellent example is that of Sunnyside Infants School. There, over the last few years, a sophisticated strategy has been adopted to create conditions in the school that support the development of the staff. At the outset was a concern with how to find time to observe children in the classroom for the purposes of new assessment requirements. With this in mind a staff development day was led by an external consultant. This event had an enormous impact on staff thinking. Specifically, the consultant led the staff through a series of problem-solving processes focusing on the arrangement of one classroom. Gradually the teachers rearranged furniture and resources in order to make the classroom more autonomous. Subsequently similar activities have been carried out in other rooms. It does seem that the impact of this approach had to do with the tangible nature of the task (i.e. rearranging equipment, etc.) and the context (i.e. the classroom).

Following on from this day the staff explored classroom management issues. This led to the formulation of a house style involving the use of learning centres in which pupils carry out assignments. By the end of the first year there was clear evidence of increased pupil autonomy in the classroom.

During the second year staff began to question the quality of learning going on in the learning centres. Their concern was that pupils might simply be completing tasks without any significant learning taking place. With this in mind they decided to work in small teams to observe in one another's classrooms. Observation focused on the quality of engagement in the learning centres. To facilitate these observations the Headteacher covered classes to free teachers. She asked them to plan the observations and also allocated time to debrief what had occurred.

The evidence suggests that the strategy has had a significant impact. Specific changes in teaching style are evident in all classrooms; there is clear evidence of increased pupil autonomy in learning, even with very young pupils; and the quality of dialogue about teaching and learning amongst staff is very striking to the outsider. Indeed it does seem that the adopted strategy has brought about a significant change in the culture of the school.

A crucial element of the Sunnyside strategy is the importance placed on locating staff development in classrooms. This seems an obvious point and yet it is one that is usually overlooked. So much of in-service education occurs away from the usual context in which teaching takes place and, indeed, is led by people who have not visited the specific contexts in which their participants have to operate. Eisner suggests that this is 'akin to a basketball coach providing advice to a team he has never seen play' (1990: 102).

In recent years the work of Bruce Joyce and Beverley Showers (1988) on staff development, in particular their peer coaching strategy, has transformed thinking on staff development. Joyce and Showers identified a number of key components which when used in combination have much greater power than when they are used alone.

These major components are:

- presentation of theory or description of skill or strategy;
- modelling or demonstration of skill or models of teaching;
- practice in simulated and classroom settings;
- structured and open-ended feedback (provision of information about performance);
- coaching for application (hands-on, in-classroom assistance with the transfer of skills and strategies to the classroom).

Based on this analysis, Joyce and Showers (1988: 85) summarized their 'best knowledge' on staff development like this:

- the use of the integrated theory-demonstration-practice-feedback training programme to ensure skill development;
- the use of considerable amounts of practice in simulated conditions to ensure fluid control of new skills;
- the employment of regular on-site coaching to facilitate vertical transfer — the development of new learning in the process of transfer;
- the preparation of teachers who can provide one another with the needed coaching.

More recently Joyce (1991) has distinguished, helpfully in our opinion, between the two key elements of staff development: the workshop and the workplace.

The *workshop*, which is equivalent to the best practice on the traditional INSET course, is where we gain understanding, see demonstrations of the teaching strategy we may wish to acquire, and have the opportunity to practice them in a non-threatening environment.

If however we wish to transfer these skills that the workshop has introduced to us back into the *workplace* (i.e. the classroom and school) then merely attending the workshop is insufficient. The research evidence is very clear that skill acquisition and the ability to transfer vertically to a range of situations requires on-the-job support. This implies changes to the workplace and the way in which we organize staff development in our schools. In particular this means the opportunity for immediate and sustained practice, collaboration and peer coaching, and studying development and implementation. We cannot achieve these changes in the workplace without, in most cases, drastic alterations in the ways in which we organize our schools.

Patterns of Development

From our work with schools such as the three we have described in the IQEA project, we can begin to put together a picture of what happens in moving schools and, in so doing, point to certain patterns that seem to be connected to their success. IQEA schools are encouraged to use the school development planning process to express their developmental aspirations in the form of *priorities*. The school's development plan contains a series of priorities which are ideally supported by action plans. These are the working documents for teachers. In them the priority is subdivided into targets and tasks, responsibilities are allocated, a time frame established, and evaluation or progress checks identified (Hargreaves and Hopkins, 1991).

Through this approach to planning, priorities are then reformulated within a *strategy*. A strategy typically involves teachers in some form of collaborative classroom based action. The exact nature of the strategy, or combination of strategies, is peculiar to each school. Strategies need to take account of the priorities that have been agreed, existing conditions and the resources that are available.

Most primary schools are, of course, used to planning in this way and to establishing working groups for developmental tasks. But, as we saw in the account of Eastside School, it is as they move into action that problems tend to arise. Beginning to work on something new, to change, inevitably creates some difficulties, both for individuals and the institution. Teachers are faced with acquiring new teaching skills or mastering new curriculum material; the school is often faced with new ways of working that are incompatible with existing organizational structures.

This phase of destabilization or *internal turbulence*, as Michael Huberman (1992) calls it, is as predictable as it is uncomfortable. Many research studies have found that, without a period of destabilization, successful, long lasting change is unlikely to occur (see Louis and Miles, 1990). Yet it is at this point that most change fails to progress beyond early implementation. In these cases, when the change hits the wall of individual learning or institutional resistance, internal turbulence begins to occur and developmental work begins to impact on all staff. Often the working group continues for a while, but eventually it fragments, or another priority is found on which they can focus. The change circles back on itself and nothing much is achieved — so we start something new. This is the cycle of educational failure so well documented by Slavin (1989) in his article on faddism in education. This, we find, is the predictable pathology of educational change.

Many of the schools that we have been working with seem to survive this period of destabilization by either consciously or intuitively adapting or accommodating the *internal conditions* in the school to meet the demands of the agreed on change or priority. In order to overcome the wall, we encourage schools to diagnose their internal conditions in relation to their chosen change *before* they begin developmental work. They can then begin to build these modifications to the school's internal conditions into the strategies they are going to adopt (Hopkins *et al.*, 1994; Ainscow *et al.*, 1994).

When this happens we begin to detect changes in the culture of the school of the sort described in the story of Eastside. In this way a school's change capacity increases and the ground-work is laid for future change efforts. Instead of rebounding against the wall, a virtuous circle of change began to be established. Our experience is that schools like Riverside that have been through similar change cycles experience less internal turbulence because they have progressively enhanced their capacity to change as a result of this developmental process.

Headteachers who adopt this type of approach to the management of change seem to agree with Schein when he wrote, 'that the only thing of real importance that leaders do is to create and manage culture' (1985: 2). They realize that the impact of successful change needs to be on the culture of the school, for it is culture that sustains change and consequently enhances the achievement of students. They therefore focus on culture first. It is almost as if they begin by asking 'What cultural changes are required?' and then, 'What priorities, strategies, and changes in conditions can bring this about?' The link between setting priorities and the culture of the school is therefore of some importance. Sequencing priorities over time can help the successive shaping of school culture. In recognition of this many school leaders 'start small and think big' in their planning for development, they also sequence priorities in such a way that they build on initial good practice and then on subsequent success (see Fullan, 1991). They manipulate strategy and conditions in order to affect culture, in the pursuit of enhancing the quality of educational outcomes and experience for all pupils.

Although the conditions may be eased and the internal turbulence reduced at the school level, the pressure of individual learning on the part of teachers remain the same. The conditions in and the culture of the school are increasingly supportive of their developmental efforts. As was noted at Sunnyside School, teachers who experience a more supportive environment within the school feel more able to endure the threat of new learning. As they adapt the teaching and learning practices in their classrooms, they begin to see that the learning of their pupils is enhanced and this evidence gives them confidence in the change and increases their commitment to the new approach.

In this discussion it is the strategy chosen by the school that not only links the priority to the conditions, but also has the impact on culture and student outcomes. In the schools we are working with we have seen many strategies and combinations of strategies. The following list is not exhaustive. It is simply a composite of those strategies used by schools in the early phases of the project. Obviously no school used them all, but also no school relied on just one:

Staff Development

- staff development processes are used to support individual teacher and school development;
- teachers are involved in each other's teaching;
- where appropriate, external consultants are used to support teacher development.

Inquiry and Reflection

- there is a search for increased clarity and shared meanings;
- reflection and review activities are used to monitor progress and enhance the professional judgment of teachers.

Leadership

- staff throughout the school are encouraged to adopt leadership roles;
- temporary systems or working groups are created;
- individuals take on key roles in initiating change and supporting development work.

Involvement

- pupils, staff and parents are encouraged to be involved in school development;
- a climate that encourages access is created;
- effective use is made of external consultants.

Coordination

- efforts are made to maintain momentum;
- links are made between formal and informal structures;
- images of success are created.

Planning

- planning processes are used to legitimize and coordinate action;
- resources for school improvement are specifically allocated.

Although it may be helpful conceptually and strategically to think of these aspects of school improvement as distinct, in reality they coalesce. In practice, the priority or curriculum focus and the strategy combine in the minds of teachers to present a uniform reality. On a day-to-day basis school improvement is an amalgam of broad strategies such as self-review, action planning, staff development which link together the classroom and the school, as well as the more dynamic aspects of the change process.

In this section of the chapter we have tried to tease out the process of development as we have seen it in the schools in which we have been working. The analytical and conceptual distinctions we have made may be a necessary element in setting out the territory of school development, but they are insufficient to tell us why the process works in the way it does. In order to get a better understanding of movement in schools, therefore, we have to examine how one development cycle leads on to another.

Moving on

Schools that are successful in their improvement initiatives seem to move from one cycle of development to another through the creation of what we have called earlier *a development structure*. However, this is easier said than done. Schools often seem to find it difficult to draw a line under certain developments and to move on to something new. It certainly helps to have a clear idea of what the school wants to achieve by when and to build evaluation into the end of the work on a particular priority. What must be avoided is development work on a priority just 'fizzling out', and then the school searching around for something else to work on.

The transition from one cycle to another is greatly assisted by the creation of a development structure. Perhaps the most crucial challenge facing schools today is how to balance change and stability effectively; how on the one hand to preserve what is already successful in a school, and how on the other, to respond positively to innovation and the challenge of change. We believe that the school's internal conditions are crucial in achieving the correct balance. We are also realizing from our current work that by adapting their structural arrangements, many successful schools, such as Riverside, are finding it easier to move from one developmental sequence to another.

Schools are finding out quite rapidly, or eventually more painfully, that procedures established to organize teaching, learning and assessment cannot also cope with developmental activities which inevitably cut across established hierarchies, curriculum areas, meeting patterns, and timetables. What is required are complementary structures each with their own purpose, budget and ways of working. Our experience is that the innovative responses required for sustained development are likely to involve:

- delegation;
- task groups;
- high levels of specific staff development;
- quality time for planning;
- collaborative classroom activity.

Obviously the majority of a school's time and resources will go on its day-to-day activities, but unless there is also an element dedicated to development, the school is unlikely to progress in times of change. Decisions can then be made as to what aspect of the school requires development, and it is that priority which gets the treatment for a specified period of time. In practice, therefore, the development structure acts as a support system for the rest of the school's activities. A priority on teaching and learning, for example, will inevitably spread itself across a school's curriculum if carefully managed. After work on a particular development is completed, another aspect of the school's operation is selected, and so on. In this way, over time, most aspects of the school will have been subject to some form of development activity.

Concluding remarks

In our experience it is in these ways that successful schools respond to the challenge of imposed reform within a decentralized system. Schools will embrace some changes immediately. This will be because the school either has no other legal option, or because it has a particular expertise or penchant for that change. Other changes, where experience is perhaps lacking, are selected as development priorities and sequenced over time. Some centralized initiatives, however, are resisted, either because they are incompatible with the school's central purpose, or because they may be regarded as being wrong.

This discussion and the various examples given in this chapter go some way to explain what happens in moving schools. This analysis suggests that unless schools are able to take a more assertive approach towards external policy initiatives they will continue to suffer from 'innovation overload' and gradually lose control of their own educational agenda. It is the integration of phases of action such as those described in this chapter into the daily life of the school that keeps the process of development going.

Acknowledgments

We would like to acknowledge the contributions of our many colleagues in the IQEA project, particularly Geoff Southworth and Mel West, to the ideas presented in this chapter.

References

AINSCOW, M., HOPKINS, D., SOUTHWORTH, G. and WEST, M. (1994) *Creating the Conditions for School Improvement*, London, Fulton.

EISNER, E.W. (1990) 'The meaning of alternative paradigms for practice', in GUBA, E.G. (Ed) *The Paradigm Dialog*, London, Sage.

FULLAN, M.G. (1991) *The New Meaning of Educational Change*, London, Cassell.

HARGREAVES, D.H. and HOPKINS, D. (1991) *The Empowered School*, London, Cassell.

HOPKINS, D., AINSCOW, M. and WEST, M. (1994) *School Improvement in an Era of Change*, London, Cassell.

HUBERMAN, M. (1992) 'Critical introduction', in FULLAN, M.G. *Successful School Improvement*, Milton Keynes, Open University Press.

JOYCE, B. (1991) 'Cooperative learning and staff development; teaching the method with the method', *Cooperative Learning*, **12**, 2, pp. 10–13.

JOYCE, B. and SHOWERS, B. (1988) *Student Achievement Through Staff Development*, London, Longman.

LOUIS, K.S. and MILES, M. (1992) *Improving the Urban High School*, London, Cassell.

ROSENHOLTZ, S. (1989) *Teachers' Workplace: The Social Organization of Schools*, New York, Longman.

SCHEIN, E. (1985) *Organizational Cultures and Leadership: A Dynamic View*, San Francisco, Jossey-Bass.

SLAVIN, R. (1989) 'PET and the pendulum: Faddism in education and how to stop it', *Phi Delta Kappan*, June, 752–8.

Chapter 10

School Inspection for School Development?

Geoff Southworth and Michael Fielding

School effectiveness studies show that a broadly common set of characteristics is associated with successful schools. Although there are a number of riders to add to this statement, we now know more about the character of effective schools than we did twenty years ago. However, while we are now a little clearer about what effective schools look like, we do not know enough, as yet, as to how effective schools got to be like that. Not surprisingly school improvement has increasingly become a major area of study. We urgently need to understand more clearly and richly how schools develop and grow. In part, this explains why in this volume we have the contributions of Weindling and Ainscow. Ainscow's account of the Improving the Quality of Education for All (IQEA) project at the University of Cambridge Institute of Education, a venture we are also involved with, is just one example of the efforts now underway to simultaneously support the improvement of schools and to understand more perspicaciously the processes by which schools as organizations develop.

Interest in school improvement is not, of course, just confined to teachers, headteachers and researchers. Central government is also concerned with making schools better. Central government during the 1980s and early 1990s has sought to improve the quality of schools through increased competition for pupils and consumer choice. The Thatcher Government's macro-philosophy was based upon the belief that 'efficiency and quality are best sustained and enhanced in situations where users and consumers have choice' and information to make those choices and exercise them; in short, 'where there is a market' (Bolton, 1993: 6). If market forces is the macro-philosophy of central government, school inspections are one of the mechanisms for implementing it.

Central government, through the 1992 Education (Schools) Act, has established the Office for Standards in Education (OFSTED) to 'improve standards of achievement and quality of education through regular independent inspection, public reporting and informed advice' according to OFSTED's mission statement. These intentions are to be realized by three strategies. First, by regular independent inspections of all schools in England and Wales.

Second, by publicly reporting on each and every school's inspection, as well as by HMI providing other information about the education service by conducting surveys and noting trends. Third, by OFSTED offering advice to the DfE, SCAA, schools funding agency and other interested agencies. In one sense then, OFSTED has been established to provide publicly available information for the consumers of education, principally parents, to make informed choices about the schools to which they wish to send their children, or to alert them (and the school's governors) to the prevailing standards in the schools where their children are being taught. For the purposes of this chapter we are concerned with the first of these three strategies and to a limited extent with the second.

We have many concerns about inspection as a strategy for improving schools, but we will restrict ourselves to just four at this point. First, it remains an open question whether inspection does lead to improvement. Little or no research has been undertaken to test the hypothesis that inspections lead to improvement (Gray and Wilcox, 1993: 4). Inspection is largely a process of measuring, and measuring something does not usually affect growth or development without other actions also taking place. The inspection process includes the identification of action points in the published inspectors' report on the school and a requirement for governors to produce an action plan in the light of the report. Yet these tactics lean in favour of describing *what* is to be done rather than *how*. The emphasis is on ends rather than means.

Second, inspections are at best a portrait of a school for one week of its life. The inspection offers a snapshot view of the school at a particular point. Inspections do not show whether the school is in decline or growing. Nor do they suggest rates of progress in either direction or whether the school has become inert. Inspections cannot tell outsiders where the school is coming from or likely to be going to, only where the school is. An inspection is a snapshot not a moving picture of the recent past, present and future.

Third, the process of inspection does not encourage professional dialogue. Inspectors are required to make judgments but not to discuss these with those they observe. Judgments are to be received by the staff in the school not debated with the inspectors. The process puts teachers and other staff in a relatively passive role, presents inspectors as the powerful and makes teachers by comparison, powerless. This strikes us as too strongly weighted in the favour of inspectors. It diminishes, if not denies, the professionalism of teachers. It also impedes any critical analysis of the inspectors' views with the inspectors. Opportunities to learn with and from one another are denied. Inspectors judge and tell, teachers receive and react.

Fourth, much hinges on the capacity of OFSTED to have produced a workable, reliable and valid scheme for school inspection. It has been the task of OFSTED and HMI to characterize the quality of education and standards of achievement in schools. *The Handbook for the Inspection of Schools* (OFSTED, 1993) marks the publication of these characteristics. It is an important step that these are now made public, but there has been little discussion of their appropriateness or validity. A major concern of ours is that the handbook adopts an overly simple and tidy view of teaching and learning. Yet at no point is it suggested that learning might be conceived and viewed in other ways. Learning is taken to be unproblematical, an assumption which we do not share.

Although it is not difficult to rehearse concerns about the philosophy and practice of school inspection, we must also acknowledge that inspections are now taking place. We might wish things to be otherwise but we must also try to deal with things as they are. This outlook is not a wholly pragmatic one, as we hope some of our later points will demonstrate, nor do we wish to inhibit critique. We strongly believe that the profession should be critical of inspection every bit as much as it should be critical of all other professional practices. Critical awareness and enquiry are at the heart of learning. However, our intention in this chapter is less to do with providing an all out assault on inspection than with trying to see if the process of inspection can be harnessed with the efforts of teachers and governors to improve schools.

School development seems to us to be inherently necessary because there are never any terminal points in education. As Richmond (1971: 174) said, 'death is the only terminal behaviour'. In other words, there is always some scope for growth and development. To argue otherwise seems to us to deny the opportunity to learn and to claim to be an educator. Education is to do with journeys not colonization. In this sense then, growth is healthy and natural. Importantly, development occurs not because one is weak or poor or deficient but because learning is normal.

So saying, it is important to add that in acknowledging that learning is ever-present, this is not to confuse growth with some quest for perfection. Effective schools are not perfect schools. We make this claim because schooling is far too open-ended and uncertain to ever make perfection a desirable, let alone, realistic achievement. Teaching and learning are often uncertain and ambiguous tasks where the outcomes are provisional and unclear. Moreover, education is a value laden activity and notions of perfection in education, like effectiveness and improvement, involve beliefs about the purposes and goals of education which are not necessarily shared by others and on which there appears to be no consensus. School development is therefore a process of professional and organizational growth which involves technical improvement — in performance and attainments — and the on-going examination of professional beliefs and values (see Holly and Southworth, 1989). School development is both intensely practical and deeply philosophical.

School devlopment is fundamentally concerned with moving the school forward. Developing schools are *moving schools* (Ainscow, 1994, Chapter 9 in this volume), that is, schools which are working towards improving their practice and becoming steadily more effective. Inspection has a part to play in this process, but only a part. School development rests on much more than inspection.

Our position on school inspection and school development matches that expressed in the National Commission on Education (NCE) Report:

> Public accountability is important. Regulation and inspection have a key part to play in encouraging and maintaining high standards in schools. However, we would wish to see this balanced by a recognition that sustained commitment to raising achievement must come from within schools and that headteachers, working together with their staff, bear the major responsibility for school effectiveness. Successful schools are those which reflect on their own practice and devise and implement changes in response to the needs of their pupils. Some of the most valuable strategies for improvement are those initiated by the school community itself: by the head and teaching staff supported by the governing body and the wider community of parents.
>
> (NCE, 1993: 170)

While this statement helps to provide a sense of perspective about inspection and school improvement, it also raises the question of how might inspections play a part in developing the school? There are no easy answers to this question, but by drawing upon the experience of staff in schools which have been inspected by OFSTED teams, there are three sets of insights which we believe are significant in making the inspection a constructive exercise.

First, there is no doubt that when a school is inspected the event is a major one in the professional lives of the teachers and the heads. In our work at the University of Cambridge Institute of Education we encounter many teachers and heads whose schools have been or are about to be inspected. Almost without fail they are keen to tell us about the experience; what it was like, what was said and how they were judged. Many of these colleagues have a strong need to talk about the experience. It is as if they must tell anyone who appears interested what it was like for them. This suggests that inspections are a deeply felt experience. Inspections have an emotional dimension as well as a professional one. Teachers with whom we have worked talk about 'dreading' inspections and of being fearful of them. Others confess to being in a state of panic at the prospect of the inspectors arriving. Inspections are in every sense a critical incident for the staff of the school.

If the critical quality of inspections is to be productive, as against corrosive, to the spirit of the staff then staff in schools must try to help one another deal with the tension and anxiety that inspections create. Senior staff must offer encouragement and support to colleagues who feel under tremendous pressure. And senior staff must be helped by their staffs. Headteachers can feel under the greatest pressure of all, usually because they personally identify with the school and see its success and failure as their own. Teachers must try to recognize that their heads need to be helped every bit as much as they do. School governors have a part to play here. We have been encouraged by the way several chairs of governors and other governors have been aware of the strain inspection places upon the staff and head and have attempted to support them in the run up to inspection and during the week of the visit. We believe all governors should do likewise.

The second point follows from the first. What is being inspected is the school. The inspection report comments on the standards of achievement and quality of teaching in the school. Individual teachers are not named, although in smaller primary schools it is not difficult to attribute certain comments in the report to individual teachers. Nevertheless, since it is the school as a whole which is under scrutiny, staff in the school must try, in addition to preparing their own classrooms and teaching for inspection, to attend to the policies, schemes and procedures which make the school a cohesive organization. Staff must recognize that they are being collectively inspected and must work hard to sustain or increase professional collaboration. If inspection drives every teacher into his/her classroom in order to look after themselves, they may simultaneously harm the school because what the inspectors may see is a loosely connected group of individuals and not a team of teachers. We know from a great number of studies (Mortimore *et al.*, 1988; Nias *et al.*, 1989; 1992; Fullan and Hargreaves, 1992) that teamwork and collaboration are crucial to making the school effective for the children.

Third, the major focus of inspections is the teaching and learning in the school, as the OFSTED handbook makes plain. Although the inspectors are interested in many aspects of school organization and curriculum management, the greatest area of concern is what the children do. Inspectors will read and take account of school policies, but they will also watch and comment upon classroom practices in terms of the quality of teaching and the quality of the children's learning. Given this strong focus upon teaching and learning there are three points we wish to draw attention to.

First, what the inspectors offer is an independent view of the school's main work; teaching and learning. The inspectors should help all staff and governors to see more clearly those areas of teaching where the school is strong and those areas which might need further development. Second, the process of inspection should generally act as a stimulus to staff to keep attending to teaching and learning issues and avoid becoming side-tracked on other seemingly important matters. This point is especially pertinent to headteachers. In recent years many heads have been somewhat distracted from teaching and learning by a host of other issues, as Hayes' chapter in this volume suggests. They have been pulled away from the curriculum and teaching and required to attend to financial and administrative concerns. The process of inspection however, and the weight OFSTED attaches to teaching and learning, suggests that heads and colleagues should now reconsider the emphasis they place upon the range of tasks they perform and ensure that they devote some time to looking at the quality of learning in the school.

Third, although the inspectors are right to take a strong interest in learning, we must be cautious in accepting too readily their assumptions about teaching and learning. For example, the OFSTED handbook apparently offers a rather straightforward and unproblematic view of teaching and learning. Yet, others who have studied children's learning are less certain of encapsulating the nature of children's learning in such a way. Desforge argues that learning is complex, can be understood in a number of ways and should not be constrained within a single model (1993: 3–4). To opt for a single model of learning is too dogmatic. Yet, OFSTED and the business of inspection may exercise an irresistible influence upon heads and teachers and lead them to adopt a narrow and unproblematic view of learning.

Desforge also argues that there is a distinction between learning and work. He acknowledges that children work hard in classrooms, but is also aware that 'hard work is not necessarily associated with the mindful learning' he describes in the article (p. 6). Indeed, he suggests that mindful learning is sometimes passed by as teachers manage classroom work. Consequently, Desforge offers an important warning:

> Teachers and children alike adopt the language of production line work to characterise classroom life. Work that is intended to foster learning becomes an end in itself. Pupils when asked to describe what they are doing respond in terms of 'geting my work done' or 'it's my work' or 'the teacher gave us this work'. Teachers also frequently assume that if children are working then they are learning. Marshall has exposed the poverty of the 'work metaphor' in respect of learning. At root, the production line work metaphor distracts attention from the *intention* to learn. In seeking evidence of learning we must not be fooled by evidence of mere work.
>
> (Desforge, 1993: 6)

What Desforge brings to mind is the danger that the inspectors may conflate learning with work. In watching how the children are working the inspectors may believe they are judging how the children are learning, not least because the inspectors might tacitly accept the production line metaphor since such terms as objectives, outcomes, targets and delivery have such currency in education today. In other words, Desforge warns us not to try to simplify teaching, nor to adhere to a monocular view of children's learning. The inspectors offer us a view of learning, yet it is only their view, it is not *the* view. Inspectors' perspectives should be challenged and questioned.

These early insights into the process of inspection also suggest to us that staff in school need to think about four sets of issues. These four are: preparation, managing inspection, following-up the inspection and developing a critical culture. We will now expand on each of these in turn.

Many schools are already preparing for inspection. Heads are ensuring that the paperwork is organized and policies are written. Some schools have undoubtedly gone into policy overdrive and are trying to erect a paper wall which they hope will provide a defence against potentially hostile inspectors! For sure, check the paperwork and continue to develop policies in line with the school's development plan and priorities. However, there are many other practical things to be done. For example, use the OFSTED handbook as a source of discussion material for staff meetings and school-based INSET activities. Raise colleagues' awareness of the framework for inspection and the criteria for observing and judging lessons. As a staff try to gauge your own strengths and weaknesses so that the observations of the inspectors are less of a surprise.

Second, the week of the inspection needs to be carefully managed. Parents will be notified and the children will need to know who the visitors are. Governors also will need to be involved and kept aware of the process. However, our evidence suggests that it is the staff in the school who are under the greatest strain. They feel they are being watched and placed under intense scrutiny. The week is a time of considerable pressure. As one head told us, there was an absence of humour and the school became a more solemn, serious place. It is important that heads and deputies try to note whether the atmosphere in the school markedly alters and whether this is stifling some of the strengths of the school. If it is, it should be brought to the attention of the staff (and perhaps the inspectors who may be overly inquisitorial) with the hope that they may relax a little more. It is not unusual for individuals to try to tighten things up when they are under pressure; it is also the case that sometimes such a response can be counter-productive.

Third, in the light of the inspection feedback and report there is a clear requirement for the school's governors and headteacher to draw up an action plan for the coming year and beyond. We welcome the idea of an action plan but hope that the plan is not devised as a knee-jerk reaction to the points raised by the inspectors but is done in a more thorough and evaluatory way. Schools should have several months notice of the inspection which, in turn, means that heads and INSET co-ordinators could adjust their timetables and ensure that in the period following receipt of the report, the staff could hold an in-service day, half-day or series of after school meetings. These sessions would allow the staff the opportunity to reflect together on the report.

Reflection on the report seems to be a vital activity because we have already noted how heads and teachers tend to focus on the negative elements in a report and overlook the positive aspects. A time for staff to reflect should begin by noting the strengths in the school which the inspectors have identified. Next, staff might analyse the report as a whole and see how balanced it is and whether it matches their own self-evaluations of the school. Both these activities are likely to be necessary to overcome the defensive tendencies of the inspected. If inspections are to be used constructively then the understandably defensive instincts of staff need to be assuaged in order to create a more open discussion. Once the initial reactions have been attended to then staff might begin to analyse the implications of the report for the school's development. For example, curriculum co-ordinators and year team leaders could consider what the report means for their respective responsibilities. The head and INSET co-ordinator might focus on the staff development needs of individuals, key stage teams and the whole staff. Priorities might be established from all this analysis and discussion and these ideas might then be shared with the governors. Some schools might, of course, involve the governors in this post-inspection review. Whatever form this activity takes, we believe that it is important that time is set aside to follow-up the inspectors' report. While it is understandable that there will be a feeling of relief following the departure of the inspectors, there is nevertheless a responsibility on the staff and the governors to respond to the report in a considered and strategic way.

Fourth, all that we have said is based upon a belief that effective schools are ones where, in addition to the staff working hard, being committed and caring teachers, the staff are self-evaluatory and concerned to develop themselves as individuals and contribute to the growth of the school as an educational organization. This belief is an extension of contemporary ideas about a culture of collaboration (Nias *et al.*, 1989; see also chapters by Southworth in this volume) because while we accept that collaboration is a condition of school development, such working together needs to incorporate a capacity for critical appraisal of self and others. If school improvement is to be internally driven by teachers they need to be self-evaluatory about their work, their customs and their habits. Moreover, such evaluation needs to be conducted in groups as well as by individuals and should encompass the whole school. Collaborative, critical enquiry creates groups whose members are:

- mutually supportive;
- evaluative of self and others;
- questioning and challenging;
- reflective;
- strongly focused on their teaching and the pupils learning;
- aware of the school as a whole as well as of their own classroom;
- willing to share ideas and practices;
- concerned to develop themselves and to contribute to the development of colleagues.

In a sense this list stems from our experience with school self-evalution (see Holly and Southworth, 1989) as well as our work on school improvement projects. School self-evaluation is every bit as important in the 1990s as it was in the 1980s. Inspection does not make self-evaluation redundant, it makes it even more important.

In our terms self-evaluation involves staff in a school developing a set of policies, or their own framework if you prefer, which articulates their values, commitments and approaches to teaching and learning. Such a framework will be unique to each school in taking account of the school's locality and phase of development. The advantage of this approach is that it goes beyond the OFSTED framework which is primarily an instrument for judging professional competence according to a standardized set of criteria. There is a need for teachers and governors to transcend the OFSTED criteria and examine the educational beliefs which underpin the school's practice. This has the further advantage of enabling the school as a learning community to critique the OFSTED report as well as assimilate it.

Staff in school should be wary of merely accepting the judgments of inspectors because such behaviour will only lead to passivity and dependency. Rather, staff should be forever curious about their own development and strengths and those of the school as a whole. Then, whenever the inspectors call, their visit and their judgments can be contrasted against their own assessment of the school's work. This contrast may even reveal that the inspectors' views are rather thin and pale compared with one's own rich and detailed portraits.

Moreover, our belief is shared by the National Commission on Education who say:

> We . . . place considerable weight on self-evaluation by schools, linked to planning for future development and the effective use of the school budget to fund recognised priorities.
>
> (NCE, 1993: 170)

Inspections should add impetus and, perhaps, relevance to school self-evaluation but they should not supplant it. Indeed, we would argue that school inspections should be seen as only another component in the improvement of schools. Inspections have a part to play in helping us to develop our schools, but this part should not be over-emphasized nor allowed to dominate the other elements which are necessary for school development:

> Although inspection is a regulatory and quality assurance function, it can be seen as part of a partnership with schools aimed at continuing improvement . . . a national inspection framework, though necessary, is not enough on its own to promote continuing improvement. A range of partnerships is needed . . . there is no single recipe for improvement . . .
>
> (NCE, 1993: 172, 174)

The idea of partnership for improvement seems to us to put the inspection enterprise into perspective. Inspections should help us see ourselves a little bit better and a little bit differently. But the school will not improve unless the staff have a capacity to act upon the inspectors' report in a critical way. If inspection can be used to help staff in school create teams whose members are collaborative and critical then inspection will have a positive role to play in school development.

References

BOLTON, E. (1993) 'Imaginary gardens with real toads', CHITTY, C. and SIMON, B. (Eds) *Education Answers Back: Critical Responses to Government Policy*, London, Lawrence and Wishart, pp. 3–16.

DESFORGE, C. (1993) 'Children's learning has it improved?', *Education 3–13*, **21**, 3, pp. 3–10.

FULLAN, M. and HARGREAVES, A. (1992) *What's Worth Fighting For In Your School? Working Together for Improvement*, Milton Keynes, Open University Press.

GRAY, J. and WILCOX, B. (1993) 'Inspection and school improvement: Rhetoric and experience from the bridge', paper presented to the ESRC seminar on School Effectiveness and School Improvement, Sheffield.

HOLLY, P. and SOUTHWORTH, G.W. (1989) *The Developing School*, London, Falmer Press.

MORTIMORE, P., SAMMONS, P., STOLL, L., LEWIS, D. and ECOB, R. (1988) *School Matters: The Junior Years*, Wells, Open Books.

NATIONAL COMMISSION ON EDUCATION (NCE) (1993) *Learning To Succeed: A Radical Look at Education Today and a Strategy for the Future*, London, Paul Hamlyn.

NIAS, J., SOUTHWORTH, G.W. and YEOMANS, R. (1989) *Staff Relationships in the Primary School: A Study of School Cultures*, London, Cassell.

NIAS, J., SOUTHWORTH, G.W. and CAMPBELL, P. (1992) *Whole School Curriculum Development in the Primary School*, London, Falmer Press.

OFSTED (1993) *The Handbook for the Inspection of Schools*, London, Office for Standards In Education, 2nd ed.

RICHMOND, W.K. (1971) *The School Curriculum*, London, Methuen.

Notes on Contributors

Mel Ainscow has been a tutor at the University of Cambridge Institute of Education since 1986. Previously he was a headteacher and local authority adviser. His work bridges the fields of school improvement, teacher development and special educational needs. His recent publications include *Effective Schools for All* and *Managing School Development* (both published by Fulton). He directs the UNESCO project Special Needs in the Classroom and acts as a consultant to initiatives in a variety of countries.

Jim Campbell is Professor of Education at Warwick University and Director of Graduate Studies in Education. He is the author of *Developing the Primary School Curriculum* (Cassell, 1985); *Breadth and Balance in the Primary Curriculum* (Falmer, 1993); *Primary Teacher at Work* (with S. Neill, Routledge, 1994); and *Curriculum Reform at Key Stage 1* (with S. Neill, Longman, 1994). He is Chair of the Association for the Study of Primary Education, and editor of the journal *Education 3–13*.

Colin Conner is a tutor at the University of Cambridge Institute of Education. His particular interests are concerned with assessment, evaluation and children's learning. Over the last four years he has been engaged in researching the implementation of national curriculum assessment and has written a number of articles based on the developments observed. He is the author of *Assessment and Testing in the Primary School* (Falmer Press, 1991).

Marion Dadds started her career in primary education in Nottinghamshire and taught children from three to eleven years old. She then worked as Advisory Teacher for Language and Reading Development in Essex before moving to the University of Cambridge Institute of Education where she is now Tutor in Education 3 to 13. For several years she has been conducting research into the impact of action-research based INSET on teachers' classroom practices and the life of their schools. From this work, she believes and knows that practitioners can develop their work by studying it carefully and working together with school colleagues.

Michael Fielding with twenty years in some of the UK's pioneer comprehensive schools and wide-ranging experience through in-service work, research projects and his previous post as a senior adviser; he enjoys working with colleagues across and from all phases of education. His interests include effective INSET, staff development, teaching and learning styles, various aspects of management and the development of learning organizations. Particular interests are in the development of democratic/emancipatory practices and perspectives in education.

Denis Hayes has taught in a variety of primary schools over the past twenty years as class teacher, deputy head and headteacher. He is currently working in the Faculty of Arts and Education (School of Education) at the University of Plymouth involved in Initial Teacher Education and teaching on Masters Degree programmes. His research interests include *Decision-making in Primary Schools* and the *Role of the Primary Headteacher* (1993).

David Hopkins is a lecturer at the University of Cambridge Institute of Education where his work is mainly concerned with teacher and school development. David has previously worked as an Outward Bound instructor, school teacher and university and college lecturer. He is a consultant to the OECD on School Improvement and Teaching Quality. He was recently co-director of the DES School Development Plans Project and is currently co-director of the Improving the Quality of Education for All project, which is a network of some forty schools in England committed to school improvement. His recent books include: *A Teacher's Guide to Classroom Research* (second edition), 1994, *Evaluation for School Development*, Open University Press, 1989; *The Empowered School*, Cassell, 1991; *Personal Growth Through Adventure*, 1993 and *School Improvement in an ERA of Change*, 1993. He is also a Mountain Guide and has climbed in many of the world's great mountain ranges.

Geoff Southworth is a tutor in primary education and management at the University of Cambridge Institute of Education. Prior to joining UCIE he was a primary teacher, deputy and headteacher in Lancashire. At UCIE he has conducted research into staff relationships, whole school curriculum development, primary school leadership and mentoring. He has written numerous articles and books including *Whole School Curriculum Development in Primary Schools*, with Jennifer Nias and Penny Campbell Falmer Press 1992. He has contributed to many conferences and been a consultant to schools in England and overseas.

Dick Weindling spent ten years working in industry before entering education as a mature student. After teaching in London he joined the NFER and became Head of the Educational Management department. More recently he has been an independent consultant with CREATE for the last six years. He has conducted research at both national and local levels. With colleagues he has recently completed two projects for the DFE: *Effective Management in*

Schools (HMSO, April 1993), and *The National Evaluation of the DFE Headteacher Mentor Scheme* (DfE, December 1993). With his partner in CREATE, Keith Pocklington, he is currently involved with two major School Improvement projects, designed to change the culture of the school and to improve teaching and learning.

Index

achievement portfolios *see* portfolios
agreement trials 111, 114, 115, 117,
    118, 119
Ainscow, M. (1991) 29
Ainscow, M. (1994) 177
Ainscow, M. *et al.* (1994) 170
Alexander, R. (1984) 24
Alexander, R. (1992) 90, 92, 93
Alexander, R. (1994) 102
Alexander, M. and Campbell, J. (1994)
    97–8
Alexander, M. *et al.* (1992) 64, 91, 96, 100
Alutto and Belasco (1972) 77
Angus, L. (1989) 23
Articled Teacher Scheme 114
Ashton, P. (1975) 94
Ashton, P. (1981) 94
assemblies 17, 71, 72
assessment 7–8 *see also* self-assessment
    agreement trials 111, 114, 115, 117,
        118, 119
    Dearing Reviews 105–6
    evidence of achievement 117–18
    existing culture 108–9, 113–14
    internal discussions 118
    moderation 106–7, 110–13
    school development and support 109,
        114–17, 119
    school improvement 153
    teacher assessment 118
    teachers' reports 107
    training 106
Assessment of Performance Unit (APU)
    96
Association for the Study of the
    Curriculum 102
at-risk children 144, 151, 152
Attainment Targets 81
award-bearing INSET projects 123–4,
    126, 132, 141–3

balkanization 42
Ball, S.J. (1987) 17, 71
Barth, R. (1992) 157
basic subjects 92–4, 98, 146
Bassey, M. (1977) 92
Bates, R.J. (1983) 24
Bates, R.J. (1989) 24
Beach, R.H. (1989) 73
Beare, H. *et al.* (1980) 18
Beare, H. *et al.* (1989) 48–9
beliefs 14, 15, 17, 22, 25
Bennett, N. and Carré, C. (1993) 95,
    96
Bennett, N. and Summers, M. (1994)
    95, 100
Bennett, N. *et al.* (1980) 92
Bennis, W.G., Benne, K.D. and Chin,
    R. (1985) 73
Blease, D. and Lever, D. (1992) 70
Blyth, A. and Derricott, R. (1977) 30
Bolam, R. (1993) 38–9, 45
Bolam, R., McMahon, A.,
    Pocklington, K. and Weindling, R.
    (1993) 146
Bolton, E. (1993) 175
Bottery, M. (1990) 83
budgets 58–9
Burns, J.M. (1978) 18
Bush, T. (1981) 32, 33

Campbell, R.J. (1985) 24, 75, 100
Campbell, R.J. (1994) 92, 102
Campbell, R.J. and Neill, S.R. (1990)
    89
Campbell, R.J. and Neill, S.R. (1994)
    93, 94, 96, 98, 101
Campbell, R.J. and Southworth, G.W.
    (1992) 85
Campbell, R.J. *et al.* (1991) 89, 90
career prospects 83, 86–7

188